SVEC
2013
10

Representing violence in France
1760-1820

SVEC (formerly known as *Studies on Voltaire and the Eighteenth Century*) is dedicated to eighteenth-century research. *SVEC* welcomes work across a broad range of disciplines and critical methodologies.

www.voltaire.ox.ac.uk

General editor
Jonathan Mallinson, Trinity College, University of Oxford

Associate editors
Daniel Brewer, University of Minnesota
Michel Delon, Université de Paris-Sorbonne–Paris IV
Sarah Maza, Northwestern University

Advisory panel
Wilda Anderson, Johns Hopkins University
Matthew Bell, King's College London
Marc André Bernier, Université du Québec à Trois-Rivières
Nicholas Cronk, Voltaire Foundation
Rebecca Haidt, Ohio State University
Jens Häseler, Universität Potsdam
Mark Ledbury, University of Sydney
François Moureau, Université de Paris-Sorbonne–Paris IV
J. B. Shank, University of Minnesota
Joanna Stalnaker, Columbia University
W. Dean Sutcliffe, University of Auckland
Stéphane Van Damme, Sciences Po, Paris

Senior publishing manager
Lyn Roberts

http://www.voltaire.ox.ac.uk/www_vf/svec/svec_board.ssi

Representing violence in France
1760-1820

Edited by
THOMAS WYNN

VOLTAIRE FOUNDATION
OXFORD

© 2013 Voltaire Foundation, University of Oxford

ISBN 978 0 7294 1076 2
ISSN 0435-2866

The Voltaire Foundation is a department of the University of Oxford. It furthers the University's objective of excellence in research, scholarship and education by publishing worldwide.

Voltaire Foundation
99 Banbury Road
Oxford OX2 6JX, UK
www.voltaire.ox.ac.uk

A catalogue record for this book is available from the British Library

Eighteenth-century literature / eighteenth-century history / politics
Littérature du dix-huitème siècle / histoire du dix-huitième siècle / la politique

Cover illustration: William Hogarth, *George Taylor's epitaph: death giving George Taylor a cross buttock*, c.1750. Yale Center for British Art, Paul Mellon Collection.

FSC® (the Forest Stewardship Council) is an independent organization established to promote responsible management of the world's forests.

This book is printed on acid-free paper

Printed in the UK by TJ International Ltd, Padstow, Cornwall

Contents

List of illustrations	vii
Acknowledgements	ix
THOMAS WYNN, Introduction	1
I. Violence and the crisis of reason	15
JOHN DUNKLEY, Gambling and violence: Loaisel de Tréogate as a neuroscientist?	17
OLIVIER RITZ, Metaphors of popular violence in the revolutionary debate in the wake of Edmund Burke	35
STÉPHANIE GENAND, Dreaming the Terror: the other stage of revolutionary violence	49
PIERRE SAINT-AMAND, Gothic explosions: Révéroni Saint-Cyr's *Pauliska ou La Perversité moderne*	61
II. Violence and the (re)writing of history	73
CATRIONA SETH, The 'dix août' (10 August 1792) in literary texts	75
MICHÈLE VALLENTHINI, Violence in history and the rise of the historical novel: the case of the marquis de Sade	93
YANN ROBERT, The everlasting trials of Jean Calas: justice, theatre and trauma in the early years of the Revolution	103
PIERRE FRANTZ, Violence in the theatre of the Revolution	121
III. Violence and institutions	137
THOMAS WYNN, Violence, vulnerability and subjectivity in Sade	139
ODILE JAFFRÉ-COOK, The Bastille or the 'Enfer de Dutailli de Saint-Pierre'	161

OURIDA MOSTEFAI, Violence, terrorism and the legacy of the Enlightenment: debates around Jean-Jacques Rousseau and the Revolution — 177

IV. Violence and morality — 189

MALCOLM COOK, Violence in the work of Bernardin de Saint-Pierre — 191

REBECCA SOPCHIK, Violence and the monster: the *Private lives* of the duc d'Orléans — 203

JEAN-CHRISTOPHE ABRAMOVICI, 'Avec une telle violence que...': Sade's use of the term *violence* — 221

WILL MCMORRAN, The sound of violence: listening to rape in Sade — 229

MICHEL DELON, Violence in the novels of Charlotte [de] Bournon-Malarme — 251

Summaries — 263
Bibliography — 269
Index — 295

List of illustrations

Figure 1: *Les Amours et aventures d'un émigré* (Paris, chez les marchands de nouveautés, An VI [1797]. Private collection.   87

Acknowledgements

This volume owes an immense debt to the intellectual support, thoughtful advice and unfailing good humour of Pierre Frantz and Michel Delon, to whom I'd like to express my gratitude and esteem. They were instrumental in co-organising the conference *Violence au tournant des Lumières*, held under the aegis of the Phoenix research group at the Institut Français in London on 8 and 9 April 2011. This conference was generously supported by the Institut's Philippe Lane and Nicole Béa, the Faculty of Arts and Humanities of Durham University (thanks to David Cowling, Heather Fenwick, Andrea Noble and Ed Welch) and the Université Paris-Sorbonne (thanks to Nadine Marchand-Tollet). I should also to thank David Andress, Katherine Astbury, Linda Gil, Vincent Jolivet and Rachel Sternberg; Silas Spencer; Teresa Bridgeman, Jennifer Curtiss Gage, Matthew Smith, Jozef van der Voort and Lucas Wood; and Nicholas Cronk, Jonathan Mallinson and Lyn Roberts of the Voltaire Foundation.

Introduction

THOMAS WYNN

What does Voltaire dream of? On 30 August 1769 the writer tells the comte d'Argental of his recurring Goyaesque nightmares (D15855):

> Je ne vois de tous côtés que les injustices les plus barbares; Lally et son bâillon, Sirven, Calas, Martin, le chevalier de La Barre[1] *se présentent quelquefois à moi* dans mes rêves. On croit que notre siècle n'est que ridicule, il est horrible. La nation passe un peu pour être une jolie troupe de singes, mais parmi ces singes il y a des tigres, et il y en a toujours eu. J'ai toujours la fièvre le 24 du mois d'auguste, que les barbares Welches nomment août. Vous savez que c'est le jour de la Saint-Barthélemy.[2]

Violence cannot be repressed, ignored or disavowed. In the dead of night, the *philosophe*'s mind and body fall prey to the violence that will not stay comfortably buried in the past, and which continues to claim new victims. Behind the façade of political

---

1. Thomas Arthur, comte de Lally, baron de Tollendal, was gagged before his execution for treason on 9 May 1766. Pierre Paul Sirven was charged with his daughter's murder and hanged in effigy on 11 September 1764, although he was fully acquitted on 25 November 1771. Jean Calas was broken on the wheel, strangled and burned on 10 March 1762; on dramatic representations of his life, see Yann Robert's chapter in this volume, 'The everlasting trials of Jean Calas: justice, theatre and trauma in the early years of the Revolution', p.103-19. Martin, a farmer, was also broken on the wheel for a murder he did not commit. The chevalier de La Barre was beheaded and burned on 28 February 1766. Texts relating to all these men – bar Martin – may be found in Voltaire, *L'Affaire Calas*, ed. Jacques Van den Heuvel (Paris, 1975). On Martin, see D15808, D15824, D15828 and D15868; and 'Certain, certitude', in *Questions sur l'Encyclopédie*, *OCV*, vol.39, p.571.
2. Emphasis added. In an earlier letter to d'Alembert (29 March 1762, D10394), Voltaire had suggested that the barbarity of the French lies precisely in their frivolous and indiscriminate disregard for the massacre: 'Tous nos cantons hérétiques jettent les hauts cris, tous disent que nous sommes une nation aussi barbare que frivole, qui sait rouer et qui ne sait pas combattre et qui passe de la Saint-Barthelemy à l'Opéra-Comique.'

security ('la nation') and inconsequential social pleasures ('une jolie troupe de singes'), lurk the disruptive horrors of judicial and religious brutality. Crucially, violence appears as the agent of this gruesome projection; surging forth into Voltaire's dreams, violence presents itself rather than being managed and processed by the writer's deliberate choices. How then might explosive violence be the object of organised representation?[3]

Some of the problems inherent in the representation of violence may be perceived if we turn to a text Voltaire had written some years earlier. On 3 February 1763 the *Mémoires secrets* reported that a clandestine work was circulating in Paris: 'Il court manuscrite une tragédie de M. de Voltaire, intitulée *Saül*. Ce n'est point une pièce ordinaire, c'est une horreur dans le goût de *La Pucelle*, mais beaucoup plus impie, plus abominable. On n'en peut entendre la lecture sans frémir.'[4] This impious recounting of biblical history is drenched in violence. Samuel and his henchmen hack apart Agag, king of the Amalekites – 'tandis que je couperai un bras, coupez une jambe, et ainsi de suite morceau par morceau' (p.478) – whose remains are then served up to their followers. Two hundred men are slaughtered in advance of a wedding celebration (II.i); a man is defenestrated and left to die in a pool of his own blood (III.i); another character is exposed to enemy troops and, should he survive their attack, he is to be butchered by his own men (III.ii). Yet this violence is treated in an irreverent register, as when David tells how his son Ammon raped his own sister, and then chased her out of his room 'à grands coups de pied dans le cul' (p.516). This treatment of violence, which brings to mind *Candide*, is at its most absurdly gruesome when the poet-king David sings one of his 'chansons gaillardes' in honour of his people (p.523-54):

> Chers Hébreux par le ciel envoyés,
> Dans le sang vous baignerez vos pieds;
> Et vos chiens s'engraisseront
> De ce sang qu'ils lécheront.

---

3. On violence and dream-narratives, see Stéphanie Genand's chapter, 'Dreaming the Terror: the other stage of revolutionary violence', p.49-60.
4. Quoted in *Saül*, *OCV*, vol.56a, p.429.

> Ayez soin, mes chers amis,
> De prendre tous les petits
> Encore à la mamelle,
> Vous écraserez leur cervelle
> Contre le mur de l'infidèle;
> Et vos chiens s'engraisseront
> De ce sang qu'ils lécheront.

Violence is, of course, deployed here to expose, attack and ridicule biblical myth, but Voltaire's presentation of brutal acts in *Saül* is significant in other ways. Violence is depicted as primitive,[5] belonging to a superstitious and pre-civilised (or rather 'under-civilised') people; 'Saül ci-devant roi des Juifs, Dieu ne vous avait-il pas ordonné par ma bouche d'égorger tous les Amalécites sans épargner ni les femmes, ni les filles, ni les enfants à la mamelle?' (p.474). Endemic to these Middle Eastern tribes, violence does not invite an involved response from the reader, it does not lead towards catharsis; in short, violence is resolutely *other*. Furthermore, violence is not heroic, as illustrated in David's acknowledgement of his mendacity (p.483-84):

> J'allais dans les villages les plus éloignés, je tuais tout sans miséricorde, je ne pardonnais ni au sexe ni à l'âge [...]; et afin qu'il ne se trouvât personne qui pût me déceler auprès du roi Akis, je lui amenais les bœufs, les ânes, les moutons, les chèvres des innocents agriculteurs que j'avais égorgés, et je lui disais par un salutaire mensonge que c'étaient les bœufs, les ânes, les moutons et les chèvres des Juifs.

Violence brings no distinction or glory to its agent. Above all, violence is presented as disruptive, and indeed the manner in which it is presented is disruptive, for as the initial stage directions (p.465-66) state:

> On n'a pas observé dans cette espèce de tragi-comédie l'unité d'action, de lieu et de temps. On a cru, avec l'illustre La Motte devoir se soustraire à ces règles. Tout se passe dans l'intervalle de deux ou trois générations, pour rendre l'action plus tragique par

---

5. Indeed violence is 'primitivising', in that it appears to destroy modern society; we note that US Secretary of State Richard Armitage is alleged to have warned Pakistan, 'We'll bomb you back to the Dark Ages'.

le nombre des morts selon l'esprit juif, tandis que parmi nous l'unité de temps ne peut s'étendre qu'à vingt-quatre heures, et l'unité de lieu dans l'enceinte d'un palais.

Not only generically uncertain, this 'espèce de tragi-comédie' is an example of armchair theatre; not intended for performance, *Saül* is therefore more akin to Voltaire's clandestine pamphlets than to his plays performed at the Comédie-Française.[6] The rather tired jibe at La Motte's expense risks misleading the reader into taking this passage as no more than another episode in the long-standing debate over the unities. One might instead argue that this humour serves to contain something that is far more troubling and disturbing within the terms of a reassuringly familiar complaint (La Motte had been dead for over three decades, after all). Breaking apart the classical aesthetic, violence cannot be represented rationally, elegantly or even seriously, hence Voltaire's critique of the barbaric Shakespeare: 'C'est une belle nature, mais sauvage; nulle régularité, nulle bienséance, nul art; de la bassesse avec de la grandeur; de la bouffonnerie avec du terrible; c'est le chaos de la tragédie dans lequel il y a cent traits de lumière.'[7] Humour may temporarily make sense of violence, as it does in *Saül*, but that very gesture of containment within laughter suggests that violence is incomprehensible. Violence cannot be understood, in fact it will not be understood or even seriously contemplated; it is *unthinkable*.

Voltaire's treatment of rape, infanticide and mass slaughter in *Saül* illuminates some of the principal characteristics, issues and tensions germane to the experience, analysis and representation of violence in the latter part of the eighteenth century. Firstly,

---

6. On the work's genre and philosophical dimension, see Marie-Hélène Cotoni, 'Une tragédie de Voltaire en marge de toute règle: *Saül*', in *Marginalité et littérature: hommage à Christine Martineau-Génieys*, ed. Maurice Accarie, Jean-Guy Gouttebroze and Eliane Kotler (Nice, 2001), p.407-21; and Alain Sandrier, '"Si j'avais écrit *L'Embrasement de Sodome*": Voltaire et le théâtre manuscrit de la philosophie clandestine', *Revue Voltaire* 8 (2008), p.49-65.
7. Letter to Horace Walpole, 15 July 1768 (D15140). See also the *Lettre de Monsieur de Voltaire à Messieurs de l'Académie française* (1776), in which Voltaire attacks Le Tourneur's translation of Shakespeare, a playwright whose works he characterises as 'un chaos obscur composé de meurtres et de bouffonneries'; see *OCV*, vol.78a, p.1-53 (46).

violence occupies a paradoxical position. At once central and marginalised, violence is deployed, not interrogated; it is a gory means to a critical end. Secondly, violence is aesthetically troublesome; conventional forms of representation are inadequate and new artistic forms must be sought. Thirdly, violence is morally problematic; when the Académie française defines violence in both its 1762 and 1798 editions as 'la force dont on use contre le droit commun, contre les lois, contre la liberté publique',[8] this is a phenomenon that is nothing if not illegitimate in its disruption of the public realm. Finally, violence places the beholder in a peculiar ethical position; how is it possible to regard the pain of others? Does the beholder or reader sympathise, turn away, gawp or – as in the case of *Saül* – resolve her moral conflict through laughter?

These and other questions have been to the fore in recent debates about the role and representation of violence in late eighteenth-century French culture.[9] Although this is a vast and ever-growing field of scholarship, especially given the importance of the Revolution and its aftermath, some key points may be made. Firstly, this is a period of drastically different levels of violence. Violence was still a familiar part of many people's daily lives; just as Parisians lived in close proximity to hardship and violence,[10] so too did peasants living far from the metropolis.[11] David Andress notes that in the eighteenth century it was generally accepted that 'inferiors, such as children, domestic servants and apprentices, and also wives, could be legitimately subjected to violent punishment',[12] and Mary Trouille has examined in detail the problem of spousal abuse in the period.[13] Violence could also

---

8. See also Jean-Michel Messiaen, 'Violence et son réseau lexical (1600-1800): prémisses sémasiologiques', in *Violence et fiction jusqu'à la Révolution*, ed. Martine Debaisieux and Gabrielle Verdier (Tübingen, 1998), p.33-41.
9. For a range of studies on violence in (mostly) French culture between 1690 and 1750, see *Violences du rococo*, ed. Jacques Berchtold, René Desmoris and Christophe Martin (Bordeaux, 2012).
10. Arlette Farge, *La Vie fragile: violence, pouvoirs et solidarités à Paris au XVIIIe siècle* (Paris, 1986).
11. Jay M. Smith, *Monsters of the Gévaudan: the making of a beast* (Cambridge, MA, 2011).
12. David Andress, *The French Revolution and the people* (London, 2004), p.70.
13. Mary Trouille, *Wife-abuse in eighteenth-century France*, SVEC 2009:01.

feature as a key element in pleasurable pastimes, whether in aristocratic hunting or in popular sports.[14] The pervasive presence of violence should not blind us, however, to the very real decrease in violence that had been gathering pace since at least the middle of the previous century, as charted in recent works by Robert Muchembled and Steven Pinker.[15] Just as everyday violence decreased, so did violent warfare; there were, of course, extended periods of combat such as the Seven Years' War, but casualties were less heavy than in previous conflicts. The 'bumpy decline' of organised violence that characterised much of the century was, however, interrupted by the hemoclysm of the revolutionary and Napoleonic Wars.[16] These developments and contrasts make the late eighteenth and early nineteenth centuries an especially fascinating period of enquiry, and caution against treating the violence of the Revolution in general and of the Terror in particular in isolation. This is a period that also sees significant shifts and divergences in attitudes towards violence. The long political process by which the only legitimate exercise of violence (in its guise as 'force') is that deployed by the State was accelerated and confirmed by a cultural shift – that we can consider under the general term of *sensibilité* – whereby new modes of behaviour were prized at the expense of others, resulting in 'des types idéaux et sensibles, charitables, capables de dominer leurs pulsions et d'expurger leur vocabulaire pour éviter l'insulte et les confrontations en public'.[17] Muchembled views urbanisation as playing the crucial role in this shift; it is not so much that the police are successful in repressing violence, but rather that a new perception of the value (both symbolic and monetary) of human life serves as a different socialising force, and

---

14. Philippe Salvadori, *La Chasse sous l'Ancien Régime* (Paris, 1996), p.193-243; Tim Blanning, *The Pursuit of glory: Europe 1648-1815* (London, 2007), p.393-401; and Elisabeth Belmas, 'Jeux d'exercice, divertissement et virilité', in *Histoire de la virilité 1: L'Invention de la virilité, de l'antiquité aux Lumières*, ed. Alain Corbin, Jean-Jacques Courtine and Georges Vigarello, (Paris, 2011), p.445-65.
15. Robert Muchembled, *Une Histoire de la violence de la fin du moyen âge à nos jours* (Paris, 2008); and Steven Pinker, *The Better angels of our nature: the decline of violence and its causes* (London, 2011).
16. Pinker, *The Better angels of our nature*, p.230-31.
17. Muchembled, *Une Histoire de la violence*, p.340.

this new mentality is aped beyond the city. Like Muchembled, Pinker sees Norbert Elias's theory of the civilising process as explaining the decrease in the amount of violence and the lowering of the threshold of its acceptability.[18] Pinker underlines the role that class plays, arguing that the decline of violence in Europe was 'spearheaded by a decline in *elite violence*', and noting that while the civilising process did not eliminate violence entirely, 'it did relegate it to the socioeconomic margins'.[19] James Steintrager has shown how in eighteenth-century Britain and France the enjoyment of watching another's suffering is configured as the truly inhuman, as the sure sign of the perversion of humanity which, according to the normative codes of behaviour, ought to be characterised by pity.[20] The problem of beholding pain is at the heart of Paul Friedland's recent study of capital punishment; he argues that Damiens's execution in 1757 marks a watershed in sensibilities, not in the sense that people become more caring or compassionate but rather that it is henceforth inhuman and *horrible* (especially for women) to derive pleasure from watching executions.[21] Yet the spectacle of violence was not entirely demonised in the late eighteenth century, as Edmund Burke commends violent experiences for eliciting a sense of the sublime in his *Philosophical enquiry* (1757):

> Whatever is fitted in any sort to excite the ideas of pain, and danger, that is to say, whatever is in any sort terrible, or is

18. Pinker, *The Better angels of our nature*, p.59-85.
19. Pinker, *The Better angels of our nature*, p.82, 85.
20. James A. Steintrager, *Cruel delight: Enlightenment culture and the inhuman* (Bloomington, IN, 2004). On the ethics of violence and spectatorship in the following decades, see Ian Haywood, *Bloody Romanticism: spectacular violence and the politcs of representation* (Basingstoke, 2006).
21. Paul Friedland, *Seeing justice done: the age of spectacular capital punishment in France* (Oxford, 2012), especially p.143-91. Scholars of contemporary visual culture have considered the spectator's obligations and the very possibility of intersubjective relations with the represented suffering other; see, for instance, Lile Chouliaraki, *The Spectatorship of suffering* (London, 2006); *Beautiful suffering: photography and the traffic of pain*, ed. Mark Reinhardt, Holly Edwards and Erinna Duganne (Williamstown, MA, 2007); and Lisa Downing and Libby Saxton, *Film and ethics: foreclosed encounters* (London, 2010). This 'ethical turn' is less evident in eighteenth-century studies, where researchers appear slower to interrogate the ethical implications of both our primary material and our scholarly practices.

conversant about terrible objects, or operates in a manner analogous to terror, is a source of the *sublime*; that is, it is productive of the strongest emotion which the mind is capable of feeling. [...] When danger or pain press too nearly, they are incapable of giving any delight, and are simply terrible; but at certain distances, and with certain modifications, they may be, and they are delightful, as we every day experience.[22]

As this concept of the sublime demonstrates, violence causes an upheaval and consequent reconfiguration (if only temporarily) of traditional ethical and moral positions, and Michel Delon has already examined the ambiguity of sublime violence in the late Enlightenment.[23] Burke's loosening of the bond between mimesis and morality also denies the necessity of expository clarity, and recognises violence as a seductive and productive phenomenon; moreover, violence within the terms of the Burkean sublime is an essential element to anxious political consciousness.[24] Burke's theory of the sublime became better known in France after Diderot's *Salon* of 1767, and influenced a host of writers, perhaps most particularly Sade who found therein ample justification to valorise violence: 'Tout ce qui est violent dans la nature a quelque chose d'intéressant et de sublime.'[25]

Violence was not entirely marginalised or discredited in the late eighteenth and early nineteenth centuries. It may be abhorrent and destructive, but it can also be welcomed as a creative force, or what Howard Brown calls 'a strategic instrument and object of management'.[26] When Hannah Arendt observes that

22. Edmund Burke, *A Philosophical enquiry into the origin of our ideas of the sublime and beautiful*, ed. Adam Phillips (Oxford, 1990), p.36-37.
23. Michel Delon, *L'Idée d'énergie au tournant des Lumières (1770-1820)* (Paris, 1988), p.219-36.
24. Charles Hinnant, '"The late unfortunate regicide in France": Burke and the political sublime', *1650-1850: ideas, aesthetics, and inquiries in the early modern era* 2 (1996), p.111-36; and David McCallam, 'The terrorist earth? Some thoughts on Sade and Baudrillard', *French cultural studies*, 23:3 (2012), p.215-24 (especially 218-19). On changing notions of the sublime, see Baldine Saint Girons, *Fiat lux: une philosophie du sublime* (Paris, 1993); and Nicholas Cronk, *The Classical sublime: French neoclassicism and the language of literature* (Charlottesville, VA, 2003).
25. Sade, *Histoire de Juliette*, in *Œuvres*, ed. Michel Delon, 3 vols (Paris, 1990-1997), vol.3, p.894.
26. Howard G. Brown, *Ending the French Revolution: violence, justice and repression from the Terror to Napoleon* (Charlottesville, VA, 2006), p.50.

'violence can be justifiable, but it will never be legitimate', she suggests that it is a morally tainted use of force with (at best) a short-term instrumental character,[27] yet violence in France of this period was held to perform positive identificatory functions that aided social cohesion, as Jean-Clément Martin has proposed: 'Dans cet univers, la violence centrale demeure un élément constitutif du fonctionnement d'une société organiciste, vivant sur un mode communautaire, gérant elle-même ses conflits, où la loi compte moins que la tradition et le respect d'équilibres subtils entre des groupes humains régis dans la disparité et le privilège.'[28] In rendering visible localised codes of sociability, violence forms and binds communities. Conversely, Slavoj Žižek has recently contended that Terrorist violence is 'divine' in that it lacks an identifiable origin as well as precise and limited goals,[29] and Mary Ashburn Miller's analysis of the Revolution's use of metaphors of earthquakes, lightning and volcanoes does indeed demonstrate that such discourse attempted to legitimise violence as massive, agentless and inevitable.[30] This vision of violence risks, however, depriving the participants of their agency and responsibility, as well as marginalising or disregarding those who suffer 'divine' or 'natural' brutality.[31] Far from operating as a sourceless or divisive force, violence functions as a crucial means of self-fashioning for the Cornelian-style hero as well for the more modest individual.[32]

27. Hannah Arendt, *On violence* (London, 1970), p.52.
28. Jean-Clément Martin, *Violence et révolution: essai sur la naissance d'un mythe national* (Paris, 2006), p.21.
29. See his prefatory essay 'Robespierre, or the "divine violence" of Terror', in Maximilien Robespierre, *Virtue and Terror*, ed. Jean Ducange (London, 2007), p.vii-xxxix.
30. Mary Ashburn Miller, *A Natural history of Revolution: violence and nature in the French revolutionary imagination, 1789-1794* (Ithaca, NY, 2011). It should be noted that, as her title suggests, she emphasises the natural rather than divine character of revolutionary violence.
31. On the tensions between state violence and popular participation in the Revolution, see David Andress, 'Popular violence in the French Revolution: revolt, retribution and the slide to state terror', in *Cultures of violence: interpersonal violence in historical perspective*, ed. Stuart Carroll (Basingstoke, 2007), p.175-91.
32. Michel Wieviorka offers a typology of the five ways in which violence is bound up with the construction of the subject; see *Violence: a new approach*, trans. David Macey (London, 2009), p.144-61.

Violence does not necessarily diminish (as in *Saül*) or destroy the individual, and Arlette Farge's observation about urban violence is especially useful in this respect: 'La violence est aussi un spectacle; elle n'est pas forcément une effusion hystérique, une conduite irrationnelle de foule, faisant disparaître les volontés individuelles. Chacun peut y jouer sa partie, profitant du climat exceptionnelle qui permet à la fois l'éclosion des sentiments inhabituels et une expression gestuelle inaccoutumée.'[33] Violence allows the determined actor to participate publicly and deliberately, thereby forging or representing an individual identity within the collective. In a similar vein, Richard Clay has recently argued that the iconoclasm of the Revolution was not mindless vandalism, but rather a resource used by groups across the political spectrum to contest and assert ideas in a rapidly changing environment.[34]

Once violence is understood as regenerative and constructive, it can be celebrated as modern. Whereas some Enlightenment thinkers struggled to consign violence to the past, portraying it as barbaric and primitive,[35] it is possible to see the phenomenon, especially in its organised and spectacular form, as a mark of modernity.[36] As John Gray has observed, there are 'many ways of being modern, some of them monstrous',[37] and was the guillotine itself not intended to demonstrate the social and intellectual progress achieved by the Revolution?[38] According to a pronounced strain of revolutionary discourse, violence ushers in a new era, as evidenced in the pamphlet *Des causes de la Révolution et de ses résultats*:

> Un autre effet de sa [le despotisme de la Terreur] violence fut de détruire les anciennes habitudes, et de donner aux nouvelles

---

33. Farge, *La Vie fragile*, p.320.
34. Richard Clay, *Iconoclasm in revolutionary Paris: the transformation of signs*, SVEC 2012:11.
35. Pierre Saint-Amand, *The Laws of hostility: politics, violence and the Enlightenment* (Minneapolis, MN, 1996).
36. For a series of essays debating the link between violence and modernity in this period, see *Progrès et violence au XVIIIe siècle*, ed. Valérie Cossy and Deirdre Dawson (Paris, 2001).
37. John Gray, *Al Qaeda and what it means to be modern* (London, 2003), p.2.
38. Daniel Arasse, *La Guillotine et l'imaginaire de la Terreur* (Paris, 1987), especially p.25-54.

coutumes autant de force que l'habitude eût pu le faire. [...] Dix-huit mois de terreur suffirent pour enlever au peuple des usages de plusieurs siècles, et pour lui en donner que plusieurs siècles auraient eu peine à établir. [...] Sa violence en fit un peuple neuf.[39]

Even dreadful violence can, it seems, be recuperated as reasonable. The Revolution undoubtedly marks a moment of unprecedented violence, for as Antoine de Baecque writes in his study of cadavers, '*all of a sudden*, on the occasion of a phenomenal crisis of public conscience, the corpse rises up again at the end of the eighteenth century as a sensitive weak point in society's discourse about itself'.[40] But to sever the revolutionary years from the preceding decades is to enact another kind of violence, and greater sensitivity to the history of violence is required. Recent scholarship has indeed been attentive as much to the continuities as to the ruptures that occurred in the artistic practices and institutions of the revolutionary period,[41] and it is clear that a longer-term view that treats revolutionary violence within a broader continuum may offer new insights. One also needs to look beyond 1794, given the persistence of endemic violence in France after that date, with the Revolution arguably ending as late as 1802 with the purge of the Tribunate, the Treaty of Amiens and the fixing of the state executive's future through the Consulate for Life.[42]

This volume of sixteen inter-related studies aims to develop, to challenge and to extend these debates by addressing the problematic representation of violence; we hope thereby to shed new light on previous generations' experience and understanding of violence. Howard Brown notes that while the Revolution's dismantling of social structures provoked a rapid change in values and in systems of representations, affective responses to violence such as 'shock, horror, revulsion, fright, panic, trauma, terror'

39. Adrien Lezay, *Des causes de la Révolution et de ses résultats* (Paris, Desenne, 1797), p.44-45.
40. Antoine de Baecque, *Glory and Terror: seven deaths under the French Revolution* (New York, 2001), p.12. Emphasis added.
41. See, for instance, *Revolutionary culture: continuity and change*, ed. Mark Darlow. *Nottingham French studies*, 45 (2006); and Mark Darlow, *Staging the French Revolution: cultural politics and the Paris Opera, 1789-1794* (Oxford, 2012).
42. Brown, *Ending the French Revolution*, p.2-4.

tend to be left unmentioned in official discourses of revolutionary violence.[43] The challenge of analysing the often occluded effects of violence has recently been taken up by Katherine Astbury who uses insights from trauma theory to examine how the sentimental novels, pastorals and moral tales that dominated the literary scene throughout the 1790s respond to the socio-political turbulence of the Terror and emigration.[44] One aim of this present volume is thus to explore how unofficial writings such as pamphlets, correspondence and fiction testify to the personal responses to violence across a broader chronological reach; our period of enquiry begins in the 1760s and ends some fifty years later.[45] Examining the production, mediation and reception of violence, this volume is structured around four key research questions, although this structure should not limit the resonance of the individual chapters, which enter into dialogue with contributions elsewhere in the book.

Firstly, *what is the link between violence and reason?* Voltaire's recurring nightmare suggests that violence belongs to the realm of darkness and unreason. It seems to mark reason's crisis point, apparently lying beyond human thought and deliberation, and as a result it may be unthinkable within existing moral or aesthetic categories. Four contributors explore the problematic tension between violence and reason. John Dunkley examines how three late eighteenth-century texts, surpassing the moralistic and philosophical explanations of the day, portrayed gambling in such a way as to engage the reader's sympathy for characters otherwise considered as reprehensible agents of impulsive violence. Examining metaphors of the irrational crowd in revolutionary discourse, Olivier Ritz argues that linguistic violence played a key role in the normalisation of political life through the exclusion of

43. Brown, *Ending the French Revolution*, p.48-50.
44. Katherine Astbury, *Narrative responses to the trauma of the French Revolution* (Oxford, 2012). Similarly, Ewa Lajer-Burcharth has examined how the art of the leading French painter of the 1790s bears witness to his personal trauma; see *Necklines: the art of Jacques-Louis David after the Terror* (New Haven, CT, 1999).
45. This temporal frame is therefore a little earlier than Michel Delon's periodisation of the 'tournant des Lumières' that begins in 1770, when the Enlightenment's chief ideas had largely penetrated general opinion, and ends in 1820 with the close of the revolutionary and imperial experiences and the beginning of Romanticism; see *L'Idée d'énérgie*, p.23-31.

the brutal and unreasonable people. Stéphanie Genand examines how several late eighteenth- and early nineteenth-century writers experimented with the new literary genre of the dream in their portrayal of irrational violence. Pierre Saint-Amand unpicks the complex nexus of science, desire and sentiment in Révéroni Saint-Cyr's *Pauliska ou La Perversité moderne*.

Secondly, *how might violence be inscribed within history?* Voltaire's dream shows that violent acts cannot be securely buried in the past, but the inevitable discussion and commemoration of such ruptures pose significant challenges, as four of the volume's chapters demonstrate. Catriona Seth analyses the literary commemoration of 10 August 1792, when hundreds of people were slaughtered at the Tuileries, and she argues that these bloody events mark a moment when conventional values of friendship, heroism and allegiance are fundamentally challenged and indeed overturned. A different account of violence, history and fiction comes in Michèle Vallenthini's chapter on Sade's later novels, as she explores how violence causes the writer to flee from political actuality and to seek refuge in the past. The clandestinity of *Saül*'s initial circulation indicates that violence may be unsuitable for public representation, and two chapters in this volume explore the fraught nature of the theatrical commemoration of violence on the revolutionary stage: Yann Robert analyses the risks of remembering the violence suffered by Jean Calas earlier in the century; Pierre Frantz considers the political stakes when audiences behold violent plays, and asks if such performances stem or perpetuate violence.

Leading on from the theatre's role in commemorating and continuing violence, our third question is *what role do institutions play in producing and perpetuating violence?* Although violence seems to be a destructive force, recent theoretical writings (in particular trauma theory, and Judith Butler's appraisal of military violence) have stressed its productive quality. If violence is indeed creative, then what are the conditions of such creation, how might that violence be sustained, channelled or challenged? Thomas Wynn's chapter on Sade's prison correspondence considers how the prison apparatus and experience do not destroy the individual, but reconstitute the apparently immutable Sade as a new, different subject. A bleaker view of prison emerges in Odile Jaffré-

Cook's close reading of the correspondence between Bernardin de Saint-Pierre and his brother Dutailli, who was then imprisoned at the Bastille; she traces how ostensibly non-violent incarceration impacts upon the individual, destroying him in the process. Another Parisian institution is at the heart of Ourida Mostefai's chapter, which examines the role played by the Panthéon in the revolutionaries' attempts to commemorate, condemn and contain violence.

The fourth and final question is *how do violence and morality map on to each other*? Violence appears in both Voltaire's dream and his peculiar tragedy as a morally compromising and ethically illegitimate force. But it is not simply excessive or distorted human force, for as Malcolm Cook shows in his analysis of Bernardin de Saint-Pierre's *Etudes de la nature* and *Paul et Virginie*, it is also central to the natural world, although its moral valence is significantly different in each realm. Rebecca Sopchik demonstrates how pamphlets imputed violent acts to the duc d'Orléans with the intent of dehumanising and discrediting him so as advocate his execution or to justify his death after the fact. Given that such rhetorical violence attempts to model an appropriate response from the reader by forcefully removing her autonomy, it is clear that one needs to address how violent representations implicate and position their audience. In his analysis of the term *violence* in four of Sade's works, Jean-Christophe Abramovici shows that the marquis aims to position the reader in significantly different ways. The recent ethical turn in theoretical debates reminds us that the reading or viewing of violence is not a neutral or even innocuous act; and in his provocative essay on listening to rape in *Justine*, Will McMorran argues that critics have been reluctant to acknowledge their own involvement, indeed their complicity with Sadean violence. Michel Delon at once closes the volume and opens new avenues by introducing the perhaps unfamiliar figure of Charlotte (de) Bournon-Malarme; simultaneously offering essentialist and historically contingent explanations for violence, her novels encapsulate some of the persistent ambiguities and unresolvable contradictions of the period's thought, fiction and culture.

I

Violence and the crisis of reason

Gambling and violence: Loaisel de Tréogate as a neuroscientist?

JOHN DUNKLEY

In the light of reading Jonah Lehrer's *Proust was a neuroscientist*,[1] I wanted to bring his perceptions to bear on a few of the literary texts which I used in a study published in 1985 in order to test the hypothesis that writers on gambling in the eighteenth century perceived eccentric and often violent behaviours in gamblers, which they represented in their subjects with an accuracy supported by modern research in psychology and the neurosciences.[2]

The first phrase of my title suggests perhaps that I am pushing at open doors. The idea that gambling leads to violence seems a truism, hence not worth proving. I am not, however, setting about proving a truism; what I want to do is to look at the modern research into the neurological and cognitive triggers of pathological gambling behaviours and to suggest the bridge or bridges which link these to other manifestations of personality, including a number of types of violence. This leads to considerations of how society copes with these and other behaviours which it considers aberrant or destructive. The evidence of this investigation can be used in an examination of gambling and its behavioural concomitants as they are shown in some eighteenth-century French novels and a play, which are essentially imaginative literature with a sociological slant.

To sideline from the outset purely socio-moralistic literature, based on the premise that gambling promotes socially destructive behaviour and is therefore deplorable, is not to imply that such literature is irrelevant to the argument, but in some respects it

---

1. Jonah Lehrer, *Proust was a neuroscientist* (Edinburgh, 2011).
2. John Dunkley, *Gambling: a social and moral problem in France, 1685-1792*, SVEC 235 (1985).

clouds the issue. Though it provides evidence for the presence of some behaviours, including violence, it attributes pathological gambling (a term dating from the latter years of the twentieth century) to idleness and avarice, which is both simplistic and incorrect. The reason for the eighteenth-century moralists' invocation of these motors is that in texts written to dissuade people who believed in God as the source of morality it was a powerful tool to link the supposed motivations of a disapproved behaviour to at least three deadly sins (specifically sloth, greed and envy) and to the tenth commandment (forbidding covetousness). It was in the nineteenth century that there was a move away from this view initiated by the challenge of Darwinism to transcendentalism and of Freud to reductionist positivism. In the twentieth century, there also appeared a number of social history studies, of very unequal quality, focused on gambling, by du Bled, Mauzi, Grussi and Belmas, *inter alia*.[3] Orientated towards different readerships, some of them tend to report violence prompted by gambling but synthesise very little and place considerable emphasis precisely on *instances* of gambling and violence. Instances and anecdotes may prompt amusement and intellectual collusion in the reader, but since they are inevitably abstracted from their contexts they only serve to validate the most commonplace views on the topic without integrating gambling and violence into a broader and potentially meaningful overview.

This study will focus mainly on problem gambling, which includes pathological gambling. Violence will be taken to include physical and verbal violence, obviously, but also the moral and mental cruelty which is implied when a gambler causes the dilapidation of family fortunes. The eighteenth-century view of gambling, as it is associated with violence, focuses exclusively and insistently on its destructive power over the individual and his or

---

3. Elisabeth Belmas's *Jouer autrefois: essai sur le jeu dans la France moderne (XVIe-XVIIIe siècle)* (Seyssel, 2006) is a model of scholarship. It is Victor du Bled's *Histoire anecdotique et psychologie des jeux de cartes, dès, échecs* (Paris, 1919), and Olivier Grussi's *La Vie quotidienne des joueurs sous l'ancien régime à Paris et à la cour* (Paris, 1985) that particularly tend towards the anecdotal. Robert Mauzi's article, 'Ecrivains et moralistes du XVIIIe siècle devant les jeux de hasard', *Revue des sciences humaines* 90 (1958), p.219-56, is discussed in my study (noted above), p.152-53.

her associates. It is seldom if ever viewed as in any way creative,[4] and usually the emotional alliances which individuals form in order to counter its effects (the formation of friendships or the concerted efforts of young lovers) are not presented as the beneficial consequences of solidarity in the face of a threat but as existing independently and despite the odds.

In the drive to discourage heavy gambling, designated as *manie*, *passion* and *rage*, the moralists of the seventeenth and eighteenth centuries all mention its capacity to provoke violence and use this apparently inevitable consequence as an ethical scarecrow. Sometimes this violence is displaced – like eating the cards, since presumably they are the only physical manifestations of abstract chance available for revenge. More usually violence occurs amongst the players. Sometimes too the violence takes the form of self-harm or suicide. While these physical manifestations of violence are also present in imaginative literature, it can go further and explore the nuances of violence when it occurs in and disturbs the mind of a character.

Most eighteenth-century observers also differentiate between male and female gamblers. Usually, they devote a separate chapter to women, in the context of a more extended study, which implies that they see the typical gambler as male. This is essentially borne out by modern studies which find that men tend to indulge in extravert gambling (casinos) whereas women tend to gravitate more towards introvert gambling (slot machines, scratch cards, etc.).[5] In eighteenth-century imaginative literature, most, though not all, gamblers are young males. Two modern researchers note that epidemiological studies indicate that two thirds of pathological gamblers are, and it is on the presentation of this group that this study will principally but not exclusively concentrate.[6] This follows the trend in modern research to study

---

4. On the possibility that violence might be creative, see Thomas Wynn's chapter 'Violence, vulnerability and subjectivity in Sade', p.139-60.
5. Bingo is an exception, but it seems that its chief focus is an investment in elderly, class-specific female sociability rather than any monetary advantage. See Joseph Hraba and Gang Lee, 'Gender, gambling and problem gambling', *Journal of gambling studies* 12:1 (1996), p.83-101.
6. Jon E. Grant and Marc N. Potenza (eds), *Pathological gambling, a clinical guide to treatment* (Washington, DC, and London, 2004), p.59.

population *segments* as opposed to the general population in relation to problem gambling.

Firstly, what, if it exists, is the general, contemporary view of gambling? Here, one must necessarily be very schematic, partly through constraints of space and partly through those of ignorance of the complexities of modern sociology and neuroscience. The latter field is, as we know, developing rapidly and constantly. In contrast to the situation in the eighteenth century, gambling is now mostly a *legal* activity integrated into a *consumerist* culture. Except where it involves activities which are designated as criminal for other reasons, it is not punished, it is *taxed*, and, in its pathological manifestations, it is *treated*. It therefore figures alongside activities like alcoholism, drug misuse, internet addiction and compulsive shopping. A recent exhibition at the Wellcome Institute, entitled 'High Society', which focused on the use of drugs and the evolution of society's attitudes to them, summarised these in the exhibition guide under the heading 'A sin, a crime, a vice, or a disease?' and traced their history through education, criminalisation and medication.[7] A similar history can be observed for pathological gambling, which is variously viewed as an obsessive-compulsive spectrum disorder, or an affective spectrum disorder, or an addiction, or an impulse control disorder, or possibly a mixture of all these, among others![8]

A possible bridge between pathological gambling and violence

7. It ran from 11 November 2010 to 27 February 2011. The evolution of perspectives on gambling is more fully described by Per Binde in 'Gambling, exchange systems and moralities', *Journal of gambling studies* 21:4 (2005), p.445-79.
8. See Grant and Potenza, *Pathological gambling*, p.xiv. K. S. Leung and L. B. Cottler summarise thus: 'The efficacy of naltrexone treatment for pathological gambling has been replicated in a double-blind, placebo-controlled, confirmatory study. For mood-stabilizers, whereas carbamazepine and topiramate continued to produce positive results, olanzapine failed to show superior outcomes compared with placebo control. Two new pharmacological agents for pathological gambling, N-acetyl cysteine and modafinil, produced significant improvement for pathological gamblers. Several studies examined the outcomes of non-pharmacological treatments. Recent studies showed that cognitive-behavioral therapy failed to produce superior outcomes compared with other less costly methods such as brief interventions. Two new pharmacological treatment methods have been reported, including the use of videoconferencing in delivering ongoing supervisions after exposure therapy and the congruence couple therapy, which aims to heal the person as a system whole.' See 'Treatment of pathological gambling', *Current opinion in psychiatry* 22:1 (2009), p.69-74.

is suggested in an article (not the only one, of course) entitled 'Are Dopaminergic genes involved in a predisposition to pathological aggression?' Thomas J. H. Chen and his colleagues write:

> We hypothesize that pathological aggression, a complex behavioral disorder, in adolescents may in part involve polymorphisms of the dopaminergic system. While a number of neurotransmitter systems must be involved, due to polygenic inheritance, one major pathway should involve the dopaminergic system. Advances in our knowledge of the neurobiology of aggression and violence have given rise to rational pharmacological treatments for these behaviors. The main biological systems that are known to be involved are certain reward neurotransmitters including: serotonin, opioid peptides, γ-aminobutyric acid, and the catecholamines (dopamine and norepinephrine). *It is our notion that pathological aggressive behavior is in part similar mechanistically to other forms of impulsive behaviors such as pathological gambling.* By analogy to drug dependence, it has been speculated that the underlying pathology in pathological gambling is a reduction in the sensitivity of the reward system.[9]

Insensitivity to a reward system implies following an immediate opportunity for gratification without considering possible longer-term consequences. The bridge is, then, *impulsiveness*. Grant and Potenza write:

> Researchers [working with pathological gamblers] have reported increased rates of alexithymia, attentional impairment, impulsiveness, risk-taking, obsessionality, sensation seeking, lack of behavioural restraint, diminished ability to resist craving, poor coping, negative affect and novelty seeking in persons with pathological gambling as compared with normal samples [sources given]. These wide-ranging traits appear to describe individuals who seek excitement and new experiences, easily submit to their desires, and exercise little restraint over their impulses.[10]

And: 'Pathological gambling shares similar neural features with other disorders or conditions characterized by impaired impulse control.'[11]

---

9. Thomas J. H. Chen *et al.*, 'Are dopaminergic genes involved in a predisposition to pathological aggression? Hypothesizing the importance of "super normal controls" in psychiatric genetic research of complex behavioral disorders', *Medical hypotheses* 65:4 (2005), p.703-707 [emphasis added].
10. Grant and Potenza, *Pathological gambling*, p.48, 60, 132.
11. Grant and Potenza, *Pathological gambling*, p.132.

Like us, eighteenth-century observers recognised impulsiveness as one of the major distinguishing characteristics of young men in everyday life. Prévost's Des Grieux provides a well-known and early fictional example. He is clearly impulsive in that he abandons his plan to become a seminarist within moments of meeting Manon, with all the predictable consequences. And if one reads the novel against the grain, one sees that his typical (indulgent, patrician) father is perfectly prepared to accommodate this testosterone-fuelled spree provided that it remains within the parameters which society normally allowed to young men, probably because any other course was futile. What he balks at is the risk of *permanency*.[12] Des Grieux also gambles but, intent on making money to supply Manon's wants, he is an instrumental gambler, not a pathological one. Similarly instrumental is his involvement in violence; he is forced into violence in order to obtain something for Manon or to avoid being separated from her. He does not generally resort to violence, and his attack on G...M... is an *impulse*, prompted probably by face-saving and, in a sense, by impotence (societal, not sexual, of course). Impotence, in both its commonly received senses, is linked to gambling and violence through the notion of *male fitness*.

An observation by Wilson and Daly aligns well with Des Grieux's situation:

> Sexual selection theory suggests that willingness to participate in risky or violent competitive interactions should be observed primarily in those age-sex classes that have experienced the most intense reproductive competition (fitness variance) during the species' evolutionary history, and in those individuals whose present circumstances are predictive of reproductive failure.[13]

Though Des Grieux is presented as more physically attractive than G... M..., and (until the closing scene) is almost certainly more

---

12. See Maurice Daumas, *Le Syndrome Des Grieux; la relation père / fils au XVIIIe siècle* (Paris, 1990). In their article, 'Neurodevelopment, impulsivity, and adolescent gambling', R. Andrew Chambers and Marc N. Potenza cite 'changes in neural circuitry involved in impulse control [as having] significant implications for understanding adolescent behaviours', *Journal of gambling studies*, 19:1 (2003), p.53-84 (53).
13. Margo Wilson and Martin Daly, 'Competitiveness, risk-taking and violence: the young male syndrome', *Ethology and sociobiology* 6 (1985), p.59-73 (59-60).

potent in the sexual sense, he cannot compete with G... M... in terms of fitness because G... M... has more money than he has, and it is only money that can ensure the possession of Manon. It might be argued (perhaps sophistically) that this act is a rare example of creative violence because it affirms, or creates, fitness in Des Grieux, and promotes his dream of possession by destroying the obstacle to it. Certainly, his current circumstances are 'predictive of reproductive failure'.

In the real world of gambling as reported by the annals of the eighteenth century, the one person who stands out as exceptional is Louis XIV's courtier, the marquis de Dangeau (1638-1720). He did not chatter or flirt at the gaming table but concentrated on the game, noting the cards that had already been played. The way he gambled was seen by his contemporaries as being unusual and slightly shifty, not quite the thing to do. In other words, most people in that population segment, the Court, played inattentively, hence, by implication, impulsively.

In the imaginative texts of the later eighteenth century, what sort of characters gamble, and in what types of violence do they get involved? I am going to use as exemplars some of those which I looked at in my 1985 study, in order to take the examination of them further than the research- knowledge available when it was written allowed. Advances have naturally been made in the sociology of gambling, and the neuroscientific field hardly existed at the time when the research was done. One of the most complete portrayals, and probably the best known, is Saurin's *Béverlei* (1768). It dramatises the sorry fate of a *négociant* turned gambler. There are three very obvious instances of violence in this play. One is the hero's suicide in the first version of the ending, which is extreme, exemplary violence to the self. Another is the reported murder of the villain, Stukéli, by an accomplice, Jame. (This second instance can be left out of account because it is mainly an illustration of 'just deserts', and murder is a cliché in this milieu.) The third is the aborted violence of the imminent murder of Tomi by his gambling father. The suicide is *not* an impulsive act. Suicide is, in some instances at least, the ultimate expression of self-loathing; it is prompted here by Béverlei's reflection on his own reprehensible conduct in a situation for which he believes himself responsible, and it has been prepared by the act of self-degradation when he lies down in the street and is rescued by the family retainer, Jarvis (IV.v). He has been contemplating suicide since IV.ii and is now putting himself literally on the same level as the repulsive detritus (including decaying animal material) which typically littered the streets. By contrast, the contemplated murder of Tomi *is* prompted by impulsiveness, when Béverlei envisages the possible grim future of his son. He is succumbing to the effects of poison at this moment, hence he is acting 'while the balance of his mind is disturbed', to use the conventional phrase, and infanticide in such circumstances is from time to time recorded. Bachaumont noted the horror of some female spectators faced with this spectacle, and that they returned to see it again the next evening.[14] They could thus have the vicarious pleasure of violence witnessed from a position of safety, and appear *sensible* (twice), which implies a link between them and the female courtier who, to the disapproval of Louis XV, attended Damiens's (pornographic) execution, or the later *tricoteuses*.

Is Saurin, in that case, offering the audience an impulsive protagonist? The Tomi episode seems to imply that he is. Impulsiveness is also behind his challenge to the virtuous Leuson (his future brother-in-law) to fight a duel (IV.iii), and duelling often appears in the same context as gambling in eighteenth-century literature. A recent article by Per Binde also underlines their affinity.[15] But there is another trait present here, and it is one which modern research links with impulsiveness, and that is risk-taking. They often *are* present in the same action (a modern example might be agreeing to ride home from a party in a car driven by a drunk), and they are both more prevalent in young males than in other segments of the population. Seen from this perspective, Béverlei is a character-type which eighteenth-century audiences would have recognised instantly: he is an entrepreneur involved in risky maritime trade. His goods come into Europe from the New World via Cadiz.[16] This is gambling in

---

14. Louis Petit de Bachaumont, *Mémoires secrets, édités par P.-L. Jacob, bibliophile* (Paul Lacroix), (Paris, [1921]), p.280 (entry dated 11 May 1768).
15. Binde, 'Gambling, exchange systems and moralities' (see n.7, above).
16. The *asiento* ensured that Cadiz was not associated with the slave trade, but in 1768 slave-trading would not have tarnished Béverlei's reputation.

another form. An off-the-cuff calculation, based on the evidence of Béverlei's household, suggests that he must have made his fortune in his mid-twenties, the very age at which the characteristics mentioned above are particularly powerful.

There is another instance of violence in the play, and it is a curious one. The main setting is Béverlei's house, which has become very dilapidated. It is possible to construe this physical deprivation as both physical and emotional violence which Béverlei inflicts upon his wife, his son and possibly also his servant, Jarvis, since servants regularly faced destitution in their old age. But the play shows Madame Béverlei as infinitely patient with her husband and their deteriorating circumstances, and Henriette, Béverlei's sister, reproaches her for it (I.i). Indeed, contemporary critics also saw this as unrealistic. Only the imminent murder of Tomi rouses her to anger. One of the headings under which modern gambling-research studies examine the violence prompted by gambling is 'domestic violence'.[17] Eighteenth-century observers were clearly aware of the link, but their way of expressing this tends to vary according to the class of people involved. Jean Barbeyrac, author of the most significant study of gambling of the eighteenth century, noted, in his discussion of the effects of paternal gambling on the family: 'Trop heureux encore si, quand il vient de faire quelque grosse perte, il ne décharge sur eux sa mauvaise humeur, et ne les punit de son imprudence ou plutôt de son injustice propre!'[18] In fact, modern research proves that it is *not* primarily the gambler who goes on the attack. Given the critics' reaction to Madame Béverlei's forbearance, it may not be entirely perverse to suggest that Saurin's virtual denial of any hint of domestic violence is designed both to preserve the image of Béverlei's fundamental goodness but also, and just as importantly, to make the situation *so* incredible as to make the spectator *dis*believe it. It's a familiar strategy: prime-ministerial assurances that 'The minister has my total

---

17. Mary Trouille, in her study on *Wife-abuse in eighteenth-century France* (*SVEC* 2009:01) documents instances of domestic violence in which gambling plays a part. She describes the case of the (real) marquise de Mézières (ch.3) and cites fictional instances from *Ingénue Saxancour* and *The Wrongs of woman, or Maria*.
18. Jean Barbeyrac, *Traité du jeu*, 2 vols (Amsterdam, Pierre Humbert,1709), vol.1, p.323.

confidence and support' are standard code for 'If the press keeps up the pressure, he can rediscover his family next week.'

Madame Béverlei abstains from any verbal violence towards her husband. This conforms to her social status and to the theatrical conventions of litotes and euphemism. But verbal violence does make its appearance onstage in this context when Béverlei repeats all the shameful things which people are saying about him (*vilain, malheureux, infâme*, etc.).[19] In other words, his reputation, essential to business confidence, is undermined. (Interestingly, reputation for men was founded on what they did do, and for women on what they did not.) Calumny, such as that which follows Béverlei, is a verbal form of violence all the more insidious because it spreads, covers its tracks and does irreparable harm. Fear of this form of violence has long been used as a social regulator, and denials are counterproductive: 'No smoke without fire.' Clearly it was essential for social acceptance in the bourgeois circles of the day.

Béverlei focuses solely on the decay of a pathological gambler who is the victim of crooks. Novels, with more space at their disposal, tend to include gambling and violence in the context of lives more broadly narrated. I shall use three examples: Damiens de Gomicourt's *Dorval* (1769), Bardou's *Histoire de Laurent Marcel* (1779) and Loaisel de Tréogate's *Dolbreuse* (1783). They are all fictional life-stories and are of uneven literary quality. They do not necessarily convey a realistic account of a period in a young man's life, but they do transmit credible accounts of reactions to particular circumstances, built on believable experience. They all relate episodes of gambling, but the most striking point they have in common is their insistence on the impulsiveness of the protagonists and their rapid changes from one situation to the next. This could of course be construed as simply the narratological effect of an attempt to include as many interesting episodes as possible, but on the other hand the protagonists' abrupt changes of direction are explicitly explained in terms of the typical character of the age-segment.

To take the texts in chronological order, *Dorval* (1769) is a moralistic *roman à tiroirs* in four volumes. The most developed,

---

19. Dunkley, *Gambling: a social and moral problem in France*, p.171.

and very conventional, gambling episode comes in volume IV, where Dorval falls prey to a group of card-sharps (*grecs*). As seems common with this type of bildungsroman, the protagonist goes straight from one *égarement* to the next. Here, Dorval has passed through the hands of the fifteen-year-old prostitute, Sophie, and gone on to complete a course of serial fornication. He recounts the progress of his decline.

> Arraché, malgré moi, par le dépérissement de ma santé, à ce genre de vie, je devins la proie de ces hommes oisifs, qui, sans état, sans fortune, encore plus, sans principe[s], se font, sur le bien des dupes qui les croient, un revenu sûr. Ils sont d'abord leurs complaisants, servent leur goût, flattent leurs passions, encensent leurs défauts, obtiennent leur confiance, et finissent par avoir leur fortune. Le jeu est le grand ressort de leur machine. Quelques succès qu'ils accordent, font passer dans l'âme de leurs victimes, l'avidité et l'avarice. Ils assurent dans leur cœur, le goût du jeu, par l'espérance du gain. Quittant leur ruse, ils se servent, alors, de toutes leurs armes, et ne laissent, aux malheureux, qu'ils ont séduits, que le regret de l'avoir été. Frécour [un faux ami] s'associa d'abord à ma fortune, me quitta et devint mon adversaire. Mon bonheur le suivit huit jours de suite; je ne connus que les revers. Il me restait environ cinq cents louis; Frécour en fut bientôt le maître. Cinq cents autres furent proposés, sur une même carte, et je les perdis encore sur ma parole. L'impatience me prit, l'humeur me gagna; je devins inconsidéré dans mes propos. Frécour y répondit, par des injures. Nos épées se mesurèrent; la mienne fut plus heureuse. Frécour resta sur le carreau. Je fus arrêté et conduit à For-l'Evêque.
>
> Dans ce séjour d'horreur, je retrouvai ma raison. Je me rappelai mon père; je le vis expirant pour sa patrie, victime de son amour pour son fils. J'eus horreur de moi-même; le désespoir entra dans mon cœur. L'amour de ma gloire retint mon bras, et me sauva un nouveau crime.[20]

His course runs from fornication to gambling to duelling and then back to equilibrium. Peer-group pressure, of which both eighteenth-century writers and modern researchers recognise the influence, is discernible here. Duelling and consequent death are

20. Augustin Pierre Damiens de Gomicourt, *Dorval, ou Mémoires pour servir à l'histoire des moeurs au XVIIIe siècle*, 4 vols (Amsterdam and Paris, Mérigot jeune, 1769), vol.4, p.60-63.

commonplace, but the allusion to Dorval's father at the end of the extract refers back to an earlier episode which also illustrated extreme violence done *on impulse*. His father had found him a career as an officer in the army (they had been living in their ancestral home in Brittany) and had joined up alongside him as an infantryman. His father is killed in an engagement. The son then writes:

> Ma douleur me rendit injuste. Tout à mon désespoir, la rage s'empara de mon cœur; je lui [à son père] immolai, impitoyablement, quelques prisonniers, qui se rencontrèrent sur mon passage. Les soldats, aussi affligés et aussi animés que moi, ne marchaient plus, ils volaient à la poursuite des ennemis; tous ceux qu'ils purent atteindre, furent sacrifiés à leur vengeance. Le temps a pu affaiblir ma douleur; mais il ne l'a pas détruite. Mon cœur est encore déchiré, au souvenir de ce cruel événement [c'est-à-dire, la mort de son père].[21]

So gambling is integrated, as we have seen, into a scenario of impetuousness, risk-taking and violence, characteristics which are the hallmark of the age-segment. Frécour has also traded on Dorval's impulsiveness and desire for instant gratification and dangled Sophie and other women in front of him because Dorval had supplanted him in the popularity stakes among women of higher social standing, so the background of male competitiveness and male fitness in the purely sexual sense is present too.

The second novel, Bardou's *Histoire de Laurent Marcel* of 1779, also relates an encounter with a victim of *grecs*; this one is a young provincial from Montluçon. (According to Ange Goudar, *grecs* were particularly on the lookout for naive provincials like this one.[22]) Two of the 'good' characters, Monsieur L'Herbier and Marcel, come across the young man, sitting on a bench, in sodden

---

21. Damiens de Gomicourt, *Dorval*, vol.4, p.17-18.
22. Ange Goudar (1708-1791) led a colourful life all over Europe. His *Histoire des grecs ou de ceux qui corrigent la fortune au jeu*, is a key text on eighteenth-century gambling in France. It earned him £1,700 when it was published in 1757. According to Cl. Christin and M.-F. Luna, he obtained this from the printers of Avignon, but the title-page bears the imprint La Haye; an account of his life is given in *Dictionnaire des journalistes*, ed. Jean Sgard, 2 vols (Oxford, 1999), vol.1, p.456B-458A.

clothes, lamenting his misfortunes in the Tuileries gardens. They elicit his story. His father had originally intended to have him made into a priest. But he protests and his father indulges his desire to travel. He travels to Paris (278 km) and plunges into the pleasures of life there. So the portrayal is one which includes the risk-taking typical of the age-segment, though the decision is not impulsive. Marcel also notes that his new acquaintances in Paris 's'aperçurent que mon goût dominant se tournait vers le jeu' (p.179). In the gambling den, the crooks first let him win large sums, then make him lose heavily. Research indicates that early gains encourage higher stakes on riskier bets, even without external intervention.[23] He gets a further 400 *pistoles* from his father and chases his losses, losing yet again. When he realises that he is being cheated, he at first uses verbal violence on the *grecs*; 'Je les traite de fripons, de scélérats, de gueux à pendre', then he goes for his sword, whereupon they throw him out of the window. He makes a soft landing, but the people he calls upon to help him turn out to be crooks as well. Having led him through a labyrinth of empty rooms and courtyards, they bring him at last to a river gate, seize him, and set him adrift in a boat on the Seine, presumably to drown. At last his luck turns and he manages to swim ashore and get into the Tuileries gardens. This may perhaps have been conceived as no more than a moralistic warning (the book is full of them) on the risks of playing in dubious dens or, more generally, of trusting to luck and strangers. But there is an interesting follow-up to it, where violence is done by the virtuous characters to one of the cheats, whom they trick into a lone meeting (were eighteenth-century villains really so naive?), unmask, asset-strip and lock him in a cupboard before they leave.

This violence is not spontaneous but clearly planned in such a way as to minimise the risks to the perpetrators. Its success derives from the imbalance of numbers. The violence of the first episode is a conventional warning ('these people are dangerous'), and the second is a lesson that evil people finally get what they deserve (here, asphyxiation or starvation). The one is banal and the other an illusion. The episodes are perfectly coherent from a

23. Kenneth Abrams and Matt Kushner, 'Behavioral understanding', in Grant and Potenza, *Pathological gambling*, p.113-26.

psychological point of view, with impulsiveness, risk-taking and violence incorporated in a conventional way into a moral tale. But, while it follows a pattern familiar in eighteenth-century novels, it cannot be written off as simply a literary cliché and an outdated attempt at therapy. Examining case-studies, 'talking through the problem', comparing experiences, testing one's own experience against other people's and so on, are still used nowadays in cognitive psychology as forms of addiction therapy. They are no longer almost the *only* kind of therapy available of course (the other was incarceration for *dérèglement de conduite* in an establishment such as Saint-Lazare), but they still figure prominently.

A novel which illustrates a different kind of violence is Loaisel de Tréogate's *Dolbreuse* of 1783. It is different from most eighteenth-century bildungsromane in that its initial premise is that societal influences are capital in determining behaviour (still a current position), and that observation of man in this context is the ideal basis for ethics. The author writes in his preface that:

> Nous estimons que [les philosophes moralistes] presque tous se sont égarés dans les spéculations d'une fausse métaphysique, et qu'aucuns n'ont saisi le véritable principe des règles de la morale; c'est qu'ils ont trop négligé la connaissance de l'homme physique, et que la plupart d'entre eux n'ont pas vu d'assez près les hommes. Eloignés du grand théâtre où l'on apprend à les connaître, par ce goût de la retraite si naturel à tous les sages, ils n'ont pas pu observer l'influence de l'esprit de société sur le cœur humain; l'influence qu'il reçoit des usages, du progrès des lumières et des vices, ni par conséquent acquérir la science nécessaire pour combattre avec fruit les habitudes dépravées.[24]

He overstates the case in claiming that the majority of moralists lost sight of their object amidst a welter of theory, but his claim is what justifies the novel that follows. He underlines the influence of peer-pressure, and *de facto* takes into account the point that people act according to the prevailing norms of the social group rather than according to the *ideals* transmitted by the media of the

---

24. Joseph-Marie Loaisel de Tréogate, *Dolbreuse, ou l'homme du siècle, ramené à la vérité par le sentiment et par la raison*, 2 vols (Amsterdam and Paris, Belin, 1783), p.ii-iii.

day, such as sermons, treatises and the moralising theatre. In Hume's terms, the moralist Loaisel is tackling the *is* rather than the *ought*.

Dolbreuse marries the virtuous Ermance early on in the novel but then returns to his regiment and follows the usual pattern of misconduct. The characteristic impulsiveness also enters the picture early on, and the hero offers a justification: 'Mais une âme jeune, et douée d'une sensibilité trop grande, est aussi lente à se résoudre que prompte à céder à toutes les impulsions.'[25] Once in Paris, he writes: 'J'avais affaire à des hommes qui ne donnaient pas le temps à la réflexion de mûrir dans mon esprit [...] je m'abandonnai à mille nouveaux prestiges sans presque m'en apercevoir.'[26]

Gambling becomes one of Dolbreuse's major activities and, in the process of his own cycles of winning and losing, he notes the variety of manifestations of violent behaviour among the other gamblers: 'Troublés jusqu'à une certaine aliénation d'esprit, ils oublient les égards les plus ordinaires de la vie civile; et encore leur faut-il passer tout, paroles offensantes, manières brusques, emportements furieux, comme à ces malades qu'une trop grande dissipation d'esprits, ou un sang trop agité, fait tomber en démence.'[27] These are all standard observations no doubt, but the novelty comes in the violence of the despair which follows Dolbreuse's loss of every last thing he owns:

> La première crise de ma fureur passée, je rentre chez moi et me jette sur un lit, moins pour y chercher du soulagement à mes maux, que pour fuir la lumière dont l'obscur reflet me devient importun même au milieu des ombres. Je couvre la tête, je ferme les yeux, j'appuie fortement ma main sur mes paupières, pour ne plus voir aucun objet. Pendant une longue et pénible nuit, mon accablement fut terrible. J'éprouvais, si l'on peut s'exprimer ainsi, une sécheresse de déscspoir qui resserrait mon cœur presque au point d'intercepter ses battements. Il n'est pas de souffrance comparable à celle-là.[28]

25. Loaisel de Tréogate, *Dolbreuse*, vol.1, p.95.
26. Loaisel de Tréogate, *Dolbreuse*, vol.1, p.124.
27. Loaisel de Tréogate, *Dolbreuse*, vol.2, p.11-12.
28. Loaisel de Tréogate, *Dolbreuse*, vol.2, p.14. This can be read alongside a later episode when he imagines he has been responsible for the supposed death of a

In literary terms, the representation of emotion is of course Romantic: the emotions are not analysed or precisely described but what *is* conveyed is their intensity and their urgency – in these particular cases, their violence.[29] They isolate and distinguish the sufferer from everyone else, and at the same time invite complicity. Attention is drawn to the *physical* manifestations which they induce because, while they cannot be categorised, they can be recognised. It is taken that the implied reader, knows, or can be brought to know, what it feels like to be going through this type of experience.

The foregoing discussion suggests the following conclusion. Modern research in domains which did not even exist in the eighteenth century has analysed, synthesised and documented a mass of modern gambling practice, legitimate and otherwise, and we have come to understand and cope with it in such ways as the eighteenth century never could have envisaged. Our attitudes towards violence have likewise become more sophisticated. Though we live, in these respects, in a different world from our ancestors, we find that their observations of the proclivities of gamblers, including the proclivity to violence, are elements of the view of a particular age-segment which are still valid. But, if science is answering some of the questions to which gambling and violence give rise, this is not quite the end of the story.

This is where my reference to Jonah Lehrer comes in. In his *Proust was a neuroscientist*, there are two chapters which especially bear on what I have been saying here – the one on George Eliot

---

countess whom he had seduced. He faints with despair, and, on recovering, goes on a Rousseauian peregrination in the course of which he sees his crimes written in the skies and traced in furrows of fire along the street (II, p.35). The spontaneous involvement of brain chemicals in promoting hallucinations is now a medical commonplace but its causation, when not induced, was mysterious in the eighteenth century.

29. In his seminal study of the work of Loaisel, Raphaël Gimenez writes: 'Une lecture minutieuse de l'ouvrage permet d'y trouver tout ce qui caractérise l'âme romantique: épanchement d'une sensibilité aiguë, plaisirs de la volupté amoureuse, goût intense d'exister, effusion de mélancolie, évasion au-delà du tangible, retour à la foi chrétienne, vague des passions, tout s'entremêle dans *Dolbreuse*'; *L'Espace de la douleur chez Loaisel de Tréogate, 1752-1812* (Paris, 1992), p.9.

and the other on Virginia Woolf. What particularly emanates from these, and Lehrer's 'Coda', is that the experience of life transcends the prevailing scientific explanations for the functioning of the brain/mind. Scientifically viable and accurate until proven otherwise, they are nonetheless incomplete, if for no other reason than that we do not feel that they fully represent what we feel we are. The point is that the experience of being human is certainly the experience of social interactions and influences, but it is *not* the experience of the activity of neurons, synapses, dopamine, serotonin and so on. Except when a malfunction occurs, we are not aware of the chemical processes which ensure the functioning of the body. While we are engaged in the everyday business of living, we are aware of ourselves as a *self* with certain (often unstable) attributes, and our conception of ourselves, vague perhaps and subject to change, has nothing demonstrable or perceptible to do with neuroscience. It eludes scientific description, though it is susceptible to illustration of the kind we have found in literary texts. It is possible to conclude, then, that eighteenth-century fiction writers saw in the gamblers they described all the behavioural patterns which different branches of modern science can explain, more or less fully depending on the particular branch, and that, like George Eliot and Virginia Woolf, Loaisel and his contemporaries also ventured into that area of humanist analysis which complements and extends the scientific accounts to which we now have access, and which in doing so validates the work of the humanities generally.

Metaphors of popular violence in the revolutionary debate in the wake of Edmund Burke[1]

OLIVIER RITZ

'Dès 1789 la violence est au cœur du débat en Europe, autour des *Réflexions sur la Révolution de France* du député anglais *whig* Edmund Burke';[2] the historian Jean-Christophe Martin's observation is particularly apposite regarding Burke's comments about the people. With the onset of the Revolution, the people played a new political role, exemplified by the storming of the Bastille. This violent popular intervention was in turn linked to the institutional revolution unfolding at the Assemblée nationale. Describing popular action and protests was henceforth to become a major issue in the debate about the Revolution, with some voices condemning popular violence, others justifying it, and others passing over it in silence.

Around the *Reflections on the Revolution in France*, published in November 1790, one can identify a series of texts that intersect and dialogue with each other. Whereas the British debate has been the object of numerous studies,[3] the French debate deserves greater attention. This debate comprises not only French translations of works by Burke and his British adversaries (such as Priestley, Paine and Mackintosh), but also those French texts

1. Translated by Thomas Wynn.
2. Jean-Clément Martin, *Violence et Révolution: essai sur la naissance d'un mythe national* (Paris, 2006), p.9. Other historians of revolutionary violence allot a similar place to Burke; see Albert Soboul, 'Violence collective et rapports sociaux. Les foules révolutionnaires, 1789-1795', in *La Révolution française* (Paris, 1984), p.563-82; and David Andress, 'La violence populaire durant la Révolution française: révolte, châtiment et escalade de la terreur d'Etat', in *Les Politiques de la Terreur, 1793-1794*, ed. Michel Biard (Rennes, 2008), p.69-80.
3. See, for example, Alfred Cobban (ed), *The Debate on the French Revolution, 1789-1800* (London, 1950), and Pamela Clemit (ed.), *The Cambridge companion to British literature of the French Revolution in the 1790s* (Cambridge, 2011).

which inspired the *Reflections*, such as the *Exposé de ma conduite* by Mounier (president of the Assemblée nationale during the October Days of 1789), the *Mémoire* by Lally-Tollendal (who, like Mounier, resigned from the Assemblée after those events), and the *Etat de la France* by Calonne (the former *Contrôleur général des finances* who had left France for London following his disgrace in 1787). Burke and his opponents referred to these works, and the reactions that they provoked overlapped with the attacks against the *Reflections*. Thus, when Boissy d'Anglas published the *Observations sur l'ouvrage de M. de Calonne [...]; avec un postscript sur les derniers écrits de MM. Mounier et Lally*, he also took aim at Burke; and James Mackintosh linked Burke with Calonne in the very title he gave to his *Apologie de la Révolution française et de ses admirateurs anglais, en réponse aux attaques d'Edmund Burke; avec quelques remarques sur le dernier ouvrage de M. de Calonne*. An assessment of the French section of the debate in which Burke occupies a central place, will thus allow us to take into account those texts that inspired the *Reflections* and to draw out the importance in that debate of the events of 5 and 6 October 1789 (the October Days).

Contemporaries' evocation of public acts of violence often goes beyond merely enumerating factual matters. In describing the people, these texts use several series of metaphors, especially those of animals, natural elements or savage man.[4] These metaphors are not simply a rhetorical ornament intended to increase the reader's horror (or sometimes his admiration); by means of these metaphors, explanatory models can be constructed, and the limits of the acceptable and unacceptable in terms of popular violence can be defined. By encouraging slippages of meaning and lexical contagion, these rhetorical features create links, demarcate new boundaries and pass judgements. Thus, they themselves become the object of a crucial debate: should those texts that discuss the Revolution and its violence use violent images? Can they even refrain from doing so?[5]

This chapter will firstly explore the way in which authors

4. On violence and nature, see Malcolm Cook's chapter 'Violence in the work of Bernardin de Saint-Pierre', p.191-202.
5. On the political stakes of using a rhetoric of violence, see Pierre Frantz's chapter, 'Violence in the theatre of the Revolution', 121-35.

contrast different metaphors, before turning to the metaphors' boundaries and limits; following an analysis of the debate over metaphors, this chapter ends by considering the transformations these metaphors brought about in the language of the Revolution.

Metaphors against metaphors

The people's depiction as an animal has a long history. For La Bruyère, the people are a 'nombreux troupeau qui [...] paît tranquillement' when they let themselves be led by a 'berger, attentif et soigneux',[6] but for Courtilz de Sandras they become a 'bête brute [...] qui demeurant sans frein court à l'abandon de tous les côtés où son instinct le pousse'.[7] Lally-Tollendal repeats this rhetoric in his *Lettre écrite au très honorable Edmund Burke* (1791): 'Les démagogues ne peuvent plus retenir ces animaux féroces qu'ils ont déchaînés.'[8] When animal metaphors present the people as an instinctive and passionate being, it is clearly dangerous to leave them to their own devices.

Burke, however, rarely uses animal metaphors in the *Reflections*. His most famous example, and one of the most commented upon in British literature, is the expression 'swinish multitude',[9] which is attenuated in the French translation, where it is just a question of a 'multitude bestiale';[10] the people's specifically porcine qualities have utterly disappeared. Further on, the adjective 'quadrimanous' denounces the revolutionary leaders' animal character; in the French, this becomes the somewhat clumsy

6. Jean de La Bruyère, *Les Caractères*, X, 29 [1692] (Paris, 1995), p.385.
7. Courtilz de Sandras, *Testament politique de Louvois* (Cologne, 1695), p.393; cited by Pierre Ronzeaud, *Peuple et représentations sous le règne de Louis XIV: les représentations du peuple dans la littérature politique en France sous le règne de Louis XIV* (Aix-en-Provence, 1988), p.218.
8. Trophime-Gérard de Lally-Tollendal, *Lettre écrite au très honorable Edmund Burke, membre du parlement d'Angleterre* (n.p., 1791), p.44.
9. Edmund Burke, *Reflections on the Revolution in France, and on the proceedings in certain societies in London relative to that event: in a letter intended to have been sent to a gentleman in Paris* (London, Dodsley, 1790), p.117.
10. Edmund Burke, *Réflexions sur la Révolution de France, et sur les procédés de certaines sociétés à Londres, relatifs à cet événement: en forme d'une lettre, qui avoit dû être envoyée d'abord à un jeune homme, à Paris*, 2nd edn (Paris, [1790]), p.163.

'quadrimonse', although the translator emphasises the image by adding an explanatory note: 'N'est-ce pas dans Buffon qu'il est remarqué que la nature a donné quatre mains aux animaux, dont l'instinct semble les porter à tout détruire?'[11] One comes across many 'affreux hurlements' and 'cris perçants' in his account of the October Days, but these are associated with an image that is rather more monstrous and mythological than it is animal: 'on traînait lentement Leurs Majestés au milieu des hurlements horribles, des cris perçants, des danses frénétiques, des propos infâmes, et de toutes les horreurs inexprimables des furies de l'enfer, sous la forme des femmes les plus viles.'[12] The people, in a feminine form, are even more distanced from humanity: now infernal, they are dangerous, violent and horrid by their very nature. One of the images that Burke privileges is that of the savage, and one example may be found in his description of the people escorting the king back to Paris following the October Days: '[Ce spectacle] devait, ou je me suis bien trompé, ressembler à une procession de Sauvages Américains entrant dans Onondaga après quelques-uns des massacres qu'ils appellent leurs victoires, et conduisant dans leurs cabanes, entourées de crânes suspendus, leurs captifs.'[13] Here Burke illustrates the central idea of the *Reflections*: in breaking with tradition, the French Revolutionaries break with civilisation. Further on, he imagines the king pondering the 'transformation étrange et effrayante de ses sujets autrefois civilisés', and condemns the Parisians' 'cannibales appétits'.[14] Taken collectively, these metaphors serve to exclude certain elements and to constitute foils [*repoussoirs*] by which to situate and anathematise those now disparaged elements. The order of society is threatened by those exterior(ised) elements, or, more accurately, by those elements which are at the limits of humanity and civilisation and which burst forth to occupy a place which is not and cannot be theirs.

Metaphors, when deployed by defenders of the Revolution, allow revolutionary violence to be presented instead as a rational

11. Burke, *Réflexions*, p.366.
12. Burke, *Réflexions*, p.147.
13. Burke, *Réflexions*, p.137.
14. Burke, *Réflexions*, p.154 and 303.

and acceptable phenomenon, at least to some extent. They borrow examples from medicine and the natural sciences. Although James Mackintosh writes that outbreaks of violence are unavoidable when the people play a part in a revolution, he presents these acts as a necessary evil: 'La sensibilité qui faiblit à l'aspect d'un mal présent, sans étendre ses regards jusqu'au bien à venir, n'est pas une vertu, parce que ce n'est pas une qualité utile au genre humain: elle arrêterait le bras d'un chirurgien, qui coupe un membre gangrené.'[15] The Revolution must thus be defended, because the resultant good is greater than the evil that inevitably occurs. The Revolution, the people and violence are linked, but not without the addition of a fourth component, namely progress: 'On tenterait inutilement d'augmenter la fertilité du sol sans en favoriser en même temps les excroissances nuisibles. Celui qui, dans de semblables occasions, attend un bien sans mélange, doit se rappeler que l'économie de la nature a invariablement déterminé que les grandes passions étaient sujettes à produire les vertus et les vices.'[16] The laws of politics and nature thus follow the same paths, thereby exonerating the revolutionaries of their violent acts.

The more traditional metaphor of the human torrent, liable to unforeseen and uncontrollable flooding, could of course follow the same logic in describing the power and force of revolutionary acts. Paradoxically, however, those authors who use this metaphor appeal to the actors' responsibility. It was Calonne who first called upon the Revolution's opponents not to remain passive: 'Longtemps, trop longtemps peut-être, la partie du public qu'on peut appeler sensée, s'est tenue à l'écart et a gardé le silence, craignant d'irriter inutilement une foule aveugle, voulant laisser passer l'impétuosité d'un torrent débordé et espérant toujours une résipiscence qui n'est plus à espérer.'[17] Yet Calonne does not explain how one might confront this overflowing torrent. In his *Lettre au très honorable Edmund Burke*, Joseph Priestley

---

15. Jacques [James] Mackintosh, *Apologie de la Révolution française et de ses admirateurs anglais, en réponse aux attaques d'Edmund Burke; avec quelques remarques sur le dernier ouvrage de M. de Calonne* (Paris, Buisson, 1792), p.148.
16. Mackintosh, *Apologie*, p.182-83.
17. Charles-Alexandre de Calonne, *De l'Etat de la France, présent et à venir* (London and Paris, Laurent, 1790), p.305.

explains to his addressee how to prevent these violent torrents from forming:

> Les Rois et les Ministres seuls sont responsables de toute l'effusion de sang, de toute l'anarchie qui accompagnent ces révolutions devenues nécessaires par l'abus qu'ils ont fait de leur pouvoir. Ce sont eux qui, après avoir engorgé les canaux de la justice, sont les premiers à se récrier de ce que le torrent a rompu les digues, et à se plaindre que le pays a souffert de ses débordements.[18]

Whereas the counter-revolutionaries' nature is threatening and furious, that of the Revolution's defenders is rational and controllable; the metaphors of the first group exclude popular violence from society, whereas those of the second group reveal the attempt to integrate and to master that violence.

Metaphor's uncertain boundaries

The metaphors in the debate are not always as clearly delineated as they are in the preceding examples. Opponents of the Revolution skilfully use equivocal terms, whose metaphorical scope is uncertain. The adjective 'barbare', for instance, frequently occurs in translations of Burke's *Réflexions*, and it nearly always has the sense of 'cruel, inhumain' – which is the primary meaning allotted to it in the Academy's dictionary in both the 1762 and 1798 editions – without ever referring to the original opposition between civilised people (the Greeks and the Romans) and the uncivilised other. Only once does the expression 'conquérants barbares' explicitly evoke the barbarians in the text, although arguably the term, due to its constant repetition and its resonance with animals and savages, takes on a metaphorical value in the work as a whole.

Mounier uses few real metaphors in his *Exposé*, but the word 'brigand' takes on a comparable value. The slippage towards this metaphorical value is all the more remarkable in that his starting point is in no way picturesque or euphemistic. On the contrary, Mounier is keen to assert that, in a very real sense, numerous

---

18. Joseph Priestley, *Lettre au très honorable Edmund Burke, au sujet de ses réflexions sur la Révolution de France* (Paris, 1791), p.26.

brigands had mingled with the Parisians on 5 and 6 October. This assertion was to be repeated a great deal, by people including the defenders of the Revolution who wanted to exonerate the people of the violent acts committed at Versailles. The word 'brigand' is repeated so often in Mounier's text that it becomes a dominant motif, and it seems to serve as a metaphor for the people as a whole; thus when he writes 'Les brigands [courent] à l'hôtel des gardes, en égorgent plusieurs qu'ils y rencontrent', it is far from clear whether he is referring to just a part of the crowd or to the mob as a whole. The characteristics of a brigand, beyond the limits of society (a veritable outlaw), a troublemaker and liable to wreak fatal violence, resemble those of the animal, the savage and the barbarian.[19]

There appears in several texts the expression 'horde de brigands',[20] which combines the barbarian with the brigand. In its true sense, the horde is the 'nom que l'on donne aux Peuplades ou Sociétés des Tartares errants, et à des troupes de sauvages'.[21] It is still the only definition given in the 1798 edition of the Academy's dictionary, and when the metaphorical or figurative usage had become widespread during the Revolution.

Mounier too brings forth a veritable monster in his text: 'Deux têtes des gardes du corps furent publiquement promenées dans Versailles; et un monstre, armé d'une hache, portant une longue barbe et un bonnet d'une hauteur extraordinaire, montrait avec ostentation, son visage et ses bras couverts de sang humain.'[22] Is this also a metaphor? Not for Mounier, although the network of images he uses refers yet again to barbarity, and this monstrous figure functions more precisely as an emblem. Presented as real (and yet too good to be true, as it were), the monster becomes an image of popular violence. In this way, the frontiers between metaphors and

---

19. See *Cartouche, Mandrin et autres brigands du XVIIIe siècle*, ed. Lise Andriès (Paris, 2010).
20. See especially Trophime-Gérard de Lally-Tollendal, *Mémoire de Monsieur le Comte de Lally-Tollendal, ou Seconde lettre à ses commettans* (Paris, Desenne, 1790), p.165.
21. *Dictionnaire de l'Académie Française*, 5th edn, 2 vols (Paris, J. J. Smits, 1798), vol.1, p.695.
22. Jean-Joseph Mounier, *Exposé de la conduite de M. Mounier, dans l'Assemblée nationale, et des motifs de son retour en Dauphiné* (Paris, Cuchet, 1789), p.79.

literal expressions are blurred so as to terrify the reader all the more. Similarly, the most frequently used images seem interchangeable; the monster, the savage, the barbarian and the brigand are all variants of the same figure of the violent people.

The debate over metaphors

This way of writing was condemned by defenders of the Revolution. Jean-Baptiste Louvet's *Paris justifié* cites entire passages of the *Exposé* in order to best refute Mounier's attacks:

> Page 68. *Les femmes de Paris formaient divers attroupements, entremêlés d'un certain nombre d'hommes, couverts de haillons pour la plupart*. Hélas! à qui la faute? *Le regard féroce, le geste menaçant, poussant d'affreux hurlements*. Nous pardonnons ici l'hyperbole, en faveur du mouvement oratoire. Cependant, il importe de rétablir les faits dans leur simplicité: ces hommes, que M. Mounier va partout nommer des brigands, c'était, pour la plupart, les ouvriers du faubourg Saint-Antoine.[23]

The criticism of the oratorical effects prepares Louvet's attack against the word 'brigand', which he presents as inappropriate, artificial and utterly out of step with what he calls the 'simplicity' of the facts themselves. Louvet may have been in the margins of the debate opened by Edmund Burke, and his participation may have been limited to his crossing swords with Mounier at the end of 1789, but the questions he raised were nonetheless echoed in Paine and Mackintosh's criticism of Burke's style.

In the *Rights of man*, translated as the *Droits de l'homme*, Thomas Paine presents Burke's text as a dramatic play: 'Je ne puis guère regarder l'ouvrage de M. Burke que comme un drame; et il doit lui-même l'avoir considéré comme tel par les licences poétiques qu'il s'est permises, d'omettre les faits, d'en défigurer d'autres, et d'arranger toute la machine pour produire un effet de théâtre.'[24] The image of the 'drame' allows him to highlight Burke's artifice, and to assign a cause to it: the pursuit of effects. All the emotions

---

23. Jean-Baptiste Louvet, *Paris justifié, contre M. Mounier* (Paris, Bailly, 1789), p.40. Original emphasis, to denote the quotations from Mounier's text.
24. Thomas Paine, *Les Droits de l'homme; en réponse à l'attaque de M. Burke sur la Révolution française* (Paris, Buisson, 1791), p.45.

aroused by Burke's text are thus marked out as the result of a rhetorical 'machine' that inevitably distances the reader from the true facts.

For Mackintosh, Burke is victim to his own illusions: 'son imagination avait peuplé la France de conspirations, d'assassinats, de massacres, et de toute la race des chimères épouvantables, qui sont les fruits d'une imagination fertile, aidée d'une extrême sensibilité'.[25] By reproaching Burke for his 'imagination fertile' and 'extrême sensibilité', Mackintosh claims that his own account of the Revolution is closer to the facts and dictated by reason. The expression 'chimères épouvantables' and the enumeration 'de conspirations, d'assassinats, de massacres' serve to disqualify all of Burke's accusations. The technique used by the author of the *Reflections'* author is thus turned against him; while the contagion of metaphors gives a certain forcefulness to his condemnation of the Revolution, it also allows his opponents to refute all his accusations at once, dismissing them as nothing more than rhetorical effects or pure imagination. Nevertheless, the kind of writing that Mackintosh proposes to describe the Revolution is not devoid of effect; paradoxically, he underlines the horror of popular violence throughout his text. While Burke is accused of distorting the facts, they are, in and of themselves, no less likely to elicit a sense of horror:

> Les massacres de la guerre et les meurtres commis par le glaive de la justice, sont défigurés par la solennité qui les accompagne. Mais la justice sauvage du peuple a une horreur nue et sans déguisement. Ses plus légers efforts excitent toute notre indignation, tandis que le meurtre et la rapine, revêtus des ornements pompeux des actes de l'Etat, peuvent paraître avec impunité dans le monde.[26]

Popular violence is more revolting, it is more of an affront, but therein lies its merit; institutionalised violence provokes no horror because it is hidden, but it is no less guilty for being occluded.

Mackintosh insists upon the value of truth in writing as well as in society. Coherent in his principles, he refuses rhetorical artifice

---

25. Mackintosh, *Apologie*, p.4-5.
26. Mackintosh, *Apologie*, p.157.

and the 'ornements pompeux des actes de l'Etat' alike. The savage man thus takes on more positive connotations; closer to nature, 'nu et sans déguisement', he is closer to truth, even if he is violent and cruel. But with the adjective 'sauvage', Mackintosh reintroduces into his text one of the principal metaphors used by the Revolution's adversaries. Can the subtlety of his argument withstand the persuasive force of an image that presents the people as a threat to society?

The profusion of metaphors

The image of the savage is also found in Boissy d'Anglas's *Observations sur l'ouvrage de M. de Calonne*, whose author effects a strange combination and a significant reversal:

> Après les agitations des peuples, arrive nécessairement un calme profond: c'est le sommeil des nations, pendant lequel leurs tyrans veillent. Il faut donc qu'avant de s'y abandonner, les peuples se soient préservés d'avance des entreprises de leurs ennemis; comme le sauvage de l'Amérique, avant de se livrer au repos, prépare autour de sa demeure des barrières, insurmontables aux bêtes féroces, que la nuit pourrait amener.[27]

If the people are indeed savage, they are calm, civilised, even *civilising* savages, and far from being destructive, they are in fact constructive ('prépare autour de sa demeure des barrières'). But they must protect themselves against even greater savagery, namely 'les bêtes féroces'. The conventional accusation is thus reversed, and is now applied to tyrants, for Mackintosh and Paine both accuse the *ancien régime* of barbarity; Mackintosh states that '[le people] a été accoutumé à la barbarie par ses oppresseurs',[28] while Paine condemns the barbaric punishments of the *ancien régime*.[29] The question is thus not *if* there are any barbarians, but rather *where* they might be. And as one text follows another, these

---

27. François-Antoine de Boissy d'Anglas, *Observations sur l'ouvrage de M. de Calonne intitulé De l'état de la France présent et à venir; et à son occasion, sur les principaux actes de l'Assemblée nationale; avec un postscript sur les derniers écrits de MM. Mounier et Lally* (Paris, Le Boucher, 1791), p.22.
28. Mackintosh, *Apologie*, p.147.
29. Paine, *Droits de l'homme*, p.41.

barbarians increasingly overrun all the language that is used to describe the Revolution.[30]

The success of the word 'horde' is especially evident in the revolutionary songs; for instance, *La Marseillaise*,[31] after asking if one can hear 'dans nos campagnes / Mugir ces féroces soldats', begins the following verse with the question 'Que veut cette horde d'esclaves, / de traîtres, de roi conjurés?' The *Réveil du peuple* of Year III answers this question: 'Tu souffres qu'une horde atroce / Et d'assassins et de brigands, / Souille par son souffle féroce / Le territoire des vivants.'[32] The name of a barbaric people enters a specifically revolutionary vocabulary with the debate over vandals and vandalism from Year III onwards. Violence is firmly embedded in revolutionary discourse.

What is true for the barbarians is true for other images. The example of Louis-Sébastien Mercier reveals an evolution in the choice of words to describe the people, violence and the Revolution. At the time of the October Days, Mercier defended the people in his newspaper, the *Annales patriotiques*; he evoked violence in a very factual manner, free from metaphors and without the hint of a brigand in the text. To conclude his account, he wrote on 12 October: 'le Peuple Français ne manque jamais d'humanité et de générosité, que lorsqu'on le pousse aux extrêmes et qu'on l'insulte sans raison dans ses droits et dans son existence'.[33] Nine years later, in the *Nouveau Paris*, the same events are subject to an entirely different treatment:

> Ce monstre! Je l'ai vu: il fut longtemps esclave au Maroc, dont le souverain compte au nombre de ses menus plaisirs celui de faire sauter cinq à six têtes chaque matin avant de déjeuner. C'est là qu'il s'est exercé par force à l'horrible métier qu'il fit ensuite par goût à Paris.
>
> On rapporte qu'à Versailles, cet homme féroce, pour empêcher

---

30. On the increasingly violent language of the Revolution, see Rebecca Sopchik, 'Violence and the monster: the *Private lives* of the duc d'Orléans', p.203-20.
31. Or, to give it its proper title, *Le Chant de guerre pour l'armée du Rhin*, composed by Rouget de Lisle in 1792.
32. Cited by Pierre Michel, *Un Mythe romantique, les Barbares, 1789-1848* (Lyon, 1981), p.48.
33. Louis-Sébastien Mercier, *Annales patriotiques et littéraires de la France* 10 (12 October 1789).

que la pluie n'enlevât le sang qui colorait sa barbe (qu'il porta longtemps), la tenait à l'abri sous sa redingote. Il disait en revenant à Paris après la nuit du 6 octobre 1789: *C'était bien la peine de me faire aller là-bas pour deux têtes!*[34]

Mercier takes up Mounier's monster, transforming it into a fantastical and picturesque figure, an exemplary barbarian that can now speak the truth of the events in October. This is more than a simple change in perspective, for Mercier testifies to a profound change in revolutionary discourse.[35] However, such a way of writing about the Revolution does not date from 10 August,[36] nor from the Terror, nor indeed from the Thermidorean Reaction, for in 1790 Edmund Burke had already shown that, in Stéphanie Genand's words, 'the structure provided by dates and periods dissolves, giving way to the potency of horrific scenes'.[37]

Mackintosh condemns the violence of the language of Burke's *Reflections* and his 'harangues incendiaires contre la violence',[38] although he nevertheless recognises that such a style of writing possesses a certain force: 'Indépendant des lois ordinaires de la méthode, il peut faire avancer un groupe d'horreurs éclatantes, pour faire une brèche dans nos cœurs, par laquelle la canaille la plus indisciplinée d'arguments peut entrer en triomphe.'[39] Paine, on the contrary, claims to perceive in that violence a sign of weakness, and makes the populace (as it is conceived by Burke himself) a metaphor of his adversary's style: 'Son intention était d'attaquer la révolution Française; mais au lieu de s'avancer en ordre, il l'a assaillie par une *populace* d'idées qui sont tombées les unes sur les autres, et se sont entre-détruites.'[40]

Whether it is 'la canaille la plus indisciplinée d'arguments' or 'une populace d'idées', Burke's style has the same chaotic violence

34. Louis-Sébastien Mercier, ch.88, 'Coupeur de têtes', *Le Nouveau Paris*, ed. Jean-Claude Bonnet ([1798] Paris, 1994), p.365.
35. It should be noted that the way in which violence unfolds in *Le Nouveau Paris* of 1798 is similar to that in the fictional works studied by Stéphanie Genand; see 'Dreaming the Terror: the other stage of revolutionary violence', p.49-60.
36. For an account of the literary responses to this massacre, see Catriona Seth's chapter, 'The "dix août" (10 August 1792) in literary texts', p.79-92.
37. See Genand, 'Dreaming the Terror', p.52.
38. Mackintosh, *Apologie*, p.4.
39. Mackintosh, *Apologie*, p.6.
40. Paine, *Droits de l'homme*, p.160.

as the basest groups of society, but it is precisely that which gives it its forcefulness and its energy. Hugo may well have said 'J'ai mis un bonnet rouge au vieux dictionnaire';[41] but if we take Paine and Mackintosh's word for it, Burke had already done so.

The debate over popular violence and the debate over metaphors coincide. The people swarm into the places of power and the barbarians invade language; passions burst forth as much in the realm of politics as in the realm of discourse. What place can be given to a people driven by its passions and whose acts elicit horror? What place can be given to images produced by those passions and which are likely to propagate them further? If the debate still seems open in the first years of the Revolution, those writers who refuse metaphors in the name of the true historical facts did not prevent brigands, savages and monsters from gradually invading all revolutionary language. These images increased in number thanks to their polemical force and the slippages in meaning to which they were prone. Linguistic violence did not develop at the same pace as popular violence. The language used to describe the Revolution was already rich in violent imagery in the first texts of the debate opened up by Edmund Burke, when writers were discussing the storming of the Bastille and above all the October Days, that is to say well before 10 August 1792, the September Massacres or the Terror. After Thermidor and Robespierre's fall, linguistic violence, far from diminishing, came to a head, playing an essential role in the normalisation of political life by excluding the people. The return to political order occurred through the violent condemnation of everyone accused of threatening society; a return to linguistic order took place more slowly over the following years, during the Consulate and above all during the Empire. The French Revolution thus appears as the story of the explosion of violence in politics and language, then of its control and its gradual exploitation. Order was re-established, but political and literary passions were always ready to burst forth again.

---

41. Victor Hugo, *Les Contemplations* (1856), I.7, 'Réponse à un acte d'accusation'. On this line and the date of its composition (1854), see Tony James, 'Le "bonnet rouge" de Victor Hugo', http://groupugo.div.jussieu.fr/groupugo/89-12-16james.htm.

Dreaming the Terror: the other stage of revolutionary violence[1]

STÉPHANIE GENAND

> LISETTE
>
> Pourquoi donc a-t-il la bizarrerie d'ennuyer le premier venu du récit de ses songes. Est-il question d'un événement, se passe-t-il quelque chose d'extraordinaire, il y trouve toujours l'explication d'un de ses rêves. Ma foi, Madame, vous l'avouerez avec moi, cette manie n'annonce pas un homme très raisonnable.
>
> EMILIE
>
> Chacun n'a-t-il pas la sienne, et celle des rêves est plus à la mode que tu ne penses, Lisette.
>
> Charles-Guillaume Etienne,
> *Le Rêve, opéra-comique en un acte et en prose*[2]

If violence structures the political practices of the *ancien régime*, founded upon 'le grand spectacle de la punition physique' analysed by Michel Foucault in *Surveiller et punir*,[3] its banality paradoxically provides no key for making sense of the unprecedented radicalism of the Revolution. Sensitive to the rupture marked by the massacres perpetrated in and after 1789, contemporaries sensed the singularity of events that exceeded the existing paradigms:

---

1. Translated by Lucas Wood.
2. Charles-Guillaume Etienne, *Le Rêve, opéra-comique en un acte et en prose* (Paris, Vente, An VII), p.8. With music by Gresnich, this work was first performed at the Théâtre de l'Opéra Comique National on 8 Pluviôse An VII.
3. Michel Foucault, *Surveiller et punir: naissance de la prison* (Paris, 1975), p.21.

> La révolution anglaise des années 1640 n'avait pas rompu l'ordre éternel des révolutions politiques. Il n'en est rien avec la Révolution française, quand, contrairement à ce qui se passe dans les autres pays affectés par les mêmes mouvements au même moment, elle est comprise [...] comme une rupture affichée avec le passé et ses codes. [...] La violence ne s'inscrit plus dans les cycles historiques, elle les rompt.[4]

Overturning the humanist project of the Enlightenment and the cyclical conception of history, the Revolution demanded a new system of thought capable of ascribing a political and moral meaning to the violence that emphatically marked the collapse of the *ancien régime*. This reflection has consequences of the highest order, in that it concerns the very essence of the events; only by understanding this violence is it possible to justify the successive stages of this unparalleled upheaval.

Such a project, however, comes up against a historical problem. An analysis of violence presupposes that one can identify it, that one can determine its place in the chain of events: is it an inherent part of the Revolution, or must it be partitioned into a series of discrete days and phases? The first contemporary analyses responded to these fundamental questions in a way that privileged the hypothesis of circumscription. Far from constituting a principle of the Revolution, violence remains an anomalous parenthesis, legitimated, in the parlance of the times, by 'les circonstances actuelles' or the interests of 'le salut public'. The Reign of Terror, imputed to Robespierre alone, becomes the strategic backdrop for a historiography anxious to preserve the sense of a coherent struggle for freedom. This selective excision, which is indispensable for smothering the 'passion de la revanche' that Bronislaw Baczko calls the principle of Thermidorian politics,[5] first appears in 1796 under the pen of Germaine de Staël. *De l'influence des passions* opens with a deliberately elliptical tableau of the bloody days that had just rocked France: 'C'est donc en

---

4. Jean-Clément Martin, 'Violence et révolution', in *Historiographies, concepts et débats II*, ed. Christian Delacroix, François Dosse, Patrick Garcia and Nicolas Offenstadt (Paris, 2010), p.1276-83 (1277).
5. Bronislaw Baczko, 'Une passion thermidorienne: la revanche', in *Politiques de la Révolution française* (Paris, 2008), p.165-338.

écartant cette époque monstrueuse, c'est à l'aide des autres événements principaux de la Révolution de France et de l'histoire de tous les peuples, que j'essaierai de réunir des observations impartiales sur les gouvernements.'[6] The reality of violence seems undeniable, but it is contained within the chronological limits of Robespierre's reign. Historical localisation is combined with the designation of an individual perpetrator who 's'était identifié avec la Terreur'.[7] The boundaries of its action having been delimited, violence is assigned, in the absence of an explanation, an autonomous territory that the historian may strategically avoid.[8]

The fiction published in the wake of 9 Thermidor makes for a much more complex place for revolutionary violence. The firmly traced contours marked off in political treatises give way to a mosaic of unforgettable bloody episodes not necessarily associated with the Terror; thus the execution of Foullon and Berthier, the storming of the Bastille, the attack on the Tuileries, the September Massacres, and the beheading of the king become the new leitmotivs of the post-revolutionary novel. Rather than corroborating the historiographers' model, fiction emancipates violence from the spectre of 1793 and chooses to restore its terrible continuity. If these events are not proper to a politics of the Terror, they nevertheless participate in its 'économie émotive', based, as Sophie Wahnich has shown, on the convergence of the terrible with the sacred.[9] Beyond their chronological disparity – they range from the earliest days of the Revolution to the execution of Robespierre – these literary texts display the same shocked paralysis before the spectacle of bodies or political emblems profaned by popular fury. Whereas historiography rel-

6. Germaine de Staël, *De l'influence des passions sur le bonheur des individus et des nations* (1796, Lausanne, Jean Mourer), ed. Florence Lotterie and Laurence Vanoflen, in *Œuvres complètes (Série I: Œuvres critiques)*, 2 vols (Paris, 2008), vol.1, p.134.
7. Germaine de Staël, *Réflexions sur la paix adressées à M. Pitt et aux Français* (1795, Paris, Michel), ed. Lucien Jaume, in *Œuvres complètes (Série III: Œuvres historiques)*, 3 vols (Paris, 2009), vol.1, p.88.
8. On violence, history and commemoration in fiction, see also the chapters by Catriona Seth (p.75-82), Michèle Vallenthini (p.93-102) and Michel Delon (p.251-62).
9. See Sophie Wahnich, 'De l'économie émotive de la Terreur', *Annales HSS* 4 (2002), p.889-913.

egates the massacres to the anthropological margins of a 'monstrous' Terror, narrative fiction portrays a palpable landscape of fear in which violence is no longer defined in terms of historical criteria. The structure provided by dates and periods dissolves, giving way to the potency of horrific scenes conceived as images that resist representation. If violence, here a heterogeneous category, is no longer subject to the obstacles of chronology, it engenders a further aesthetic, philosophical and moral dilemma: how can these pictures of horror be made visible? What concepts, what language should be mobilised to think the unthinkable and to speak the unspeakable? What kind of narrative can recount the eruption of raw, frenzied passion? The first lines of *L'Influence des passions* spell out this impossible wager forced upon the writers of the Directoire:

> La génération qui nous suivra examinera peut-être aussi la cause et l'influence de ces deux années; mais nous, les contemporains, les compatriotes des victimes immolées dans ces jours de sang, avons-nous pu conserver alors le don de généraliser les idées, de méditer les abstractions, de nous séparer un moment de nos impressions pour les analyser? Non, aujourd'hui même encore, le raisonnement ne saurait approcher de ce temps incommensurable. Juger ces événements, de quelques noms qu'on les désigne, c'est les faire entrer dans l'ordre des idées existantes, des idées pour lesquelles il y avait déjà des expressions.[10]

Only just extricated from the operations of history, violence, incomprehensible and unnameable, slips away from the authors who would try to reconstruct it.

This series of impasses leaves those who hope to represent the horror of the Revolution no other choice but to wait for the passage of time to dull memories and to allay grief. Thanks to an effect of artificial distantiation, such a strategy of postponement makes it possible to sketch a picture of events whose awful power demands either the veil of retrospection, or else the reassuring fragmentariness of the epistolary form. Writing *a posteriori* and filtering the narrative through the perspective of an affective subject means that the unity of the whole canvas is suppressed,

---

10. Germaine de Staël, *De l'influence des passions*, p.134.

and that only the lurid sparks of historical violence shine forth. However, this technique, which characterises certain great (partly historical) novels including *L'Emigré* and *Delphine*, does not exhaust the avenues of representation available at the turn of the century. Torn between the polarised prerogatives of history and fiction, the paradoxical programme outlined in prefaces conjures up another stage upon which these violent tableaux can take form. This writing, where narrative may unfold unfettered by reason or time, adopts as its model the world of dreams. The dream, a genuine genre of the late Enlightenment operative well beyond its consecration by Mercier, was established as the aesthetic equivalent and mirror of events that defy both chronology and thought. Although its utility for imagining alternative histories makes the dream an ideal vehicle for the sort of political reflection particularly acute at the beginning of the Revolution – such an agenda animates, among others, *Le Génie conciliateur, rêve d'un citoyen*,[11] *Le Rêve d'un homme de bien, adressé aux illustres représentants de la nation française*,[12] and *Le Rêve d'un patriote éveillé*[13] – this literary form progressively dons a more sombre countenance and abandons the ideological sphere to become a transposition of horror. Inseparable from a historical moment marked by the increasing difficulty of distinguishing reality from illusion, reason from madness, the dream narrative constitutes a privileged field of inquiry in the search for violence's subterranean traces. Reinhart Koselleck emphasises the need to plumb this source when analysing contexts dominated by the protagonists' fear:

> Les rêves sont les témoins de formes d'expérience *in eventu*. Ils nous parlent des rapports qui se nouent dans la synchronie entre persécuteurs et persécutés, rapports inhérents à la terreur agissante. Plus qu'aucune image extérieure, aucune photographie, aucun film même ne pourrait jamais le faire, ils nous montrent l'état de l'homme soumis à la terreur. C'est en cela qu'ils sont un témoignage infiniment supérieur aux notes prises au jour le jour dans des perspectives changeantes par définition, comme aux mémoires rédigés *ex post factum*. La source si difficilement access-

---

11. Anonymous, *Le Génie conciliateur, rêve d'un citoyen* (1789).
12. Anonymous, *Le Rêve d'un homme de bien, adressé aux illustres représentants de la nation française*, par M. Tri*** (Paris, Prudhomme, 1789).
13. Anonymous, *Le Rêve d'un patriote éveillé* (1790).

ible qu'est le rêve ne doit donc pas être totalement écartée du domaine de l'historien, si délicate qu'en soit, par ailleurs, l'interprétation.[14]

Exempt from the laws of linearity, and authorised both to represent the unrealistic and to meld history and fantasy, the dream serves the Terror as the only narrative model capable of rendering its unprecedented violence.

Before the dream's emergence as a free-standing genre, focused on a character's nightmare, its strategic possibilities were exploited by novelists writing under the Directoire. *L'Emigré*, published in 1797 but set during the Terror, repeatedly interrupts its epistolary dynamic to evoke the paralysing effect of the execution of political figures. These scenes, linked to the bloody executions that punctuate the early months of the Revolution, immobilise onlookers' reason and impose themselves as unbearable but recurring visions. Saint-Alban's mother succumbs to their dreadful effects after coming upon the gory heads of Foullon and Bertier being paraded around Paris:

> Le hasard avait fait rencontrer à ma mère la troupe de cannibales qui promenait les têtes sanglantes de Bertier et Foullon, avec lesquels elle avait eu quelques liaisons; à cet effroyable aspect elle tomba évanouie dans sa voiture, on la ramena chez elle, et sa santé déjà languissante ne résista pas à l'atteinte que lui porta ce hideux spectacle; elle se réveillait en sursaut, poursuivie en rêve par l'aspect des visages affreux et déformés de ces malheureux victimes des fureurs populaires.[15]

Although the violence of the scene renders the character unconscious, it bypasses the defences of oblivion to mobilise another register of representation. The disappearance of realistic details – the names of the victims, the individuality of their faces – allows for the production of a 'spectacle' whose imagery compensates for the insufficiency of descriptive language. This process of transference, whereby the dream is substituted for the narrative of the event, becomes even more explicit when it affects the letter-writer himself. The marquis does not witness the execution

---

14. Reinhart Koselleck, 'Terreur et rêve', in *Le Futur passé: contribution à la sémantique des temps historiques* (Paris, 2000), p.249-62 (261).
15. Gabriel Sénac de Meilhan, *L'Emigré*, ed. Michel Delon (Paris, 2004), p.81.

of the wardens of the Bastille, but he does watch his fiancée fall victim to the sack of her estate:

> J'abrège un récit affreux, qui ne pourrait exciter que l'horreur; je me bornerai à dire qu'elle fut inhumainement traînée dans un cachot, après avoir vu brûler son château; qu'elle y expira dans des convulsions affreuses excitées par la terreur. [...] L'image de Mme de Grandville expirante au milieu d'une multitude furieuse était sans cesse présente à mon esprit, ses cris douloureux retentissaient dans mes oreilles, et ce terrible souvenir pénètre encore en ce moment mon âme, d'un sentiment qui la déchire.[16]

Paralipsis, combined with the acceleration of a narrative transformed into a lapidary summary, discovers in the 'image' the most effective means of transmitting the horror aroused by the lynching scene. Placing reason in abeyance, the nightmare embraces the spectator's terror while distancing him from the objective reality of the murder. This oscillation between dread and denial prevails when events overwhelm the onlooker's emotional resistance. The beheading of the king, recounted by the président de Longueil, stands out in *L'Emigré* as a particularly intense paroxysm of historical violence. The political incomprehensibility of an act literally unthinkable to a pillar of the aristocracy is magnified by the horror of beholding the sacred body's agony (p.115):

> Mais la plus atroce barbarie fait retentir l'air d'un bruit affreux qui couvre ses faibles accents; enfin le crime comble l'intervalle immense qui est entre le trône et l'échafaud, entre le supplice et l'innocence. Cette affreuse image me revient sans cesse dans la pensée, et le jour, et la nuit. A tout ce qu'elle a de déchirant pour le cœur, se joint un tel étonnement pour l'esprit, que je suis quelquefois tenté de croire que cette terrible catastrophe n'est qu'un songe affreux.

The président is cognisant of the paradoxes of representation, but they conceal from him the more disturbing aspect of this 'dream-writing'. Louis XVI's death does not simply defy thought and feeling; relayed by an aristocrat with a prestigious place in the *ancien régime*, it symbolically prefigures the old order's disappear-

---

16. Sénac de Meilhan, *L'Emigré*, p.81.

ance inscribed in the monarch's decapitation. The image is a mechanism that sustains its shock effect by forcing upon the protagonist a projection of his own identity, rendered porous by a tragic end in which his own fate is mirrored. The doubling of the subject, which is fundamental to the dream, communicates the unparalleled dread and dismay inspired by the death of the royal couple. If Longueil manages to master the nightmare of the loss of the self, it takes absolute hold of the comtesse de Lowenstein, who dies imagining her own head on the block in place of Marie-Antoinette's (p.428):

> Le médecin avait un habit noir; elle l'a pris pour un prêtre: 'Je meurs innocente, Monsieur, donnez-moi l'absolution.' Elle a voulu couper ses cheveux; nous nous y sommes fortement opposés, et elle les a relevés, ensuite prenant le portrait du Marquis. [...] Cette scène a fini par un long assoupissement, et à son réveil elle a été encore plus agitée; toujours parlant de bourreaux et de guillotine, comme s'ils étaient sous ses yeux.

Displaced from the stage of history to that of fiction, violence is written in the script of dark dreams, crazed identification and decapitated doubles.

The aesthetic power of this disturbance, which so fascinated writers at the turn of the century, progressively dismantles the narrative structure. Deploying a form of writing that flouts realism and the principles of composition, the nightmare swamps the formal limits within which Sénac had succeeded in keeping it provisionally contained. Dreaming the Terror means accepting an unrestrained text in which fear is the dominant principle, and not simply a feature of tangential episodes. Such a programme defines the corpus of 'rêves effrayants' that crop up around 1800. These fifteen or so narratives, each centred on a narrator's historical nightmare, construct an imaginary space symptomatic of the literary landscape after the Terror. Mme de Staël emphasises in *De l'Allemagne* (1810) that 'vingt ans de révolution ont donné à l'imagination d'autres besoins que ceux qu'elle éprouvait quand les romans de Crébillon peignaient l'amour et la société du temps'.[17] The transposition of horrifying images answers this new

---

17. Germaine de Staël, *De l'Allemagne*, ed. Simone Balayé, 2 vols (Paris, 1968), vol.1, p.258.

demand, the outline of which Sade also traced in his *Idée sur les romans*. Bringing the Terror to the fore seems to be the watchword of a literature compelled to devise an aesthetic commensurate with the magnitude of the era's historical upheavals. Two texts are particularly illustrative of the ways in which the nightmare's potential is tapped along these lines: *Le Comte d'Artois à l'agonie à la suite de sa confession, rêve d'un membre du clergé*, published anonymously in 1789,[18] and the *Descente de Louis Capet dans la région des ombres, ou rêve d'un citoyen philosophe*, authored by a certain 'Dufey' in 1800.[19] Although separated by the revolutionary decade, both works consist of tales of the horror experienced in their protagonists' dreams, as their titles suggest, and despite the chronological gap, they share important motifs. Fear originates in each from the spectacle of a violent episode of the Revolution, the deaths of Foullon and Bertier, and the execution of the king in 1793. Rather than being contemplated at a distance, narrated by a third party or in a retrospective letter, these scenes take place directly under the gaze of characters who are witness to these memorable events. The filter of ideology only intervenes when history clashes with the convictions of the observers. The comte d'Artois remains a fervent enemy of the Revolution, and in his eyes, the attack on the Bastille is the first chapter of an unimaginable history that returns regularly to haunt him with the vision of two severed heads:

> Voilà la Bastille qui tire, aux armes, avançons, nous allons voir beau jeu... Ah, dieux! Quel spectacle...! Les têtes de mes amis au bout des piques! Ah, de Launay! Comment t'es-tu laissé prendre? Je te croyais intrépide, je croyais que tu aimais le sang. [...] Après un instant de repos, sa rage s'est rallumée, il croyait entendre la Bastille s'écrouler, il la voyait tomber, et il craignait d'être écrasé sous ses ruines. 'Ôtez-moi, ôtez-moi, disait-il, périrais-je sous ces tours faites pour me défendre, et qui auraient dû écraser les monstres devant qui elles se courbent. Enlevez donc ce cadavre, qu'ai-je besoin de voir ce Delaunay; quelle tête hideuse; eh bien, que me veux-tu? Est-ce moi qui ai répandu ton sang?'[20]

---

18. Anonymous, *Le Comte d'Artois à l'agonie à la suite de sa confession: rêve d'un membre du clergé* ([Paris?], 1789).
19. Dufey, *Descente de Louis Capet dans la région des ombres, ou rêve d'un citoyen philosophe* (Paris, chez les marchands de nouveautés, An VIII).
20. *Le Comte d'Artois à l'agonie*, p.10-11.

The monologue of the hallucinating narrator, convinced that he is buried beneath a ruined building, adopts a nightmarish dissolution of the distinction between the living and the dead, reality and illusion, that ultimately drags his discourse down into madness. Although the event is never represented objectively, the techniques of literary fantasy allow its violence (displaced from Artois's memory) to glare forth all the more brutally. The same strategy of ellipsis and transference reappears in the *Descente de Louis Capet dans la région des ombres*. Curiosity impels the narrator, who lives withdrawn from the capital by choice, to return there on the day appointed for Louis XVI's execution: 'Mais le dénouement de la catastrophe, qui fit monter Louis Capet sur un échafaud, après être descendu du plus brillant trône de la terre, m'inspira la curiosité d'aller à Paris, pour être spectateur de son exécution, et examiner s'il subirait la mort en héros.'[21] Despite being advertised as a fascinating spectacle, the king's death disappears from the narrative, which omits it and privileges instead the dream that comes to the main character upon his return home (p.6):

> Je revins dans ma retraite occupé de mille réflexions, et quelques moments après un repas frugal, je me couchai tout épuisé de la fatigue que j'avais essuyée par cette frappante journée, et je m'endormis profondément. Pendant six heures que dura mon sommeil, je fus travaillé par un rêve qui me fit suer extraordinairement. J'en fus si singulièrement frappé, qu'à mon réveil je pris la plume pour le mettre par écrit, et le communiquer à mes amis. Le voici.

This detour turns out to be less an ellipsis than a kind of transposition, or rather 'transcoding'. Strikingly absent from the objective stage, the royal execution inspires and underpins a nightmare based on the subject's imaginative projection (p.7):

> Ayant vu tomber la tête du coupable Louis Capet sous le couteau de la loi, il me sembla que la mort impitoyable avait aussi tranché le fil de mes jours avec sa faux. Mon ombre descendue dans la région des morts, aperçut des yeux une foule d'autres ombres sur les bords du Styx, qui présentaient à Caron leur pièce de monnaie pour passer ce fleuve dans sa barque.

21. *Descente de Louis Capet dans la région des ombres*, p.5.

Elaborating on the anxiety that was only hinted at by the président de Longueil, the narrator undertakes a full-fledged descent into Hades and accompanies 'l'infortuné Louis Capet' (p.14) to the tribunal that will judge him in the underworld. Surrounded by the trappings of Greek mythology, including Minos and Rhadamanthus, whom he meets beyond the Styx, the character moves across a stage upon which the obscure episodes of history are replayed. Confronted with the spectre of his crimes and with a host of intransigent ancestors who condemn his weakness, the king has no choice but to remain in this funereal domain. The narrator, who is allowed to leave the realm of shades, wakes up bathed in sweat the moment he reaches the surface. For all that the nightmare ends with a final restitution of identities, it nevertheless disorients reason in its exploration of an alternative knowledge (p.2): 'Ce n'est que quand on a quitté la vie terrestre, que l'on n'a plus les yeux fascinés, et que l'on voit les choses telles qu'elles sont en elles-mêmes.' Hell holds up to revolutionary violence the mirror of an unsettling and upside-down world. The infernal journey is a lesson in the confusion of eras and generations, the impotence of reason, and the paralysing, transfixing effect of the image. It is such terms that in the *Considérations sur la Révolution française* (1818) Mme de Staël describes 'le gouvernement appelé le règne de la terreur':

> On ne sait comment approcher des quatorze mois qui ont suivi la proscription de la Gironde, le 31 mai 1793. Il semble qu'on descende comme le Dante de cercle en cercle, toujours plus bas dans les enfers. [...] Les faits se confondent à cette époque, et l'on craint de ne pouvoir entrer dans une telle histoire, sans que l'imagination en conserve d'ineffaçables traces de sang.[22]

Never have considerations ('*considérations*') and fascination ('*sidération*') been separated by so tenuous a margin.

Violence may, from 1795 onwards, constitute a historiographical and philosophical challenge – within which dates might we circumscribe it, how might we think about it? But in the wake of the Revolution, fiction undoubtedly (and paradoxically) offers

22. Germaine de Staël, *Considérations sur la Révolution française*, ed. Jacques Godechot (Paris, 2000), p.303.

another stage on which to recount violence. From the epistolary novel that privileges the characters' interior agonies and the fragmentation of consciousness, to the 'rêves effrayants' that liberate storytelling from the burden of verisimilitude, another stage takes shape, upon which violence finds its truest means of expression.

Gothic explosions: Révéroni Saint-Cyr's
Pauliska ou La Perversité moderne[1]

PIERRE SAINT-AMAND

In *Mesmerism and the end of the Enlightenment in France*, Robert Darnton recreates the climate within which mesmerism took root in French culture in the period around the 1780s, the decade preceding the Revolution. He shows how magnetism was enmeshed within an utterly original landscape mixing the scientific with the pseudoscientific. At the heart of the theory that Mesmer applied to medicine, Darnton writes, was the 'discovery of a superfine fluid that penetrated and surrounded all bodies'.[2] Mesmerist experiments consisted of trances and other 'performances'.[3] As is well known, mesmerist treatments quickly took on an erotic flavour. The description of the 'crisis room' (p.6) with its collection of gadgets, including the doctor's famous wand, imbues magnetism with this erotic element, to say nothing of the magnetisers' laying on of hands: 'they sat with the patient's knees enclosed between their own and ran their fingers all over the patient's body, seeking the poles of the small magnets that composed the great magnet of the body as a whole' (p.4). Darnton also describes the suggestive décor of Mesmer's clinic; he is intrigued by the architecture of the rooms where patients were treated: 'Heavy carpets, weird, astrological wall-decorations, and drawn curtains shut him off from the outside world and muffled the occasional words, screams, and bursts of hysterical laughter that broke the habitual heavy silence. Shafts of fluid struck him constantly in the somber light reflected by strategically placed mirrors' (p.8). For Darnton, Mesmer's success can be understood

1. Translated by Jennifer Curtiss Gage.
2. Robert Darnton, *Mesmerism and the end of the Enlightenment in France* (Cambridge, 1968), p.3. See also Barbara Maria Stafford, *Body criticism: imaging the unseen in Enlightenment art and medicine* (Cambridge, MA, 1991), p.450-56.
3. Darnton, *Mesmerism*, p.4.

in the context of the increasingly 'baroque' proliferation of pseudosciences, each one vying to outdo the others in esoteric extremes (p.44). Above all he operated at the crux of science and fiction, necessarily invoking imagination to convey discoveries that were inadequately expressed in the purified language of fantasy. Widespread interest in mesmerism and the success of the movement thus occupied the gap left by the deficiencies of official science.

It is against this backdrop that vestiges of magnetism would emerge, in the following decade, in the text of *Pauliska ou La Perversité moderne* by Jacques-Antoine de Révéroni Saint-Cyr (1798). Michel Delon, recalling in his preface to *Pauliska* the context of scientific progress in the eighteenth century, linked Révéroni's text with the famous German doctor and described as follows the milieu in which Mesmer and his teachings met with such success: 'L'engouement de l'opinion, la caution de certains savants, la constitution d'un réseau européen pour soutenir et diffuser les thèses de Mesmer frappèrent l'imagination. Il semblait qu'il y eût là un pouvoir occulte s'exerçant sur les individus mais risquant de s'exercer sur les Etats.'[4] But in Révéroni's text, mesmerism, with its amalgam of the erotic and the bizarre, is primarily employed in the service of violence inflicted upon the body. The elements of mesmerism that are adopted and exploited by the novelist are its power structure and supremely fantastical inventions along with its imaginary leanings.[5]

This unusual post-Terror *roman noir*, which transposes the French political scene to an Eastern European setting, indeed serves as a vessel for a number of pseudosciences; it even acts them out in a terrifying manner. The story of Countess Pauliska, who flees her native Poland after the Russian invasion, portrays a geography ravaged by episodes of war: she travels from Ust to Buda, passes through Italy, and finally takes refuge in Lausanne. But various stops in the course of this perilous journey through

4. Michel Delon, preface to Jacques-Antoine de Révéroni Saint-Cyr, *Pauliska ou La Perversité moderne: mémoires récents d'une Polonaise* (Paris, 1991), p.13. All references to the novel will be noted parenthetically in the main body of the text.
5. On turn-of-the-century novels and violence, see the essays by Stéphanie Genand (p.49-60), Catriona Seth (p.75-92), Michèle Vallenthini (p.93-102) and Michel Delon (p.251-62) in this volume.

war-torn Europe provide the occasion for bizarre scientific experiments, through which the beautiful Pauliska discovers, as Michel Foucault explains, 'modern perversity', which he characterises as 'an evil very close to the body and meant for it', a fatal materialism. Foucault, while clearly identifying Révéroni's text as a 'novel of terror', also saw in the events of Pauliska's journey a timeless plot, beyond the specifics of history, genre, and geography: 'In this underground world the misfortunes lose their chronology and link up with world's most ancient cruelties [...] an ageless cycle.'[6] Nevertheless, *Pauliska* can be situated among a group of turn-of-the-century works that were written under the influence of a crisis of Reason, transmitting not only an emerging irrationality but also a violence never before imagined.[7] The novel exhibits a similar link to science and its technological excesses as that found in other fin-de-siècle novels, including Sade's work. Révéroni's constellation of machines and products of scientific invention can be read in this context.[8]

Magnetic Venus

The story of the Countess begins at the residence of Baron Olnitz, with the elderly Hungarian preparing to magnetise her. In a strange rite of initiation, he introduces his guest to a whole system

6. All quotations, Michel Foucault, 'So cruel a knowledge' in *Essential works of Foucault, 1954-1984*, vol.2, *Aesthetics, method, and epistemology*, ed. James D. Faubion (New York, 1997), p.53-67 (54).
7. In this connection see, particularly regarding Sade, Marcel Hénaff, 'Sade, the mechanization of the libertine body, and the crisis of reason', in *Technology and the politics of knowledge*, ed. Andrew Feenberg and Alistair Hannay (Bloomington, IN, 1995), p.209-31.
8. Béatrice Didier, writing about the machines in *Pauliska*, aptly recalls: 'Scientifique, officier du Génie, Révéroni semble avoir suivi avec intérêt le progrès de son siècle. Quand il écrit, l'introduction du machinisme en France est relativement récente. La première machine à vapeur de Watt fut la pompe à feu de Chaillot, construite en 1789. Quelques "fabriques" commencent à se servir de machines. Les premières machines à vapeur, les premières machines-outils rencontrèrent d'énormes difficultés [...]'. See the chapter 'Du roman noir à la science-fiction et au roman d'initiation: *Pauliska* de Révéroni Saint-Cyr', in *Ecrire la Révolution: 1789-1799* (Paris, 1989), p.229-43 (239). Didier also mentions the advent of electricity and various experiments in which it was applied, such as Jean-Antoine Nollet's electrically-charged Leyden jars.

of his own devising. She is immersed in a world of vapours that he attempts to explain as follows: 'L'effervescence se manifeste, votre front est brûlant. Les vapeurs du résidu agitent votre imagination, votre rêverie est tout amour' (p.60). The baron's seduction takes the form of a systematic inoculation, the creation of desire by means of an electromagnetic device. The Countess's initial response to this first manipulation, which affects her senses and jars her perceptions, is euphoric: 'Dois-je convenir que cet état était presque délicieux, que le passé avait disparu, que mes songes étaient enchanteurs, et qu'un être âgé et hideux me semblait paré des grâces de la jeunesse et de la beauté?' (p.60). Pauliska is then drawn into scenes of torture, of the uttermost degradation, such as a scene of biting that culminates in the calcination of the patient's skin: the flesh bitten off the victim is subjected to a thermal process of decomposition.

Pauliska's seducer is an exalted but strict materialist: he sees desire as no more than physical transmission from one being to another. One of the baron's learned manuscripts offers a recipe to demonstrate that 'everything is physical': *'L'amour étant l'union physique de deux êtres, pour que les masses se confondent, donnez l'impulsion aux atomes. Opérez une irritation sur les fibres avec des cendres de cheveux et des cils de l'opérateur. Forte inspiration par les pores; friction multipliée sur la peau. Pour breuvage, l'opérateur donnera son haleine convertie en fluide'* (p.58, original emphasis). Pauliska is horrified to read in his writings that *'L'amour est une rage, il peut s'inoculer comme cette dernière maladie'* (p.58, original emphasis). Fragments of the body must therefore be made to pass from the patient to the initiator. The 'inoculation des désirs' (p.62) cannot take place without this intimate transmission. All sorts of mixtures can serve the purpose. The baron himself, aiming to transmit a part of his own person, combines bits of skin, hair and breath vapours.[9] This strange concoction is heated and pulverised. Later in the novel, the episode in Rome shows the intensification of torture to which

---

9. The elements of parody linking Révéroni's text to *La Nouvelle Héloïse* – think of Saint-Preux's desire to share Julie's illness through inoculation – have already been noted; Révéroni adds a sadistic dimension to this transmission. See Valérie Van Crugten-André, 'Syncrétisme et dérision parodique dans *Pauliska ou La Perversité moderne* de Révéroni Saint-Cyr', *Revue d'histoire littéraire de la France* 6 (2001), p.1551-72 (1557).

Révéroni subjects his heroine, as the baron's powers are escalated. Valérie Van Crugten-André, who also points out the novel's allusions to mesmerism, its link with magnetic trance sessions, recalls Condorcet's critical observation about the effect of magnetism on female patients: 'The effects attributed to magnetism are the products of pure imagination [...] the fantastical equipment, bizarre or forced postures, unusual language, large groups of people, superficial palpation, which in sensitive individuals produce an effect that shocks and arouses their imaginative processes.'[10]

At the beginning of the novel Countess Pauliska is imprisoned in a chemist's laboratory which, by means of a hidden switch, also becomes a library in which she encounters her torturer's 'système atroce' (p.64). The baron's doctrine comprises a bizarre physics of fluids that combines air and gas. Olnitz is seeking the subtle state, the ultimate phase change, which he explains through his theory of celestial air; he emphasises the lover's 'souffle', the subject's highest form of exhalation. The elderly libertine's manuscript describes his theory thus (p.64-65):

> L'existence de cet air est prouvée par la jouissance même, comme l'est celle de l'air vital par ses effets sur la vie animale. Mais manque-t-il, cet air céleste, quand notre être s'évanouit? Non, il n'a fait que quitter sa place pour aller se réunir à sa masse éternelle. De là, par sa loi expansive, il pénètre en de nouveaux corps qu'il anime, fait jouir et anéantit par sa disparition, pour se reproduire encore. Il circule, se dégage, et suit dans sa carrière plus subtile les mêmes lois que l'air vital. [...] Mais si cet air céleste, le plus subtil de tous, échappe à tous les procédés chimiques et ne peut être recueilli, le gaz personnel, qui n'est autre chose que la combinaison de ce même air céleste avec le souffle de chaque individu, peut être recueilli, condensé, échangé, porter des effets identiques, et par conséquent créer le désir chez l'objet aimé...

In the spirit of this delirious science, Révéroni Saint-Cyr orchestrates extravagant machines, placing his own imaginative stamp on these contraptions that are ubiquitous in popular literature.[11]

---

10. Van Crugten-André, 'Syncrétisme et dérision', p.1559.
11. These machines are discussed by Michel Delon in his article 'Machines gothiques', *Europe* 659 (1984), p.72-79.

In this hyperbolic version of the libertine plot, Annie Le Brun sees 'an unprecedented device of provocation'.[12]

Such a feat of imagination is illustrated by Pauliska's journey to Buda and her stay in a distillery, an establishment that harbours an astounding print shop used to produce counterfeit money. This underwater abode, a cavity located beneath the river Danube, becomes the locus of all sorts of terrors, overseen by a certain Talbot. At first the narrator is seduced by the apartment to which she is confined; she is enchanted by the incongruous opulence of the place, and curious about its owner (p.90):

> Je me vis dans un appartement sombre à la vérité, mais d'une richesse et d'une élégance dont il est impossible de se faire une idée. Il fallait que cet homme eût déjà amassé des sommes immenses, pour se procurer, sous les eaux, des objets d'un luxe aussi fini. Meubles, bijoux, l'or semé sur la cheminée, sur le parquet, tout donnait à mon réveil l'air d'une féerie.

Pauliska conveys her enchantment in bizarrely rococo terms sprinkled with Gothic allusions.

But from her cohabitant, a Frenchman named Durand, the Countess will quickly learn the secret of this terrifying institution: 'C'est ici le foyer des agences du machiavélisme anglais; c'est d'ici que partent les ordres d'assassinat, les sommes destinées à les payer et à décréditer le trésor de France' (p.91). The description includes dimensions spelled out in dire detail: 'Ce cabinet est l'ancien caveau du trésor des Cordeliers; les murs ont six pieds d'épaisseur en tous sens [...] ce caveau est absolument enveloppé des eaux du Danube [...]' (p.95). Pauliska is assigned to bookkeeping. The printing press of this workshop-cave is transformed into a torture machine, with Durand caught up in the production line of the banknote press. The workings of the press are fatefully set in motion by the horrified Pauliska: 'je vois l'infortuné Durand, étendu sous la presse, que je viens d'étrangler par une corde attachée au levier. Sur sa poitrine est un papier, où j'ai gravé moi-même ces mots: *mort, damnation pour les traîtres!*' (p.98). Pauliska had earlier begun to work at a frightful desk, 'un secrétaire noir, marqué de taches rouges en bois incrusté, et qui jouaient le sang à

---

12. Annie Le Brun, *Les Châteaux de la subversion* (Paris, 1982), p.205.

faire horreur. J'ouvre ce secrétaire, quel spectacle, grand Dieu! L'encre dans un crâne d'ivoire, les chandeliers... des faisceaux d'ossements, portant une petite bougie lugubre, et les tablettes couvertes d'une série de poisons en fioles et étiquetés!' (p.92). Révéroni Saint-Cyr has manifestly succeeded in constructing a dark tableau of Gothic *vanitas*, with all the elements of the *roman noir* and the suggestion of blood. In these macabre shadows, which recall the *Madeleines pénitentes* painted by Georges de La Tour, Pauliska is doomed to horror, doomed to the industrial labour of violent death.

Antiphysics (love as a cage)

In a novel in which 'everything is physical' and obeys the laws of magnetism, Révéroni proffers a story-within-a-story that seems to depart at least superficially from this pattern. This is the tale of Ernest Pradislas, the Countess's young lover. In the garden of a Gothic castle, the officer makes the acquaintance of a young woman who leads him within the walls of a strange sect of Amazons, the Misanthrophiles. He ends up violently imprisoned by a group of twenty women who act out a parody of erotic desire, of the attraction between opposite sexes. This academy of women engages in a complex cult of anti-desire for men, of bitter detestation of everything male. Ernest becomes the negative model of their lessons in comparative anatomy, natural history, and figure drawing, all aimed at confirming the participants in their dogmatic beliefs and reinforcing their insensitivity. But the torture inflicted upon Pradislas (he is enclosed in an iron cage) converges in a strange way with the bodily experiments found elsewhere in the novel. Here we find the same meticulous analysis of a system of knowledge in the litany of manuscripts meant to direct the cultists' works: *Imperfections morales et physiques des hommes, Crimes des amants, Code des plaisirs des misanthrophiles.* Eschewing the progress of electromagnetism, the Misanthrophiles regress instead into the baroque world of representation. For example they recast the taxonomy and hierarchy of species, assimilating men to the animal category, redrawing the chart of living beings. Pradislas in his cage is placed next to a monkey and a parrot; cast as a sloth, he is included for comparison in a small zoological collection. The Amazons subject their victim to the technological equivalent of what Pauliska's persecutors have perfected in order to exploit their desire: isolated experimental laboratories, watertight underground compartments where free will is crushed. In this part of the text, erotic desire itself enters into another logic: in contrast to the physical underpinnings that it had in Olnitz's lascivious enterprises, where it was associated with 'procédés chimiques' (p.185), the Misanthrophiles' desire takes shape in an imaginary structure; it corresponds to a constitutional illusion that seeks to deceive the senses.

Elsewhere, these women are bent on worshipping sculpted models of the gods of Mount Parnassus. The sect has acquired various mannequins for use in their experiments. One of their particularly cherished academic sessions is inspired by the society of Berlin, which abjures relations with men. Antique portable dolls accompanying this society's shipment to their sisters form a virtual gallery of ancient masterpieces: Apollo, Antinous, Aeneas, Phaon. To complete the illusion, we learn that these statues could be artificially heated. But Pradislas, taking the place of these divine models, turns the women's illusion on its head, exploiting the very artifice that they had created, and runs off with one of their recruits, Julie de Molsheim, known to her fellow worshippers as Nircé. It could be said that, in the end, the physical trumps the fictive representation; anatomical nature supplants the simulacrum-statue: 'une idée me vient; je la saisis: je m'empare de l'arc d'Apollon et me place dans les bras de Nircé, qui est censé apporter un fantôme, tout en tenant une douce réalité' (p.123). The affected iciness of Mademoiselle Fisher, the high priestess and guardian of the place, who had ordered the mannequin and sought its embrace, is transmuted into vapour, vanishing in the jouissance of the antique. As for Ernest, the false statue, he softens and tries out his recovered lightness. Far from the castle, Julie ends up maimed by the war. Her fateful blow comes from the explosive element itself, the disfiguring effect of powder.

Gas and smoke

At the novel's end, in Rome, Pauliska once again encounters the Baron of Olnitz, whom she first met at Ust. She immediately recognises her former torturer, whose character has not altered with his geographical shift. The Baron immediately resumes his seduction of Pauliska, who is to meet him in another laboratory. The narrative lays before us all the chemist's paraphernalia: alembic tubes and flagons all await Pauliska. The Baron wishes to pick up where he had left off earlier: in Pauliska's words, 'Je crus être environnée de glaces; mais je m'aperçus bientôt que j'étais sous un vaste récipient pneumatique' (p.186).[13] He shows his victim his perverse system along with his confidence in a fearsomely powerful chemistry. The Baron puts forth a theory of rejuvenation by injection of a gas obtained from the breath of children. Pauliska describes this strange pneumatic process: 'Il me fit observer un soufflet d'ébène, garni en argent, placé sous une niche et qui paraissait puiser son aliment dans la pièce voisine. De l'extrémité de ce soufflet partaient cinq petits tuyaux en gomme élastique, terminés par un tube d'argent fort aigu et recourbé' (p.187). The container in which he encloses Pauliska is itself a complex part of a sophisticated architectural contraption (doubled by a second, identical pneumatic machine in a neighbouring room, which contains other victims). Like the machine in Ust, this is a baroque mechanism complete with trap door and various compartments.

In Rome, Olnitz joins forces with an illustrious magnetiser named Salviati along with a motley entourage including the painter Paolo Guardia, his sister Zephirina and the surgeon Taillandino. The group gives Révéroni the opportunity to recount further fantastical experiments. The magnetism practised by the Italian Salviati is equally grim. Through this posse of imposters the text stages a scientific duel, a technological rivalry whose excesses breach the bounds of the appalling. Salviati proposes replacing Olnitz's pneumatic machine with what he considers a 'bien plus simple' (p.189) device. But what he unveils is an 'immense machine électrique', a torture apparatus that is nonetheless conceived as 'voluptueux' (p.189). To the Baron's

13. Julia Douthwaite relates this procedure to the painting by Joseph Wright of Derby, *An Experiment on a bird in the air pump* (1768), in her book *The Wild girl, natural man, and the monster* (Chicago, IL, 2002), p.200. In a footnote in his novel, Révéroni describes this experiment as all the rage in Europe and pronounces it 'le comble de la folie' (p.218).

system of gasses and distilled air, Salviati adds the effectiveness of electricity produced by rubbing: as he remarks to Olnitz, 'Que sont vos gaz sans la matière du feu qui les dilate? Je tiens donc le principe, quand vous rampez encore sur les composés' (p.190). With an eye to this excess of magnetic efficiency, Salviati proposes other experimental subjects. The above-mentioned children (including Pauliska's son, Edvinski) are replaced by Zephirina and Pauliska herself (p.193):

> On nous attache chacune à un poteau de la grande roue, on lie nos cheveux ensemble par-dessus nos têtes, penchées en arrière; on pose nos reins en contact, et séparés par la seule épaisseur de la roue de verre. Salviati se place alors avec délices sur le pain de cire, et ordonne de charger. Le frottement brûle bientôt nos chairs, les étincelles scintillent.

Michel Foucault, who discovered Révéroni's novel in 1962 and shed light on its subversive nature through comparisons to the libertine novel, in particular *Les Egarements du cœur et de l'esprit*, made a distinction between *machinations* (peculiar to libertine technology and the novel of the eighteenth century) and *machines*.[14] He exposed the particular constitution of erotic desire embodied by the machine and how it intervened between the scientist-tormentor and the victim. Foucault even saw it as a cruel 'ruse of knowledge', 'a heartless mechanics' whose workings he sums up as follows:

> the electric current [...] gives rise to all the physical movements of desire in the victim. The desirability the fluid conveys to the persecutor is the persecuted's desire, while the inert, enervated tormentor receives, as if in a first suckling, that desire which he immediately makes his own; or rather, which he transmits, without retaining it, to the motion of the wheel, thus forming a simple relay in the persecuted desire that comes back to itself as an accelerated persecution.[15]

At the end of his novel Révéroni places a tribunal scene that pronounces judgement on his perverse protagonists. He stages it

---

14. Foucault, 'So cruel a knowledge', p.62. See also Béatrice Didier's distinctions in *Ecrire la Révolution*, p.239-40.
15. Foucault, 'So cruel a knowledge', p.63-64. See also Foucault's comparison with Sade's machine and his distinctive economy.

in Rome's labyrinthine underground, beneath the Castel Sant'Angelo, upon which the author projects a richly Gothic atmosphere redolent of obscure Piranesian architecture;[16] he emphasises the cavernous topography (p.197):

> Je ne m'arrêterai pas à décrire les antres sombres, les ponts voûtés en fer, sous lesquels des bras du Tibre s'éloignent en bouillonnant; [...] Quelques lampes rares projetant des ombres immenses sous ces voûtes; des sbires qui, n'ayant vu le jour depuis vingt ans, ont la pâleur des spectres; des gouttes d'eau qui, coulant des murs des cachots sur nos têtes, semblaient être l'infiltration des pleurs des malheureux prisonniers, sont les seuls tableaux dont le souvenir me reste [...].

Salviati transforms his dungeon into a chemical laboratory. He enters the Castel Sant'Angelo smuggling all his experimental instruments (box of phosphorus, electrical device, magnet) like so many keys to hell. Salviati's interrogation is transformed into a chemical process. The ink that is used to trace his name metamorphoses into blood, in the clerk's eyes, and in the end the letters burst into flame (p.201). When judgement is passed and Salviati is condemned to eternal incarceration in the oubliettes of the Castel Sant'Angelo, Révéroni describes the event in accord with his character. The physicist's very voice is enough to blow the dungeon to smithereens (p.207-208):

> une explosion épouvantable se fait entendre; l'air comprimé des cachots nous suffoque. Les voûtes fendues, brisées à l'extrémité du souterrain, laissent arriver un jour rouge à travers une fumée épaisse, et plusieurs soldats et prisonniers passent en criant que le bastion du magasin à poudre du château avait sauté en l'air, au moyen de mèches disposées par Salviati et ses aides'.

Révéroni's chaotic mix of elements explodes in this apocalyptic ending of fire, flames, inferno. The Roman fortress is vaporised, atomised by the powder magazine in a chemical blast. It is through this chemistry of evaporation, a hideous sublimation, a terminal detonation – an echo of the revolutionary 'explosion' with which the novel begins (p.32) – that Saint-Cyr renders the

---

16. See Le Brun, *Les Châteaux de la subversion*, p.130-31.

spectral or Gothic dimension of these final pages, as well as of the consummation of these evil characters, especially the enshrouding of Salviati. Zephirina collapses in a trail of smoke which dissipates before Pauliska's horrified gaze: 'cet être de feu, au physique et au moral, s'évanouit comme un songe en tombant en poussière' (p.209). The retribution of the evildoers, at the end of the text, can be justified by a vengeful hermeneutics, a sacrificial eradication of perversity in a dismal succession of scapegoats; but the author favours the chemical, materialist interpretation. It is as if he elevates the very matter of the novel to the level of horror only to explode it artificially in a cloud of smoke. After the 'orages' (p.211), Pauliska rejoins her own people, and the novel closes with a sentimental opening: peace regained, marriage to her friend Ernest Pradislas, the heroine's maternal fulfilment. The erotics of illusionism, the terrifying and artificial chemistry of bodies, is replaced by a eudaemonia shaped by love and friendship. And Pauliska dries her tears.

II

Violence and the (re)writing of history

The 'dix août' (10 August 1792) in literary texts[1]

CATRIONA SETH

Both inside and outside France people have no difficulty in identifying the country's national day and remembering the date of the storming of the Bastille. Another date that in many respects might also have warranted an important place in the calendar and in subsequent commemorations is 10 August 1792. That day's events led to the deposition of the king, and thus to the birth of the first republic,[2] yet despite that date's significance, it is generally forgotten. Contemporary novels provide a reminder of the importance of events to which official history has given a reduced place. After a brief reminder of the facts themselves, I shall argue that contemporary accounts characterised that day by violence, that this violence led to traditional points of reference being overturned and inverted, but also that unexpected acts of humanity occurred in the face of this violence.

For many contemporaries, 10 August 1792 was a momentous wrench, bringing to an end weeks if not months of political manoeuvring and drama. The arrest of the fleeing royal family at Varennes on 20 June 1791 had discredited the king who until that point had continued to enjoy a certain amount of affection from his subjects. War was being waged on all fronts and on 5 July 1792 it was declared that the *patrie* or fatherland was in danger. Citizens were invited to take up arms and to join the National Guard, a step that was to prove crucial to the storming of the Tuileries

---

1. Translated by Thomas Wynn.
2. Jeanne Françoise Polier de Bottens refers to this in her *Mémoires d'une famille émigrée*, 3 vols (Hamburg, Fauche, 1798), vol.2, p.38-39: 'La journée du dix août, en manifestant les intentions des révolutionnaires d'établir une république sur les débris du trône, avait porté l'alarme et le désespoir dans les cœurs des royalistes. L'attentat odieux que les factieux avaient osé commettre sur la famille royale, en la retenant prisonnière au Temple, révoltait tous les bons esprits des deux partis.'

Palace. The revolutionaries, now increasingly radicalised, were to set up a whole series of measures, in particular against non-juring priests (*prêtres réfractaires*). Speaking before the revolutionary assembly on 9 July 1792, Brissot called for an attack on the palace, the symbolic seat of the executive power:

> Et moi je dis que frapper sur la cour des Tuileries c'est frapper tous ces prêtres d'un seul coup! On vous dit de poursuivre partout les intrigants, les factieux, les conspirateurs [...] Et moi je dis que tous disparaissent si vous frappez sur le cabinet des Tuileries, car ce cabinet est le point où tous les fils aboutissent, où se trament toutes les manœuvres et d'où partent toutes les impulsions!
> La nation est le jouet de ce cabinet, c'est-à-dire de quelques intrigants qui le dominent; voilà le secret de notre position, voilà la source du mal, voilà où il faut porter le remède, et un remède vigoureux.[3]

Another step towards the surge of great revolutionary violence on 10 August came on 1 August when Paris heard of the Brunswick Manifesto, that is to say the allies' intention to reinstall the French monarchy in all its original force. The idea of actually attacking the palace in which the king was held was widely discussed. Lioncel, a fictional monarchist depicted by Louis de Bruno, describes the atmosphere of the time: 'on m'écrivait de Paris, qu'il s'y tramait des complots contre le château des Tuileries; qu'on agitait violemment l'esprit de la populace; que la famille royale était menacée.'[4] All but one of Paris's revolutionary sections voted in favour of storming the palace. When the tocsin sounded at midnight on 9 August, the building was surrounded by 'braves sans-culottes et intrépides Marseillois', as the caption of one engraving puts it. Such engravings are akin to propaganda, whether revolutionary or royalist; their vocabulary is similar, as are the scenes they depict, although their captions

---

3. 'Discours de M. Brissot sur les causes des dangers de la patrie, et sur les mesures à prendre, etc. (Séance du 9 juillet 1792, An IV de la liberté)', in *Choix de rapports, opinions et discours prononcés à la Tribune Nationale depuis 1789 jusqu'à ce jour*, 21 vols (Paris, 1819-1825), vol.9, p.199.
4. Louis de Bruno, *Lioncel ou L'Emigré, nouvelle historique* (1800), in *Romans de l'émigration (1797-1803)*, ed. Stéphanie Genand (Paris, 2008), p.155-287 (222). See also Malcolm Cook, *Fictional France: social reality in the French novel 1775-1800* (Oxford, 1993), p.134-38.

differ. Confusion took hold of Paris from the early hours of 10 August, and one of that day's defining characteristics is the opacity of the events, which remain difficult to read and interpret. The marquis de Mandat, commander of the National Guard and responsible for protecting the Palais des Tuileries, was killed, and replaced by Santerre.

In a climate of suspicion and uncertainty the king left the Tuileries with his family at around seven o'clock on the morning of 10 August, claiming that he wanted to avoid 'un grand crime' and thus to protect the French. Everything seemed to proceed peacefully and harmoniously, and several Swiss Guards threw down their cartridges to show that they were abandoning their weapons. Then a shot rang out, the source of which was unclear; the battle would be interpreted by the revolutionaries as resulting from the Swiss Guards' treachery. The professional and very experienced forces of the Swiss Guards clashed with the much bigger crowd of rebels, backed up by cannons. Hand-to-hand combat ensued, and all kinds of weapons imaginable were used, including of course pikes and halberds. The king's handwritten request to the Guards to withdraw, so as to stop the bloodshed, arrived in the middle of the battle and was ignored. Both sides suffered great losses; more than two thirds of the 950 Swiss Guards died, along with over 400 rebels, a total of over a thousand. These deaths, compared to the hundred killed at the storming of the Bastille, give an initial objective indication as to the violence that occurred that day; those figures do not include the even greater number of surviving Swiss Guards who were to die a month later in the September Massacres. The event lived on as a kind of deep wound, the truth of which Jacques Mallet du Pan wished to re-establish several years later. Recalling one of the most tragic dates in French history, he evoked a 'nouvelle Saint-Barthélemy préparée par un Comité de scélérats et exécutée par le rebut de la nature', and added:

> Après deux mille attentats sur des personnes désarmées; sans distinction de sexe ni d'âge; après avoir exercé les raffinements de leur barbarie accoutumée sur les cadavres; après avoir couvert les rues de victimes, peuplé les cachots de gens de bien, épuisé les expédients d'un despotisme effréné, abreuvé d'opprobres, déposé, enfermé, raillé au milieu de ses affreuses douleurs, ce roi qu'ils

nommaient en 1789, *restaurateur de la liberté*, les conducteurs de ces bêtes féroces ont porté leurs soins à couvrir de ténèbres l'histoire de leurs tragédies.[5]

Mallet du Pan's remarks are extreme, but he was not alone in recognising in that day a moment of excess and inhumanity that was to change the perception of the Revolution (both at home and abroad), and thus to mark out an essential stage in the emergence of modern times in political terms. In his *Détails particuliers sur la journée du 10 août 1792 par un bourgeois de Paris, témoin oculaire* (1822), Camille-Hilaire Durand uses the word 'violence' nine times, but only twice when describing the date in question. One of the instances concerns the memory of an eyewitness, a 'témoin oculaire' who, at the very moment of the Restoration of the monarchy, has been called to welcome the princes back into the palace from where Louis XVI, their closest relative, was hounded with 'la violence et la révolte'. The other instance occurs in a remark attributed to a pessimistic military leader who, before the battle, feared that the people would be led astray 'par séduction et par violence'. One should note that in both cases it is individuals who characterise mass movements as violent. In the period's novels, as in its engravings, the terms 'massacre' and 'massacré' frequently recur in descriptions of 10 August – that 'journée d'horreur', as one of Mme Polier de Bottens's characters puts it. Those terms are used to refer to rebels and Swiss Guards alike; Oswald's French friend in Germaine de Staël's *Corinne* was, in Mme d'Arbigny's words, 'massacré au[x] Tuileries en defendant son roi', and the hero tells how he suffered in learning of 'mon ami massacré, sa sœur au désespoir'.[6] In Mme Polier de Bottens's tale *Félicie et Florestine* the Swiss Guards are described as having been attacked by an inhuman mob:

5. Mallet du Pan accused the rebels of spreading false rumours about these events before closing down journals which were still able to maintain some independence; see the *Lettre de M. Mallet du Pan à M. D. B. sur les événemens de Paris du 10 août* ([Paris], 1792), p.3-4.
6. Germaine de Staël, *Corinne ou L'Italie*, ed. Simone Balayé, in *Œuvres complètes (Série II: Œuvres littéraires)* (Paris, 2000), p.304, 305.

la manière dont cette valeureuse troupe fut assaillie, ne prouva que trop qu'on était décidé à l'anéantir. Rien n'égala la bravoure de ce malheureux corps. Officiers, soldats, tous étaient décidés à périr pour sauver la famille Royale. Mais que peut le courage contre la force animée par la plus aveugle fureur? Bientôt ils virent qu'ils ne pouvaient échapper au massacre.[7]

Other terms and phrases have the same import. The Tuileries palace becomes a 'théâtre de carnage' in *Félicie et Florestine*,[8] and a 'lieu de carnage' in *Les Amours et aventures d'un émigré* where it presents an 'épouvantable tableau' to all those present.[9] The intentions of authors and illustrators alike are ambiguous: are these violent scenes being celebrated or condemned? For the most part, engravings, destined to be circulated widely and addressed to literate and illiterate publics alike, seem to be triumphalist and in support of the Revolution;[10] fiction, on the other hand, deplores and implicitly screens the reader from the horror, while nonetheless allusively summoning it forth in texts often destined to circulate amongst foreigners and indeed adversaries of the new regime.

It is fratricide that leads to characterising the events of 10 August as a 'combat terrible'. As the hero of *Les Amours et aventures d'un émigré* puts it, 'des Français allaient égorger leurs frères, ou recevoir la mort de leurs mains'.[11] Heroism itself is a bloody affair, as Francœur tells Lioncel (whose very name speaks of valour, of a lion who faces the Revolution's tigers) during a conversation about his activities in 1792: 'monsieur d'Oursonvilliers [...] avait dit que vous vous étiez trouvé au

7. Jeanne Françoise Polier de Bottens, *Félicie et Florestine*, 3 vols (Geneva, 1803), vol.3, p.156-57. On the mob, see also Olivier Ritz's chapter, 'Metaphors of popular violence in the revolutionary debate in the wake of Edmund Burke', p.35-47.
8. Polier de Bottens, *Félicie et Florestine*, vol.3, p.159.
9. A.-J. Dumaniant, *Les Amours et aventures d'un émigré*, in *Romans de l'émigration (1797-1803)*, ed. Genand, p.71-154 (81).
10. The numerous deaths are also alluded to in the captions to pro-revolutionary engravings, such as: 'Incendie de la caserne des Suisses, au Carrousel, le 10 août: le Carrousel était comme une vaste fournaise ardente; pour entrer au Château, il fallait traverser deux corps de logis incendiés dans toute leur longueur; on ne pouvait y pénétrer sans passer sur une poutre enflammée ou marcher sur un cadavre encore chaud.'
11. Dumaniant, *Les Amours et aventures d'un émigré*, p.81.

château des Tuileries, près du Roi, que vous vous y étiez battu, comme un lion, et que vous ne vous étiez échappé, qu'en sabrant deux *sans-culottes* qui avaient voulu s'opposer à votre retraite.'[12] In a sort of parallel calculation, Lioncel remarks that he was 'témoin du massacre de ces Suisses intrépides et fidèles, et de la mort de deux de mes camarades qui furent tués à mes côtés'.[13] Two friends for two sans-culottes; this equation is typical of a literary arithmetic that often pairs up adversaries against their victims (whether they survive or not), as if it were impossible to decide between them. I shall return briefly to this point later on.

In *L'Emigré*, one of Sénac de Meilhan's characters imagines a series of scenes which could be painted to summarise the main episodes of Marie-Antoinette's life, from her joyous arrival in France, via her marriage to the Dauphin, to her final moments on the scaffold. Also represented are the tragic events of 10 August – the eponymous hero of the novel had already alluded to this fateful day in an earlier letter, in which he told of his arrival in Germany: 'la journée du 10 août et la captivité du roi remplirent mon esprit des plus noirs pressentiments'.[14] The date is marked not only by its effects, but also by the terrible violence which characterised it and which is repeated by memoir- and fiction-writers alike.

Félicie et Florestine's Eugène de Valbreuse, thanks to whom the two heroines' emotional tangle will be unravelled, is a Swiss Guard, and like other fictional characters he was present at the Tuileries on that momentous day. He managed to escape to safety through one of the palace's basement windows, and he recounts his story in the extended letter LIX, in which violence bursts forth into his compatriots' seemingly idyllic world. The astonished Florestine records in writing what she has been told, and she begins her letter to her friend Mlle de Saint-Alme in terms that betray her urgency in transmitting the tale: 'J'avais bien raison, ma bonne amie, de vous promettre des récits intéressants; j'en suis encore toute émue; et j'ai besoin de vous faire part de ce que M[onsieu]r Eugène vient de nous raconter.'[15] If the storyline is

12. Louis de Bruno, *Lioncel ou L'Emigré*, p.221.
13. Louis de Bruno, *Lioncel ou L'Emigré*, p.225.
14. Gabriel Sénac de Meilhan, *L'Emigré*, ed. Michel Delon (Paris, 2004), p.97.
15. Polier de Bottens, *Félicie et Florestine*, vol.3, p.153.

hardly affected by revolutionary events, except when the wicked marquis de Fonrose, an émigré, arrives on the scene and stirs up trouble in rural Switzerland, the novelist relates facts that marked her readership and perhaps echo exactly the experiences of a Swiss Guard who escaped the massacre.[16] The heroine who relays the story is amazed that Valbreuse had not spoken to her about this before. It is as if, in this privileged corner of Switzerland, there was a kind of ban on the subject of the Revolution, as if it had been excluded from discourse, so as to keep it at a distance:

> je me rappelle à présent, qu'il [M. de Valbreuse, le frère d'Eugène] n'aime point à parler des malheurs de la révolution; toutes les fois qu'on a traité cette matière, je l'ai vu éluder la question; c'est par bonté, parce que nous lui avions dit que ce sujet nous attristait. Ma bien-aimée mère ne pouvait en entendre parler de sang-froid; il lui faisait la plus cruelle impression.[17]

The scenes witnessed by the Swiss Guard are described as 'affreuses' and branded as unspeakable: 'je vais tâcher de vous les rendre à mon tour. Je voudrais me rappeler ses propres expressions, mais c'est impossible.'[18] Rather as in Sénac de Meilhan's *L'Emigré*, where mediation occurs by means of tableaux,[19] horror is distanced from the readers: it is offered to us indirectly in a woman's letter that relates the account of a man who was present at the 'affreuse journée du 10 août'.

The memory of the Swiss mercenaries' tragic fate probably explains why the events are remembered more vividly in Switzerland than in France. It was following the massacre of the Swiss Guards and the deposition of Louis XVI that the Swiss cantons broke off diplomatic relations with France. Isabelle de

---

16. The hero's experience more or less matches that of Victor de Constant, the youngest son of Samuel de Constant, who at that time was serving as a Swiss Guard at the Tuileries; see Maud Dubois, 'Le roman sentimental en Suisse romande, 1780-1830', in *La Sensibilité dans la Suisse des Lumières: entre physiologie et morale, une qualité opportuniste*, ed. Claire Jaquier (Geneva, 2005), p.167-256 (172).
17. Polier de Bottens, *Félicie et Florestine*, vol.3, p.153-54.
18. Polier de Bottens, *Félicie et Florestine*, vol.3, p.154.
19. See Catriona Seth, 'Dire l'indicible: description et peinture dans *L'Emigré* de Sénac de Meilhan', in *Destins romanesques de l'émigration*, ed. Claire Jaquier, Florence Lotterie and Catriona Seth (Paris, 2007), p.188-203.

Charrière herself stopped writing her novel *Henriette et Richard* on hearing the news from France in 1792.[20]

In 1796, with the renewal of diplomatic ties between France and Switzerland, Charrière distanced herself from her initial reaction in her *Réponse à l'écrit du colonel de La Harpe, intitulé De la neutralité des gouvernans de la Suisse depuis l'année 1789*: 'Le massacre du 10 août ne fut reproché, par les Suisses aux Français, que pendant les premiers moments d'une douleur amère. La nation française s'est montrée sensible à notre deuil, ainsi que le dit le colonel de La Harpe.'[21] However, apparently still smarting in 1803, Mme Polier de Bottens – who unlike Charrière was born Swiss – claimed that 'la fureur de la populace armée' was targeted above all against the Swiss Guards during the attack on the Tuileries. Danish sculptor Bertel Thorvaldsen's gigantic statue of the Lion of Lucerne (1819), described by Mark Twain in *A Tramp abroad* (1880) as 'the most mournful and moving piece of stone in the world', which commemorates the events tends to suggest that the massacre of Louis XVI's guard remained a deep wound in the Swiss national conscience.

10 August, as a moment of violence, also offers authors a potent force that can redirect the novel's plot. In what is undoubtedly one of the first emigration novels, namely August Lafontaine's *Claire Duplessis et Clairant, histoire d'une famille d'émigrés* (a German work which soon appeared in at least two French translations),[22] 10 August is the primary reason for several characters' departure from France, as it is for the unnamed hero of *Les Amours et aventures d'un émigré*. When, in turn, Mme de Genlis came to describe an émigré's destiny in a chaotic Europe, she implied that no monarchist could stay in France after that fateful day and that foreigners (especially the Swiss) were to mistrust those

---

20. See Valérie Cossy, 'Des romans pour un monde en mouvement. La Révolution et l'émigration dans l'œuvre d'Isabelle de Charrière', *L'Emigration en Suisse (1789-1798): événements, récits, représentations*, Annales Benjamin Constant 30 (2006), p.156.
21. Isabelle de Charrière, *Réponse à l'écrit du colonel de La Harpe, intitulé De la neutralité des gouvernans de la Suisse depuis l'année 1789*, in *Œuvres complètes* (Amsterdam, 1979-), vol.10, p.280.
22. See Katherine Astbury, '*Claire du Plessis* d'Auguste Lafontaine, ou histoire d'un roman d'émigration allemand', in Jaquier *et al.*, *Destins romanesques*, p.53-66.

expatriates who arrived later and whose exile was motivated by less noble reasons. They were considered to be the assassins of the Swiss if they had emigrated later than the immediate aftermath of 10 August as her fictional baron de Kerkalis states: '[les] paysans soupçonnaient tous les Français nouvellement émigrés, d'avoir combattu à Paris, le 10 août, journée sanglante où tant de Suisses perdirent la vie.'[23]

The storming of the Tuileries has serious consequences in Mme de Staël's *Corinne*; the valiant count Raimond, Oswald's French friend, loses his life when defending his king, and the death of this marginal yet sympathetic character has significant repercussions. Moved by his friend's misfortune, Oswald hastens to help the deceased's sister, Mme d'Arbigny, who depicts her personal and financial difficulties as resulting directly from this tragic event in a 'fatale lettre' (note that the addressee endows the missive with a weight comparable to that of the day itself), every word of which the Scot claims to recall: 'Hier, dix août, disait-elle, mon frère a été massacré au[x] Tuileries en défendant son roi. Je suis proscrite comme sa sœur, et obligée de me cacher, pour échapper à mes persécuteurs.'[24] Mme d'Arbigny says that she received a final letter from Raimond (when he was at the Tuileries), asking her to contact his friend from across the Channel. The deceitful widow is lying, but the young Scot is bewitched by her and remains in France, hoping to marry her, to the despair of his father, old Lord Nelvil, who dies before his son's much-deferred return. Oswald does not hesitate in attributing his father's death to his delaying tactics and to the worries brought on by his behaviour. In some respects, Lord Nelvil is thus arguably a collateral victim of the violence of 10 August, of which the 'curse' that bears upon his son, who was absent when his father died, is an indirect though no less real consequence.

10 August is also associated with violence in part because of an upheaval whose characteristics derive from a grotesque carnivalesque spirit, and which is marked by a complete disso-

---

23. Félicité de Genlis, 'Le malencontreux, ou mémoires d'un émigré, pour servir à l'histoire de la Révolution', *Nouveaux contes moraux et nouvelles historiques*, 3 vols (Paris, Maradan, An XI) vol.1, p.392.
24. Germaine de Staël, *Corinne*, p.304.

lution of conventional points of reference. In *Corinne*, that Mme d'Arbigny's treachery replaces her dead brother's honour is indicative of the complete inversion of values once emblematic of France. One might add the reversal that is implicit in Adrien de Valbreuse's behaviour in *Félicie et Florestine*; he is an officer with the Swiss Guards and his regiment has resolved to perish in saving the royal family, yet, seeing several of his comrades die around him, 'comme il n'y avait aucune gloire à gagner dans une lutte aussi inégale, il résolut de s'y soustraire'.[25] The very man who is treated by his compatriots as a hero is a soldier who could be charged with desertion. His glory is a result of dishonourable conduct, in military terms, though none of the characters reflect on this – it is as though extreme violence eliminates any consideration of such questions. On the contrary, his use of native wit to escape from certain death is a cause for celebration amongst them. Just as Germaine de Staël observes, traditional values are overturned in the wake of 10 August.

When Adrien de Valbreuse flees, he discards the uniform that once made him so proud – 'l'habit honorable qu'il porte, hélas! Pour la dernière fois' – and buries it alongside his sword in a cave; the gesture symbolises the burial of the monarchy and of the values of chivalry, symbolically killed by the violent and unruly mob. He changes his appearance by covering his face and clothes with soil and, shaking a stake (a plebeian weapon which acts as a substitute for his noble sword), 'pouss[e] des cris semblables à ceux qu'il entendait autour de lui', cries which a few lines earlier are described as 'les hurlements féroces d'un peuple enivré de rage'.[26] The former Swiss Guard, abandoning his aristocratic demeanour, shrieking like a madman, passes for a *Marseillais*. The defender of the monarchy is mistaken for a freedom fighter. Whilst he used to draw prestige from his name and individual merit, he now becomes anonymous to blend in with the crowd.

Heroism's fluctuating boundaries are also illustrated in Dumaniant's novel *Les Amours et aventures d'un émigré* (1797), whose hero was present at the Tuileries on 10 August 1792, and who

---

25. Polier de Bottens, *Félicie et Florestine*, vol.3, p.157.
26. Polier de Bottens, *Félicie et Florestine*, vol.3, p.158.

recounts those events from a personal perspective.[27] Thus History is linked to an important episode of an individual's own history. Successive reversals and upheavals during the day demonstrate the impossibility of making sense of events. The main character says he witnessed the start of the 'combat terrible', which he seems to have envisioned at the time as a sort of Armageddon, with a 'serrement de cœur inexprimable'. He is unable to flee but even if this had been possible, he adds, 'un faux point d'honneur m'aurait retenu parmi les combattants'. The reference to this misplaced honour is interesting: at the beginning of the fight, the character has no doubt where his loyalties lie and what he has to do. Part way through, he abandons his principles and shows that individual survival and personal ties are more important than abstract values. On narrating events he refers, as mentioned, to a *faux* point d'honneur';[28] he has clearly changed and is no longer the man he was when the first shots were fired. Perhaps because he has learned fear;[29] certainly because he has had to make stark choices and has reacted as a human being rather than as the representative of one or other of the opposing sides.

At the outset, a *volontaire* pursues the hero at the Tuileries. They seem to be alone. The single combat comes to a rapid end in the narrator's favour: 'il [le volontaire] me tire à bout portant, le coup manque, le mien part et l'étend à mes pieds'.[30] The *volontaire* dies through bad luck; he fired the first shot and should have killed the narrator who, unharmed, shuts himself in a room with the corpse. He is only saved by his quick-witted decision to take up both the dead man's clothes and his role as the leader of a group of rebels who force entry and charge in. The hero's attempt to send them

---

27. On this particular aspect see Malcolm Cook, 'Histoire ou fiction? *Les Amours et aventures d'un émigré*', in Jaquier *et al.*, (ed.) *Destins romanesques*, p.181-87; and Catriona Seth, 'L'Histoire dans le roman', *Le Tournant des Lumières: mélanges en l'honneur du professeur Malcolm Cook*, ed. Katherine Astbury and Catriona Seth, (Paris, 2012), p.233-43.
28. Dumaniant, *Les Amours et aventures d'un émigré*, p.81. Emphasis added.
29. On this point, see Geneviève Lafrance's chapter, 'La Terreur aux trousses: représentation de la peur dans les romans d'émigration' in *Le Tournant des Lumières*, p.245-56.
30. Dumaniant, *Les Amours et aventures d'un émigré*, p.82.

away from the crime scene – he has, after all, killed a man, even if it was in self-defence – almost leads to a worse crime being committed. Faced with a door which closes as he arrives, as if in answer to the one with which he vainly tried to shut out the mob, he witnesses it being forced by his newfound 'comrades': 'A notre approche, une porte à demi-ouverte se ferme rapidement; on la pousse avec rudesse; elle cède au premier effort: ma position était horrible; c'était moi qui avais servi de guide à ces furieux; ils allaient massacrer quelque infortuné sans défense, et je ne pouvais le secourir' (p.82). He has become one of the attackers and is no longer the victim. The tables have been turned on him. If this moral dilemma is in itself terrible to bear, matters worsen for the hero when he discovers a touching scene: 'Un domestique mourant était étendu sur un grabat. Un vieillard encore robuste, au regard fier; une jeune personne dans l'abandon de la douleur, à genoux, les cheveux épars, les bras tendus, demandant la mort, mais implorant la grâce de son père' (p.82).

It is no longer just a matter of a struggle between two armed representatives of opposing factions (as when the young nobleman killed the *volontaire*), for now it is a potentially violent and much more awkward situation; not only are these people civilians, they are a young woman, an old man and an invalid, three categories of individuals who are normally offered immunity from attack. The narrator's direct address to the reader brings with it a sense of urgency: 'Lecteur! Mets-toi à ma place, peins-toi mon état. Le génie des auteurs invente-t-il une scène plus dramatique que celle que le hasard amenait?' (p.82). According to a phrase which was popular at the time (and attributed sometimes to Ducis and sometimes to Lemierre), 'le théâtre court les rues'; drama also bursts into the novel with this unexpected meeting, for these people are the narrator's fiancée, her father and their wounded valet. The hero then changes sides once again, his affections prevailing over his politics: 'éperdu, désespéré, je jette mon arme meurtrière. Je me mets au-devant de ces infortunés. Je m'écrie: 'C'est mon père, c'est mon épouse: immolez-nous tous trois' (p.82).[31] The invalid servant – an

---

31. It is this specific moment which is represented on the frontispiece; the image is reproduced on the next page.

Figure 1: *Les Amours et aventures d'un émigré* (Paris, chez les marchands de nouveautés, An VI [1797]). Private collection.

anecdotal character whose purpose in the narration is to show a sort of solidarity between the classes (even among noblemen) and to create a new category of innocent victims of revolutionary violence – has disappeared from the engraving. The scene is focused on the couple – Sophie is dressed in white, and her fiancé has thrown down his gun – who are surrounded on one side by her noble father, the old baron de Nangis, and on the other the armed revolutionaries, who form an anonymous group. The illustration functions as a metonymy of their life to come, caught between the two possible reactions to the Revolution, namely democratic acquiescence or aristocratic refusal. Whereas this episode ends happily for the trio, the same cannot be said for a couple of friends who fought together in the palace and were forced to take refuge under a bed. In yet another inversion, one of the men turns against his comrade when the rebels arrive: 'il saisit par les cheveux son malheureux compagnon qui n'avait pas eu le temps de sortir de sa cachette et le frappant à coups redoublés, il crie aux spectateurs: "Camarades, voilà un aristocrate que j'ai découvert, et que je viens d'exterminer". Cette horrible ruse lui conserve la vie: il s'échappe à travers la foule' (p.83). The friend is stabbed and thrown over to the 'camarades', yet, as if immanent justice were at work, the injured man survives and encounters his attacker two years later in Germany, *a priori* in the forces of the *émigré* princes; 'ils se battirent, et l'assassin reçut la juste punition de son crime' (p.83). The supposed victim returns, in a sense, from the dead, to exact revenge; the would-be assassin gets his just desserts. The two parallel scenes in which characters appear to change sides in order to survive, with their different outcomes, seem to show that history sometimes hangs by a mere thread. They implicitly invite us to reflect on whether, in extreme circumstances, one can exercise violence against an innocent. They also tend to suggest that ideas are not worth dying for.

Like Dumaniant's characters, *Félicie et Florestine*'s Adrien de Valbreuse has an implied double, namely M. de Chaumont, the young man from Neuchâtel after whom Mme de Terville enquires and who perished on that dreadful day: 'il était mon parent et mon meilleur ami, et si je ne vous en ai pas parlé tout de suite, c'est que je n'ai pas voulu mêler les détails qui le concernent, à ceux qui m'avaient pour objet'.[32] Chaumont had just arrived in the régiment when 'le 10, il périt victime du serment qu'il a fait la veille de ne pas abandonner son drapeau'.[33] Valbreuse cannot hold back his emotion when recounting the fate of this man whose conduct was so very different from his own: 'Je le vois encore dans une des salles des Tuileries, entouré de quelques-uns des siens; sans doute s'il eût jeté la bannière qui l'exposait à être remarqué, il eût peut-être échappé comme quelques autres, mais il préféra mourir à manquer son serment...'[34] His friend tried three times to shield him but was repulsed by the 'assaillants furieux', and he only managed to save himself by fleeing. The fate of young Chaumont may touch Valbreuse and his listeners, but it also illustrates a kind of vain heroism; Valbreuse, safe and sound, can find love, whereas Chaumont has died, leaving behind a tearful fiancée who temporarily loses her mind, before seeking refuge in a German convent. It is as though the author wanted to show us two possible paths for the young men caught up in the revolutionary violence: to remain true to one's pledge like Chaumont is to act honourably, but also, in a world turned upside down, to court death; to forfeit honour when common sense tells you to run off is to ensure that you make it into the future, but it is a future which requires more compromise.

When the hero of *Les Amours et aventures d'un émigré* casts down his weapon and announces that he is a relative of the baron and the young woman to whom he has led the rebels, the response is one of common humanity: 'Les bras prêts à frapper s'arrêtent.' This shows that, even in the initially dehumanised crowd, diminished by the language used, there can be collective and generous gestures; just as violence is often a mass effect, so too can its interruption be a collective act. Another double of the hero then appears, confirming the inversion of the anticipated narrative: 'Un jeune homme de dix-huit ans, c'est l'âge des vertus et de la sensibilité; ce jeune homme court à Sophie, la relève, et s'adressant à moi, il me dit: "Camarade, nous sommes armés pour combattre la tyrannie, nous ne sommes pas des assassins".'[35] This

32. Polier de Bottens, *Félicie et Florestine*, vol.3, p.163.
33. Polier de Bottens, *Félicie et Florestine*, vol.3, p.167.
34. Polier de Bottens, *Félicie et Florestine*, vol.3, p.168.
35. Dumaniant, *Les Amours et aventures d'un émigré*, p.82.

individual is a not only a spokesman for this particular group of combatants, he also functions metonymically for the French people, who can encompass, so it seems, the hero and those whom he loves: 'Non, le peuple français n'est pas un peuple cruel, il s'irrite comme un enfant, il s'apaise de même: il pleure comme lui.' The new regime is like a young child, without prejudice. Violence is transformed into emotion, tears flow, and embraces replace threats. The trio had previously been hunted down, and now they are led in a triumphal procession back to their *hôtel*, and the combatants' gesture of generosity arouses the sympathy of the people they meet on the way: 'La foule qui grossissait à chaque pas, apprenant notre aventure, bénissait nos libérateurs, les couvrait d'applaudissements.'[36] The reversal is now complete: the bloodthirsty mob has become a sensitive crowd. Whereas the hero and his family were once excluded due to their proximity to the Crown, they are now firmly reintegrated into the crowd whose only value is that of family loyalty. The 'scène dramatique' of the unexpected meeting of the hero with the baron and his daughter, a scene that took place in a context where death seemed inevitable, now concludes in a denouement worthy of a *drame larmoyant*.

The eponymous hero of *Lioncel ou L'Emigré*, a man who had fought and murdered, is also saved by a chance meeting. Having escaped from the Tuileries, he sticks close by the walls of the Louvre when he is accosted by a sans-culotte characterised by his 'état hideux', and who cries out to him: 'Camarade, s'écria-t-il, combien as-tu tué d'aristocrates? Je t'ai vu te démener, comme un diable. Que fait-on au Château? Pille-t-on? – Non, répondis-je, on massacre.' It transpires that this is none other than Laurent, Lioncel's servant. Laurent saves the hero by continuing to talk and by pretending to lead away not his master, but *'un patriote blessé* pour la *cause du peuple'*.[37] Here again identities are reversed, along with social strata: the servant takes control, and the aristocrat (now termed 'un patriote') is saved through language. That language might stand in stark contrast to appearances was a problem raised by the royalist journalist Mallet du Pan who

---

36. Dumaniant, *Les Amours et aventures d'un émigré*, p.82.
37. Louis de Bruno, *Lioncel ou L'Emigré*, p.225. Original emphasis.

lamented the loss of life at the hands of the rebels: 'c'est à la pointe des piques, ornées de crânes humains, qu'ils portent l'étendard de la philosophie; ils vous enseignent le droit de la nature en égorgeant leurs concitoyens'.[38] The complex link between violent acts and linguistic violence is implicitly foregrounded.

The case related in *Lioncel* of the monarchist's unexpected rescue is not, however, unique. The hero of *Les Amours et aventures d'un émigré* presents the reader with other examples:

> Cette journée éclaira tout à la fois des scènes touchantes et des scènes d'horreur, des traits d'humanité et des actions d'une barbarie atroce. Des hommes couverts de haillons rapportaient avec fidélité de l'or et des bijoux qu'ils avaient trouvés dans le château, et qu'ils pouvaient s'approprier. Un jeune garde national, conduisait à la barre de l'assemblée un soldat suisse qu'il avait arraché à la mort, se chargeait de son entretien et l'adoptait publiquement pour son frère.[39]

A little further on, the hero tells how a monarchist who was stabbed and left for dead by a friend in the attempt to save his own life, was then recognised by a man charged with cleaning the palace after the terrible events that took place there: 'il lui avait des obligations, il le transporta chez lui, il le soigna et le vit se rétablir en peu de temps'.[40] The man once believed dead is resuscitated; the loyalty of a plebeian rectifies a so-called friend's betrayal; the man who should have saved in fact attacks, while the commoner who could have finished off the injured aristocrat brings him back to life.

Scenes of this type are also related in the period's memoirs, such as those of Marie-Victoire Monnard who was an apprentice in Paris at the time.[41] These texts show the people's eagerness to assert their solidarity against the king. As indicated in certain engravings (which fulfil a propagandistic rather than simply

---

38. *Lettre de M. Mallet du Pan*, p.6.
39. Dumaniant, *Les Amours et aventures d'un émigré*, p.82-83.
40. Dumaniant, *Les Amours et aventures d'un émigré*, p.82.
41. See her 'Souvenirs' in Catriona Seth, *La Fabrique de l'intime. Mémoires et journaux de femmes du XVIIIe siècle* (Paris, 2013), p.1051-1131 (esp. 1091-94).

representative function), it aimed to show the events of 10 August for what they truly were, that is to say the founding act of the new republic, leading as they did to the fall of the king. The people wanted a new and united nation to rise from all the blood spilt by enemies and patriotic heroes alike, an intention demonstrated in the pensions paid to the victims' families, the funerals worthy of great men organised for the dead, and indeed the allegorical engravings of the events. The Terror, of course, was to treat the storming of the Tuileries not as an essential ritual of purification, but rather as the clarion call to further violence, as the reign of Louis XVI gave way to that of 'Roberspierre',[42] as Trophime-Gérard de Lally-Tollendal puts it in his *Défense des émigrés français adressée au peuple français* (1797). The great historical panorama of the Revolution – which continued even under Bonaparte to commemorate the 'journée trop fameuse en France', as Hippolyte de Laporte described 10 August – has downplayed the memory of this crucial day when, in spite of the king *and* the revolutionary elites, the blood of the Parisians and the blood of the Swiss Guards flowed together. This was a day when a moment of liberating violence was transformed into the beginning of a bloody terror. Perhaps this moment of uncommon savagery, in the very heart of Paris, was a necessary step towards the unprecedented surge of violence that was to come. This is certainly what we are given to believe by *Félicie et Florestine*'s Adrien de Valbreuse, who was present at the Tuileries on 10 August:

> L'on se blase sur les scènes d'horreur qui se renouvellent tous les jours, et ce *bon* peuple, ces femmes surtout, qui ne voyaient pas sans frémir il y a quelques années, conduire un criminel à la place de grève, se rendent en foule à celle de la révolution, pour voir périr chaque jour un grand nombre d'innocents. Paris n'est plus le centre de l'urbanité, de la sociabilité, des vertus aimables. Il est devenu celui de la cruauté et de la licence, décorées des beaux noms de justice et de liberté. Ô! Mon ami, on frémit en voyant ces changements effrayants, que quatre années d'anarchie ont apportés dans ce bel Empire.[43]

---

42. Trophime-Gérard de Lally-Tollendal, *Défense des émigrés français, addressée au peuple français* (Paris, Cocheris, 1797), p.150.
43. Polier de Bottens, *Félicie et Florestine*, vol.1, p.50. Original emphasis.

Violence in history and the rise of the historical novel: the case of the marquis de Sade[1]

MICHÈLE VALLENTHINI[2]

A psychological disturbance usually occurs suddenly and descends without any forewarning. It is preceded by a sense of self-confidence, which gives way to a feeling of disillusionment as events unfold. The subject overestimates his or her own strength, living under the necessary illusion that such a thing could never come to pass.

Sade writes the following in his literary notebook: 'De Thou, dans son cinquième livre, rapporte que, le lendemain de la Saint-Barthélemy, les femmes de la Cour de Catherine de Médicis sortirent du Louvre pour contempler les corps nus des Huguenots assassinés et dépouillés sous les murs. Au 10 août, les Français de Paris vinrent de même contempler les corps des Suisses jonchés sous les Tuileries.'[3] This single quotation, with its two apparently unconnected sentences, conveys the full violence of the shock brought on by historical events as well as all the anguish experienced by those affected. It reflects the intensity of the three political upheavals experienced by the author and at the same time demonstrates the extent of his resistance to historical progression. Sade is first and foremost a traumatised victim of history.[4] His works can be read as attempts to come to terms with the historic shock that he could neither avoid nor confront. To track the traumatic effects brought on by the violence of history, it is especially helpful to consider Sade's so-called historical

1. Translated by Jozef van der Voort.
2. The author would like thank the Fonds national de la Recherche Luxembourg for its generous financial support.
3. *Œuvres complètes du marquis de Sade*, ed. Annie Le Brun and Jean-Jacques Pauvert, 15 vols (Paris, 1986-1991), vol.11, p.20.
4. For other accounts of Sade and violence, see the chapters by Thomas Wynn (p.139-60), Jean-Christophe Abramovici (p.221-28) and Will McMorran (p.229-49).

works, namely *La Marquise de Gange*, *Adélaïde de Brunswick, princesse de Saxe* and *Histoire secrète d'Isabelle de Bavière, Reine de France*. One might thereby answer the following questions: What do these three novels represent? Where are the traces of violence and history located? What conception of history do they portray, and how does this conception develop over the course of the works?

One can argue that Sade's historical novels reflect experiences of violence, and that they suggest that historical changes do not allow any real experience of time; rather, they are nothing more than the endless repetition of a trauma made more acute by its meaninglessness. As a result, the hysteria that characterises these novels is arguably a consequence of the author's own traumatisation from history. In light of this hypothesis, let us turn back to the period under consideration (that is, the Empire), or more accurately its pre-history. The Revolution, a time when History and Violence mingled to an unparalleled degree, endowed the latter with a distinctive temporal dimension, together with a distressing banality, which Dr Guillotin perfectly illustrated, stating that 'Le criminel sera décapité. Il le sera par l'effet d'un simple mécanisme', and that 'La mécanique tombe comme la foudre, la tête vole, le sang jaillit, l'homme n'est plus'.[5] At this point the spectator is cheated; everything takes place in the blink of an eye. Something that used to take hours now happens in a matter of seconds. A significant temporal collapse takes place, which simultaneously brings about a shift in the relationship between observation and torture. Not only does violence become insistently all pervasive, but the steady gaze is replaced by the ephemerality of the split second.

In the same way, the period on which this chapter focuses saw events and changes in the political regime pile atop one another at a dizzying rate. The beginning of the eighteenth century was characterised by fixed and inflexible intellectual schemata; however during the period under consideration these began to be replaced by a more open and dynamic understanding of the world: the passage of history quickened its pace; time was reconceptualised as a space for reflection and experience; history

---

5. Quoted in Daniel Arasse, *La Guillotine et l'imaginaire de la Terreur* (Paris, 1987), p.26, 34.

was seen as being driven by events; and both time and history came to be problematised as literary subjects – hesitantly at first, but more and more frequently as time went on. Ultimately this led to the discovery of the historicity of personal identity. The turn of the nineteenth century (when Sade wrote his historical novels) was a key period for this reconceptualisation of the past, and it is precisely at this time that what we call the historical novel first appeared.

The historical novel is related in complex ways to other genres such as the gothic novel, the courtly romance, the adventure story and the historical tale, and as such it is a hybrid genre that is difficult to pin down. The Revolution – along with the periods immediately before and afterwards – represented a veritable maelstrom of events that left people searching for guidance, and at this time a plethora of novels were written with a historical emphasis. These were principally by women, such as Madame de Genlis and Madame Cottin; however there were also male authors such as Lamartelière or, a little earlier, d'Ussieux and Baculard d'Arnaud, who tried to make sense of the chaos in their own way by presenting it as a historical narrative.[6]

Published in 1813, *La Marquise de Gange*[7] appears to be the most accessible of Sade's historical novels, to judge from the number of articles that have been written about it.[8] The novel recounts the

6. Madame de Genlis's historical novels may be read as reminiscences for chivalric times in the framework of a plea for the monarchy. Fervently interested in the Middle Ages, she searches in Charlemagne's world for a feudal morality that privileges the construction of the moral being. Here, history validates fiction in that it maintains moral interest and appears as the source for regeneration after violent upheavals. The 1797 version of the *Essai sur les révolutions* presents history as cyclical, whereas the 1826 version presents a different vision of history; the spiral replaces the circle. To take an earlier example, Prévost's aim was to present a personal history within the frame of a generalised history, his principal concern being to re-establish the thread broken by events while still staying true to reality. For criticism of the historical genre, see Germaine de Staël's *Essai sur les fictions*, which argues that the invention on which the historical novel is founded necessarily thwarts history's moral pedagogy.
7. All page references to this novel will be to the edition in *Œuvres complètes du marquis de Sade*, vol.11, p.169-379.
8. Jacques Proust, 'La diction sadienne: à propos de *La marquise de Gange*', in Michel Camus and Philippe Roger (eds), *Sade: écrire la crise* (Paris, 1983), p.31-46; Alice

misfortunes of Diane de Rossan, marquise de Gange, and is based on a true story of persecuted virtue that had been a popular literary theme for several centuries. Set in a feudal idyll at the end of the seventeenth century, the action is driven by common Sadean plot devices: a Machiavellian scheme is put into action, various traps are set and a fatal denouement is achieved. The plot merges with the libertine machinations that are its main driver. The result of this is a binary narrative structure that, like history itself, oscillates with disorienting frequency between scenes of intrigue periods of calm, driven by the victim's naivety and the aggressors' villainy.

Euphrasie de Gange's beauty seems to announce its own fate, in a deterministic manner typical of Sade's work: 'Plus un être est favorisé de la nature et de la fortune, plus on voit bien souvent le sort l'accabler de toutes ses rigueurs' (p.180). In short, Euphrasie – the most beautiful woman at Court, glowing with a pure, angelic charm that catches the eye of the King himself – 'n'était pas née pour être heureuse' (p.180). In this way the stage is set for the plot that will inevitably lead to the death of the beautiful victim, whose life is bound up with the changing of the seasons, as indicated by the abundance of natural metaphors in the novel.[9] Madame de Gange arrives on her husband's gloomy estate in *autumn*, after having injured her shoulder in a coach accident. It is *winter* when the abbot Théodore, the marquis de Gange's brother, contrives a plan to sow discord between the marquise and her husband in

---

Laborde, 'La dialectique du regard dans *La Marquise de Gange*', *Romanic review* 60 (1969), p.47-55; Jamel Guermazi, '*La Marquise de Gange*, un récit et un mélodrame', in Simone Bernard-Griffiths and Jean Sgard (eds), *Mélodrames et romans noirs, 1750-1890* (Toulouse, 2000), p.99-112; Raymond Trousson, 'Histoire d'un fait divers du marquis de Sade à Charles Hugo', on http://www.bon-a-tirer.com/volume9/rt.html (24 Decembre 2003); Lawrence W. Lynch, 'Sade and the case of *La Marquise de Ganges*: sources, adaptations and regressions', *Symposium* 41 (1987), p.188-99; Hans-Ulrich Seifert, *Sade: Leser und Autor* (Frankfurt, 1983), p.118-32; Hans-Jürgen Lüsebrink, *Kriminalität und Literatur im Frankreich des 18. Jahrhunderts* (Munich, 1983), p.134-52; Mary Trouille, *Wife-abuse in eighteenth-century France*, SVEC 2009:01, p.213-42.

9. On the subject of natural metaphors, see Olivier Ritz's contribution to this volume, 'Metaphors of popular violence in the revolutionary debate in the wake of Edmund Burke', (p.35-47).

revenge for her rejection of his amorous advances. He sets his traps, hatches a scheme, writes false letters and orchestrates imprisonments, abductions and cases of mistaken identity, all to punish the marquise for her aloofness. Madame de Gange, as beautiful as the *spring*, does not live to see the *summer*. She dies at sword point, stabbed to death by Gange's brothers who covet her fortune.

The narrative of the novel is driven by violence on an individual basis rather than historical fact. While the text is based on the historical incident of the murder of the marquise de Gange, Sade makes a number of changes which suggest that he is not particularly interested in the facts of the case: the marquise's first name is altered, along with the spelling of the name 'de Gange'; new fictional characters are introduced throughout; the denouement is altered (although the informed reader would be aware of the abbé's true fate); and the narrative is presented formally and thematically in a manner reminiscent of the Gothic. It is clear that Sade is not overly concerned with History.

At certain points, Sade depicts his heroine tenderly but at other times he cannot prevent himself from insulting her chastity. Although he claims that 'ce n'est pas un roman que nous offrons ici' (p.177), this does not prevent him from altering the facts of the case to give them a particular spin. Sade states in the preface that his changes were carried out with a view to protecting the reader's virtue. In this case, do we see his subversiveness not in the absence of gruesome detail, but in his tipping the delicate balance between fact and fiction in favour of the latter? Sade always offers us a dark and disturbing vision of the future as a spiral of brutality, in which the materialism of Enlightenment philosophy collapses in a pathetic depiction of the world before being ultimately replaced by the fascination of Christian imagery, embodied above all by the martyr-figure of the persecuted wife, who is typically presented as a virgin. Nonetheless, we should remember for now that this, the first of Sade's historical novels, constitutes a kind of literary alibi intended to justify his depiction of violence. History is not the main driver of the plot; rather it merely provides the basic inspiration for the story in the form of the historical incident.

The second novel *Adélaïde de Brunswick, princesse de Saxe*, which

Sade began to write in 1812,[10] depicts a Germany that is torn apart by civil war. In this context, violence is, as Sade tells us, acute and frequent, and the plot features bandits' caves, secret trials, kidnappings, necromancers, libertines, confused identities, and knights in search of a fleeing woman. *Adélaïde de Brunswick* takes up the vision of history as a downward spiral that was presented in its predecessor *La Marquise de Gange*, but also takes the form of a mosaic, a tale assembled from disparate parts. While the story is derived from an entry in Moréri's dictionary, it is clear that Sade has violently distorted historical reality. Despite its frequently light-hearted tone, the story of a woman tumbling from one misfortune to another conveys a fatalistic view of history, albeit one that also embodies a certain openness towards the future. Here too, history is presented as a violently chaotic jumble of discrete actions, directed only by misunderstandings and evil designs that take on the appearance of abstract forces. There is no longer anything certain or fixed about the future; it has slipped beyond all human influence, and it may be that the only way to regain control is to resort to trickery or to adopt a stoically fatalistic attitude, as does Adélaïde. Thus the princess learns from the violence to which she has been subjected to develop self-protective mechanisms that allow her to view the future with a glimmer of confidence, albeit a confidence born of experience that is a world away from Euphrasie's naive faith. Nonetheless, the end of the novel (an exercise in disillusionment) sees Adélaïde stoically retreat from the future and from the mausoleum that the world has become, and sequester herself in a convent.

Isabelle de Bavière (1813)[11] is, as it were, a new Juliette with

10. *Œuvres complètes du marquis de Sade*, vol.12, p.267-435. The novel was not published in Sade's lifetime. It has appeared in an English translation (*Adelaïde of Brunswick*, trad. Hobart Ryland [Washington, DC, 1954]), before being published in French in the fifteenth volume of Jean-Jacques Brochier's edition of the *Œuvres complètes du marquis de Sade* (Paris, 1964). There appears to be no scholarly article on the novel, although Hans-Ulrich Seifert does discuss it (*Sade*, p.132-40).
11. *Œuvres complètes du marquis de Sade*, vol.12, p.1-265. Like *Adélaïde de Brunswick*, this novel was published posthumously; *Histoire secrète d'Isabelle de Bavière, reine de France, publiée pour la première fois sur le manuscrit autographe avec un avant-propos par Gilbert Lely* (Paris, 1953). See Chantal Thomas, 'Isabelle de Bavière:

historical padding. Sade's sources are dubious, in that he refers to documents that have been destroyed by the 'imbécile barbarie des Vandales du XVIIIe siècle' (p.21). This dark episode in France's history takes place during a period riven by the Hundred Years War, the Cabochien revolt, and the war between the Armagnacs and the Burgundians. As with the two other novels examined in this essay, the depiction of a turbulent backdrop serves only as a reminder of the violence to come. One can either submit naively to this violence (as does Euphrasie), use it to one's own advantage (like Adélaïde), or alternatively set it in motion (like Isabelle).

In the novel's preface, an exercise in pure royalist patriotism, Sade writes that what he finds most appealing about history is the opportunity to depict criminal acts, and that the particular charm of the historical novel (a term he never uses, referring to himself as a 'romancier' or 'historien') lies in the fact that it gives licence to imaginatively elaborate on those acts. By drawing out the key themes of the narrative he is able to uncover the hidden motives behind the story, and unlike his predecessors, Sade develops a particularly malevolent version of Isabelle. The novel's conception of history offers a vision of universal criminality, to such an extent that at certain points the text resembles an encyclopaedia of violent acts. Sade's Isabelle commits a list of crimes, unlike the Isabeau whom modern studies consider as involuntarily implicated in history. Sade's interest in the fifteenth century seems to be for its non-dialectical aspect of criminality. *Isabelle de Bavière* plays an important part in de Sade's representation of history, which, as Michel Delon argues, 'identifie régénération, anarchie et progrès dans les ordres d'une violence qui serait la nature même de l'homme'.[12]

There are many possible reactions to a violent experience: one can fight against it, remain immobile, flee – or one can write historical novels. At any rate this is suggested by the last three novels by the old man of Charenton, who had also experienced a

---

dernière héroïne de Sade', in *Sade: écrire la crise*, p.47-65; and Seifert, *Sade*, p.140-46.

12. Michel Delon, 'L'invention sadienne et les pamphlets révolutionnaires', in *Le Travail des Lumières, pour Georges Benrekassa*, ed. Caroline Jacot Grapa et al. (Paris, 2002), p.557-68 (566).

great deal of hardship during his life. I have argued that in these novels, as in the rest of Sade's oeuvre, there is an inherent connection between history and violence. It appears as though history is used to justify the depiction of criminal acts; abjection replaces dignity.[13] History is a useful store of ideas, which the Sadean machine fashions into an endless succession of discrete units conveying a pessimistic world-view: a rapidly descending spiral of repetitions upon repetitions; a surrender to the apparently inevitable, or in Schopenhauer's terms '*eadem, sed aliter*'. Historiography becomes a vast game in which Sade emphasises the serial aspects of reality and manoeuvres his pawns as he pleases in order to lose himself in a pseudo-historical spasm.

While Sade lacks historical consciousness in the strict sense of the word, as Michel Delon and Jean-Claude Bonnet have suggested,[14] the traumatised marquis has a keen understanding of contingency, of how it is to be an aberration, to be left to one side. He has, in short, a hysterical consciousness. He remains hemmed in and excluded, while history advances past the bars of his prison and erects a scaffold below his window. According to the interpretative framework advanced by Sade the displaced aristocrat, history does not move towards any identifiable destination. Instead it is a barren phenomenon, giving rise to many different regimes but not sustaining any of them. History is portrayed as a wound, a bout of madness, a disaster; and it is, in the novels we have examined, feminine. Might we regard Sade's historiography as a kind of '*hyster*iography'? The so-called historical novels appear to indicate as much.

History, for Sade, is much more than a mere pretext. His representation of history develops over the course of the three novels through the depiction of the three female protagonists, and just as all humour is in part serious, so there is also a grain of truth in Sade's historical alibi. Throughout these novels the markers of history make themselves felt more and more strongly.

---

13. Sade's taste for these kinds of intrigue was no doubt inspired by Deport du Tertres's *Histoire des conjurations*.
14. Michel Delon, 'Les historiennes de Silling', in *L'Histoire au XVIIIe siècle* (Aix-en-Provence, 1980) p.101-13; and Jean-Claude Bonnet 'Sade historien', in *Sade: écrire la crise*, p.133-48.

Starting out from a specific incident, they become incoherent historical facts that are difficult to pin down before ultimately developing into the chronological depiction of a reign. Moreover, although historical facts are rarely directly tackled in the text, they are always present. Authors writing in the wake of 1789 all make sense of events prior to this date through horror-stricken reference to the bloody wounds of the Revolution, and Sade is no exception. At the core of each novel there is a catastrophic event that develops into a lengthy upheaval extending to the very end of the work. These catastrophes are, moreover, a reflection of Sade's own personal calamity, which is also that of an entire class; the decline of the aristocracy goes hand in hand with the decline of an aristocratic world vision. Sade's disinterest in contemporary events and his retreat into a version of the Middle Ages redolent of the *Chevalier du cygne* convey in full both his resistance to history and his traumatised immobility in the face of progress, which he sees only in terms of decline. As he himself said, his was a strange age in which an honourable gentleman could be prosecuted for having lightly mistreated a prostitute.[15]

Sade remains a conservative. Nothing can reassure him more than what he already knows; the concrete wins out over the abstract, the known over the unknown. What is and what has been are preferable to what will be. From this perspective the representation of time in his novels takes on a nostalgic and conservative character. Progress is not shown as a positive force but as an inevitable movement towards loss – a loss that is much the same in the Middle Ages as it is in the modern age. Sade is no precursor to Walter Scott; his so-called historical novels dramatise the disconnect between history and fiction, and place him in a grey area in the literary canon. As well as borrowing heavily from the Gothic novel, the Sadean historical novel draws upon older genres such as *la nouvelle historique* which had been so utterly used as to provide nothing more than stereotypes. In the grip of his fond attachment to the past he waxes nostalgic for better times, rejects the future, and wishes to restore the world to the way it

---

15. See for example his letter to the marquise de Sade (dated roughly to 1781), in *Correspondance du marquis de Sade et de ses proches enrichies de documents, notes et commentaires*, ed. Alice Laborde, 20 vols (Geneva, 1999-), vol.16, p.252.

should be. He is shaped by his resistance to reality, by the strength of the material world and by the violence of history. As Jean-Claude Bonnet says: 'on ne saurait écrire l'histoire de la même façon depuis Charenton et depuis le Collège de France'.[16]

---

16. Bonnet, 'Sade historien', p.142.

The everlasting trials of Jean Calas: justice, theatre and trauma in the early years of the Revolution

YANN ROBERT

On 17 December 1790, the ill-fated Jean Calas was brought back to life at the Théâtre du Palais Royal, just long enough to be tried yet again for the murder of his son. Indeed, the play premiering that night, Lemierre d'Argy's *Calas, ou Le Fanatisme*,[1] re-enacted on stage with great precision all of the key incidents of that famous affair, from the discovery of Marc-Antoine's body to the ensuing inquest and trial of Jean Calas, led by the intolerant Capitoul David de Beaudrigue,[2] and ending with Calas's torture and execution on the wheel in 1762.[3] The very next day, the actors of the Théâtre de la Nation staged their own re-enactment of the trial – a tragedy written by Jean-Louis Laya.[4] All told, in the space of only seven months, three distinct plays, including one by the most celebrated playwright of the Revolution, Marie-Joseph Chénier,[5] transplanted to the stage the final days of Jean Calas, and two more, by Jean-Baptiste Pujoulx and François-Jean Villemain d'Abancourt,[6] depicted the successful appeal by Calas's wife to clear her husband's name.

1. Auguste-Jacques Lemierre d'Argy, *Calas, ou Le Fanatisme, drame en quatre actes, en prose* (Paris, Imprimerie des Révolutions de Paris, 1791).
2. The capitouls were municipal magistrates unique to the city of Toulouse. Along with military and administrative duties, they also held the right to act as examining judges, as they did during the Calas affair.
3. Inexplicably, Jean Calas's alleged accomplices were dealt much lighter punishments. His son, Pierre, was banished; his two daughters were briefly incarcerated in a Catholic convent; and his wife, servant and old friend, Lavaisse, were all acquitted.
4. Jean-Louis Laya, *Jean Calas, tragédie en cinq actes et en vers* (Avignon, chez Jacques Garrigan, 1791).
5. Marie-Joseph Chénier, *Jean Calas, tragédie en cinq actes* (Paris, Moutard, 1793).
6. Jean-Baptiste Pujoulx, *La Veuve Calas à Paris, ou Le Triomphe de Voltaire* (Paris, Brunet, 1791); François-Jean Villemain d'Abancourt, *La Bienfaisance de Voltaire* (Paris, Brunet, 1791).

Such a flurry of plays on the Calas affair[7] undoubtedly reflects the Revolutionaries' profound admiration for Voltaire, a mania which reached its peak in July 1791, with the transfer of his remains to the Panthéon. I would like to argue, however, that the Calas plays also bear witness to a widespread fascination in the early years of the Revolution with the theatrical re-enactment of trials, a craze that has yet, to my knowledge, to be studied.[8] Indeed, between 1789 and 1793, many illustrious victims of legal injustices, from age-old martyrs, like Socrates, to contemporary ones, like the chevalier de La Barre,[9] were exhumed from their everlasting sleep. The craze for 'courtroom dramas', as I will refer to them, extended even to lesser-known cases, as playwrights dug through collections of past *causes célèbres*,[10] as well as through the daily press, in search of *faits divers*.[11] So popular was this particular genre that it threatened to displace in the public's mind some of the then standard references to classical myths and history – or so

---

7. In yet another example, the playwright Desforges announced, in a letter to *La Feuille du jour*, that he would resume work on his own adaptation of the Calas trial, a task he had abandoned upon being informed of Chénier's parallel undertaking (*La Feuille du jour*, 27 December 1790).
8. In his utopian *L'An deux mille quatre cent quarante* (first published in 1771), Mercier foresees not only the Revolution itself (as he often boasted later), but also its effect on theatre. In the novel, the protagonist attends a theatrical re-enactment of the Calas trial so lifelike that he is made to feel ashamed of his own contemporaries, the men and women of the eighteenth century; Louis-Sébastien Mercier, *L'An deux mille quatre cent quarante* (London, 1772), p.186-87.
9. *Le Chevalier de la Barre, fait historique*, by Benoît Joseph Marsollier des Vivetières, was unfortunately never published. From newspaper reports, however, it is possible to ascertain that the play premiered on the same day as Chénier's *Jean Calas* and that it included many of the exact expressions reported to have been uttered by the Chevalier during his trial.
10. Hence, Laya readily acknowledges, in his preface to *Les Dangers de l'opinion*, having borrowed aspects of his play's intrigue from Nicolas-Toussaint des Essarts's voluminous *Causes célèbres, curieuses et intéressantes de toutes les cours souveraines du royaume, avec les jugemens qui les ont décidées*. See Jean-Louis Laya, *Les Dangers de l'opinion: drame en cinq actes* (Paris, chez Maradan, 1790), p.xi.
11. For instance, the unpublished play *Gertrude ou Le Suicide* stages the recent, tragic death of Gertrude Mainville, a young woman who had killed herself upon discovering that her name had been added, libellously, to *L'Almanach des filles de Paris*. On 27 January 1792, *La Chronique de Paris* praised the play, and asked that its performance initiate a trial against the author of *L'Almanach des filles de Paris*.

is suggested by the amusing misunderstanding which saw spectators riot during a performance of *Le Jugement de Pâris*, so disappointed were they that the play dramatised the tale of the Trojan prince and not the trial of Philippe de Pâris, the murderer of Louis Michel Le Peletier.[12] In fact, as early as July 1790, the insertion into dramatic works of legal affairs, such as crimes, trials and executions, had grown into enough of a vogue to elicit scathing criticism in the press.[13] In spite of these condemnations, however, courtroom dramas continued to attract considerable audiences, a popularity that, I will argue, grew out of the ability of such plays to serve as a necessary response to two traumas: first, the psychological scars caused by the inequity and secrecy of the legal system under the *ancien régime*, and second, the psychic wounds produced by the violent crimes at the origin of the trials being re-enacted.[14]

There is much to indicate, indeed, that the Calas plays were immediately perceived as inhabiting an ill-defined space between a theatrical performance and a ritualistic exorcism. A letter preserved at the Bibliothèque de la Comédie-Française shows that Grammont, the actor most commonly charged with playing villains at the Théâtre de la Nation, turned down the role of the

12. Victor Fournel, 'Le parterre sous la Révolution', *Revue d'art dramatique* (July-September 1893), p.12. Le Peletier instantly became one of the most illustrious martyrs of the Revolution when, soon after casting his vote at the National Convention in favour of Louis XVI's execution, he was assassinated by a former guard of the king. The painter Jacques-Louis David composed a famous portrait of Le Peletier, the original of which is regrettably not extant today, having been destroyed by Le Peletier's own daughter.
13. Hence, on 13 July 1790, *La Feuille du jour* asks, 'La Melpomène française nous fera-t-elle bientôt grâce des échafauds et des roues?' Almost a year later, on 8 July 1791, a similar critique appears in *Les Affiches, annonces et avis divers*: 'Nous n'avons plus de réflexions à faire sur ce genre de pièces, auquel il est malheureux que des gens de lettres estimables se livrent: il faut bien prendre son parti sur les tortures, les échafauds, les confesseurs, les exécuteurs, etc., qu'on nous offre maintenant sur la scène. Nous dirons seulement, qu'il est bien désagréable de ne pouvoir plus oser mener des dames au spectacle sans craindre de les voir s'évanouir.'
14. On the problems of cultural and political commemoration during the Revolution, see the chapters by Catriona Seth, 'The "dix août" (10 August 1792) in literary texts', p.75-92; and Ourida Mostefai 'Violence, terrorism and the legacy of the Enlightenment: debates around Jean-Jacques Rousseau and the Revolution', p.177-87.

Capitoul, despite Laya's best assurances that 'l'odieux de ces sortes de rôles ne reflue jamais sur le comédien qui les représente'.[15] This maxim may be accurate for fictional antagonists, but the Calas plays were re-enactments which devoted several acts to the meticulous re-creation of a real trial, quoting the exact words, or so the playwrights claimed, that had once been spoken by the various members of the Calas family.[16] As Grammont well understood, this amounted to an invitation to the spectators to re-judge the case and, inevitably, to direct a very real anger towards the Capitoul and thus, towards him.

Like Grammont, in fact, the press pondered the wisdom of re-enacting such a traumatic injustice, both for the Calas family and for the nation as a whole. On 20 December 1790, *La Feuille du jour* expressed the concern that 'tous les théâtres retentissant du nom de Calas r'ouvriront inévitablement la blessure de sa misérable veuve. Elle est à Paris depuis quinze ans, et demeure dans la rue Poissonnière avec ses deux filles. Madame Calas n'a pas quitté le deuil depuis la mort de son mari. Sa montre, arrêtée sur l'heure de son supplice, n'a pas été remontée.' The powerful image of the stopped watch hints at the inability by the Calas family to move beyond the legal murder of Jean Calas. The wound is partly closed (how else could it be reopened?), and yet it remains everywhere visible, as in the widow's black clothes and frozen watch. For better or for worse, the plays threatened to unsettle this uneasy stasis by prompting a new confrontation with the repressed event at the origin of the trauma.

Yet *La Feuille du jour* had already responded to this criticism two days earlier:

> J'entendais à côté de moi demander avec humeur: 'Pourquoi rappeler sur le théâtre ces effroyables événements?' Pourquoi?

---

15. See Laya's letter to the Théâtre de la Nation on 1 December 1790. The letter is unpublished, but can be consulted at the Bibliothèque de la Comédie-Française (in the 'Dossier d'auteur Jean-Louis Laya').
16. Hence, Laya notes explicitly that 'Tout ce que lit le greffier a été copié dans l'enquête même' (Laya, *Jean Calas*, p.29); Laya and Lemierre preface their plays with a detailed account of the trial (by Voltaire); and all three plays include variants of a number of quotes popularly attributed to Jean Calas (for instance, his response, when asked to name his accomplices, 'Où il n'y a point de crimes, il ne peut y avoir de complices').

Pour empêcher que le sang de l'innocence ne teigne encore l'échafaud. Il est utile de montrer ce cadavre à tous les siècles, de faire saigner à jamais la plaie que reçut l'humanité, quand des hommes cruels, quand des lois peut-être encore plus cruelles, ordonnèrent cet infâme attentat.

The Calas plays are thus praised precisely for their ability to reopen the wound, so as to ensure the theatre's role as a *lieu de mémoire*. Paradoxically, however, this *reopening* also serves to provide a much needed sense of *closure*. *Le Journal de Paris* described the Calas plays as 'une révision de ce fameux procès'[17] – that is, as a second viewing ('re-vision') and as a correction of it. Indeed, the plays seek to cope with a traumatic event (the unjust execution of Jean Calas) by re-enacting it and in so doing asserting control over it. In 1790, Calas's innocence was well known, but never before had he been exonerated in a trial conducted before an audience of his peers. By resurrecting the past, the Calas plays amended it from the perspective of the present, by providing Jean Calas with the fair and public trial that the 'cruel laws' of the *ancien régime* had denied him.

Indeed, the popularity of courtroom dramas derived less from the revelation they contained (that Calas was innocent) than from the opportunity they gave the spectators to confront the trauma produced by the cruel and unfair legal system of the *ancien régime*.[18] Of course, in light of the nearly three decades separating the Calas affair from its theatrical re-enactments, it may strike us as rather unlikely that anyone besides the victim's family could still be traumatised by Jean Calas's execution. Yet one should not

17. 'On peut appeler les premiers actes la révision de ce fameux procès devant le tribunal du public; rien n'y est oublié. Le spectateur est presque témoin de la mort d'Antoine Calas; il voit successivement l'accusation, l'effervescence du peuple, le fanatisme des juges, la scélératesse du capitoul et de son assesseur [...] L'auteur n'a, pour ainsi dire, voulu rien soustraire aux yeux des spectateurs' (*Le Journal de Paris*, 19 December 1791).

18. Scholars have recently argued for the existence of a profound and pervasive trauma in the years of the French Revolution, although they have presented this trauma as the result of revolutionary events, and not, as I am doing, as the result of *ancien régime* injustices and inequalities. See Barry M. Shapiro, *Traumatic politics: the deputies and the king in the early French Revolution* (University Park, PA, 2009). See also Katherine Astbury, *Narrative responses to the trauma of the French Revolution* (Oxford, 2012).

forget that the Calas trial was the first to genuinely reach – and affect – a truly broad audience, thanks to fictitious trial briefs which deeply moved and outraged men and women throughout France.[19] According to *Le Moniteur* of 29 December 1790, this pity and indignation had lost none of its intensity twenty-five years later: 'Vingt-cinq ans n'ont pas affaibli le sentiment de l'exécrable injustice qui a fait périr Calas sur l'échafaud.' That five different playwrights would have chosen, in less than a year, to write on precisely the same trial certainly suggests that it retained a powerful hold on the French imagination. More than any other trial, it was seen as symbolic of the secrecy, inequality and heartlessness of the legal system under the *ancien régime*.

As a result, even if many of the spectators lacked any association with the Calas affair, perhaps even any direct experience of the inequities of pre-revolutionary justice, it remains possible – indeed likely, given the debate in *La Feuille du jour* described above – that the audience experienced the plays as offering relief from what the sociologist Jeffrey Alexander has described as a 'cultural trauma'. In *Cultural trauma and collective identity*, Alexander distinguishes between psychological trauma, which is personal and results from direct exposure to a specific originating event, and cultural trauma, which is rooted in the collective memories of a group and results from a cultural construction.[20] While few spectators of the Calas plays likely had a direct cause for psychological trauma, the grounds for developing a cultural trauma were plentiful in the first years of the Revolution. As Jean-Clément Martin has noted, the early Revolutionaries, in an attempt to promote changes in the justice system, frequently reminded the general public, often with great hyperbole, of the barbaric trad-

19. That tears were shed throughout France for an obscure Protestant merchant owes much to Voltaire's gifts as a publicist. By means of trial briefs, fictional memoirs, hundreds of letters, printed images and the parading of Jean Calas's grief-stricken widow and daughters, Voltaire succeeded in arousing considerable pity for the Calas family and in transforming their suffering into a national *cause célèbre*. See Elizabeth Claverie, 'Procès, affaire, cause: Voltaire et l'innovation critique', *Politix* 26 (1994), p.76-85. See also Sarah Maza, *Private lives and public affairs: the causes célèbres of prerevolutionary France* (Berkeley, CA, 1993).

20. Jeffrey Alexander, 'Towards a theory of cultural trauma', *Cultural trauma and collective identity* (Berkeley, CA, 2004).

itions of *ancien régime* tribunals. For instance, soon after the storming of the Bastille, hundreds of pamphlets were published describing (and often inventing) victims of *ancien régime* injustices, found rotting in dark cells despite having committed no crime.[21] Few Frenchmen had in fact faced such injustices, but it was politically advantageous, from the Revolutionaries' point of view, that all feel the same wounds as those who had. This explains why it was so important to the playwrights, theatre directors and journalists that the spectators be made aware of the presence of Calas's actual daughters in the parterre. The reality of the daughters' wounds, coupled with the belief that the re-enactment of their father's heroism might offer them some closure, gave a sense of concreteness and specificity to what was, for most of the spectators, a rather undefined, collective trauma. Indeed, what is fascinating about the Calas plays is that they show that trauma need not consist of a personal wound, the result of a single, inexpressible event. Rather, the Calas plays seek to heal a cultural trauma, and do so by condensing the many injustices of the *ancien régime* into a representative event (the trial and execution of Jean Calas). In doing so, they participate in the construction of said cultural trauma, summon it into being, in fact, but only so as to then exorcise it publicly, by allowing the spectators to correct the unjust verdict issued against Calas.

The Calas plays are also particularly interesting because they are not only the trial of an individual; they are the trial of his trial. They suggest that the trauma of Calas's execution survived even after his posthumous exoneration in 1765, because legal proceedings under the *ancien régime* were incapable of dealing with a second trauma, the one produced by the act of violence at the origin of a trial. Shoshana Felman has argued that the ability to translate a traumatic act into a controlled and controllable narrative constitutes a significant meeting point between literature and the law.[22] Modern trials, according to Felman and Antoine Garapon,[23]

21. Jean-Clément Martin, *Violence et révolution: essai sur la naissance d'un mythe national* (Paris, 2006), p.62.
22. Shoshana Felman, 'Forms of judicial blindness, or the evidence of what cannot be seen: traumatic narratives and legal repetitions in the O. J. Simpson case and in Tolstoy's *The Kreutzer sonata*', *Critical inquiry* 23 (1997), p.738-88.
23. Antoine Garapon, *Bien juger: essai sur le rituel judicaire* (Paris, 1997).

unfold according to a particular logic of representation – a dramaturgy – that aims to make mute deeds and sufferings expressible, so as to allow a definitive judgment upon them, thereby laying them to rest as historical past. To that end, legal 'actors' (lawyers, witnesses, accuser and accused) are assigned roles in an agonistic clash between two passionate, spontaneous and diametrically opposed narratives, thus publicly re-enacting the conflict at the heart of the trial. Such a ceremonial re-enactment serves two purposes: first, it provides its participants and spectators with a performance through which to purge themselves of dangerous emotions, such as the desire for vengeance (an aim that is evocative of catharsis),[24] and second, like the Calas plays, such a trial reopens the wounds of the victims, but does so only to then be able to close them once and for all.

By contrast, legal procedures in the *ancien régime* were designed precisely to prevent such a public re-enactment. Prior to the Revolution, a trial did not unfold in the form of an agonistic debate, but consisted instead of a series of secret, one-sided interrogations. Following the discovery of a crime, an examining judge was dispatched to the scene, where he conducted and transcribed private interviews of the suspects and witnesses. These transcripts were then sent to the king's prosecutor, who constructed an initial narrative of the accused's guilt, without having met him or her, and ordered a second round of interrogations. The ensuing dossier reached its final destination in the hands of the magistrates, who arrived at a verdict by mechanically applying pre-existing formulas to the written texts presented to them. Testimonies and expert reports were given numerical values (near 'full-proof' for a confession, 'half-proof' for a reliable testimony, 'quarter-proof' for a variety of other clues), fractions of proof which were then added together to compose a verdict. Only once did the accused appear in court, less to articulate a competing account of the truth than to respond to the narrative

---

24. Readers interested in the thorny question of catharsis should consult Pierre Frantz's chapter 'Violence in the theatre of the Revolution', p.121-35; his contribution complements this one beautifully, in that it offers a broader analysis of the many different ways that violence (in all its forms, not just legal ones) is represented in revolutionary drama, and to what aims.

pre-drafted by the magistrates and already largely accepted as fact.[25] Such reliance on writing and on fixed formulas was motivated by the desire to eradicate to the greatest extent possible the human, and thus arbitrary, element in the workings of justice,[26] but in eliminating physical presence, speech, emotion and spectators from the courtroom, it diminished the ability of early modern trials to provide any catharsis following a traumatic event. The Calas plays can thus be understood as an attempt to tell a story that Calas's trials – including the successful appeal in 1765 – could not, in fact were designed not to, tell: an account of the trauma of loss, intolerance and estrangement from one's own nation.

Indeed, the Calas plays contend quite explicitly that they, and more broadly theatre, display a form of justice preferable to that of the closed tribunals of the *ancien régime*.[27] The subtitle of Chénier's tragedy, *L'Ecole des juges*, indicates one of the main objectives of the Calas plays, which is to instruct their spectators in a new mode of judgement. 'La salle' (that is, the auditorium) is presented in all three plays with an ideal image of 'La Salle', as the actual judge who defended Jean Calas was named, and thus given every incentive (including homonymic ones!) to identify with him. In the plays, the judge La Salle takes it upon himself to visit Calas in jail, to interact with him and listen to his story, and to rely, when reaching a verdict, on his own emotions and instincts rather

---

25. For a more detailed description of the modus operandi of criminal courts under the *ancien régime*, see Richard Mowery Andrews, *Law, magistracy and crime in Old Regime Paris, 1735-1789* (New York, 1994). See also Michel Foucault, *Surveiller et punir: naissance de la prison* (Paris, 1975), p.45-46.
26. Dès le XVe siècle, certains juristes ont proposé que le procès soit supprimé, ne donne pas lieu à une action physique et langagière et que tout passe par l'écrit [...] On a éliminé les avocats du pénal pour les mêmes raisons, afin d'éliminer le spectacle et de se concentrer sur la preuve'; *Représentations du procès: droit, théâtre, littérature, cinéma*, ed. Christian Biet and Laurence Schifano (Nanterre, 2003), p.14.
27. The Calas plays explicitly and repeatedly invoke the *philosophes*' by then standard critique of legal proceedings under the *ancien régime*, including the use of indices or clues as partial proofs (Lemierre, *Calas*, p.94) and the absence of defence witnesses (Laya, *Jean Calas*, p.28), defence attorneys (Chénier, *Jean Calas*, p.33) and juries and spectators (Chénier, *Jean Calas*, p.91).

than on transcripts and equations – an example that 'la salle' ought also to follow in the future. In an earlier pamphlet, Laya had even expressed the desire that 'l'homme de justice [vînt] puiser [au théâtre] des leçons d'éloquence et d'intégrité',[28] suggesting thereby that the theatre might serve as a form of re-education for men of justice trained for most of their adult lives to distrust eloquence, physical presence, instincts and emotions as the basis of a sound judgement.

Although perhaps partly tongue-in-cheek, Laya's suggestion derives from a sincere faith in the ability of a more performative mode of justice to disclose signs of innocence and guilt frequently obscured by the legal practices of the *ancien régime*. Hence, in the Calas plays, the facts of the case remain largely unchanged (though Laya and Lemierre are prone to poetic licence), but they are given less weight by the playwrights than are emotional indicators of virtue often drawn directly from the conventions of eighteenth-century sentimentalist drama.[29] For instance, the peacefulness of Jean Calas's sleep, indicative of a mind untroubled by guilt, remorse or uncertainty, is inadmissible in court, and yet, in Chénier's play, it single-handedly convinces a Catholic priest of Calas's innocence.[30] Likewise, in Lemierre's play, the fundamental expressiveness of the sleeping body prompts Madame Calas to tearfully call out, 'Que ses juges ne le voyent-ils en cet état? Est-ce là, leur dirions-nous, est-ce là le sommeil d'un criminel[?]'[31] Time and again, the three playwrights call attention to physical and behavioural traits – Calas's lack of anger or tears, his devotion, to the very end, to the welfare of his family, his stoical countenance upon learning of his imminent death – as precisely the sort of universal and unmediated evidence that

---

28. Jean-Louis Laya, *Voltaire aux Français, sur leur constitution* (Paris, chez Maradan, 1789), p.54.
29. For instance, in all three plays, Jean Calas's friends and kin throw themselves at the feet of the *capitouls* and implore them to share the accused's fate. Such a dramatic gesture ought at least to be taken into consideration when reaching a verdict, the playwrights implicitly argue, for would a truly wicked man, in particular one accused of exercising a tyrannical rule over his family, be likely to inspire such profound devotion?
30. Chénier, *Jean Calas*, p.53.
31. Lemierre, *Calas*, p.105.

should be granted a greater influence in the courtroom, as it would if the accused were allowed to re-enact his or her story, to call on character witnesses and to confront orally and publicly his or her accusers. Only such a performance, in which the plaintiff and accused are given leading roles, and their bodies, made visible, and as a result legible, would convince the judges to trust in their instinctual compassion, as well as in their reason. In true sentimentalist fashion, the playwrights argue that the experience of pity does not pose any threat to a judge's equity, because human beings experience an instinctual sympathy only in favour of persecuted virtue. Hence, compassion can act as a reliable indicator of innocence. Just as significantly, the Calas plays show that by allowing a controlled re-enactment of the conflict at the origin of a trial, public legal proceedings can encourage not only the judges but also the spectators to feel pity, terror and anger, to re-experience, to some extent, the traumatic event, but to do so this time in the belief that justice will be dealt, and the wound closed at the end of the trial.

It is striking, even if not, perhaps, entirely coincidental, that in the same seven-month period marked by the huge success of the Calas plays, the National Assembly debated and ultimately enacted a new legal code, which brought into the courtroom the brand of performative justice that had already taken hold of the theatre. As several members of the press observed, the Calas plays, by exposing the flaws of the pre-revolutionary justice system, contributed directly to the shift to a more theatrical and cathartic conception of justice: 'On a su gré à [Chénier] d'avoir rappelé un sujet bien propre à nous attacher au nouvel ordre judiciaire, en nous faisant frémir à la vue des suites horribles de la jurisprudence de nos ci-devant cours de justice.'[32] Just as the authors of the Calas plays had wished, the legal code of 1791 transformed the performance of justice to resemble more closely the one in the theatre, by introducing in France the institution of the jury, the publicity of trials and the right of the defence to an attorney, witnesses and counter-examination.

---

32. *Les Révolutions de Paris*, 26 February to 5 March 1791, no.86, p.390.

This chapter began with the resurrection of Jean Calas, that is, with the revival of a deceased body, and so it seems fitting to end it now with the very opposite: the burial of a live body. In what follows, I contend that the trial of Louis XVI and his subsequent execution constitute a telling inversion of the Calas plays, one that reveals the rise of a competing conception of justice and explains the almost complete disappearance of courtroom dramas starting in 1793.

Seeking, for his famed report to the National Convention, an illustration of the historical right of Frenchmen to try their kings, J.-B. Mailhe exhumed an unexpected tale: 'Un citoyen français arrêta, sur les bords de la Seine inférieure, le cercueil de Guillaume-le-Conquérant, en l'accusant de lui avoir pris son champ, et ne laissa porter le corps de ce prince dans le lieu de sa sépulture, qu'après qu'on lui eût restitué sa propriété.'[33] By describing not only the trial of a king, but more specifically, the trial of a dead king, Mailhe affirmed, inadvertently, the ability of legal proceedings to suspend death itself by interrupting funeral ceremonies – two rituals in many ways perfectly opposed, insofar as trials seek to unearth the past, and memorial services to bury it. Interestingly, it was precisely this resurrective power of legal proceedings, implicitly praised by Mailhe, which inspired the Jacobins' opposition to the trial of Louis XVI. Instead of a trial, the Jacobins argued that the Convention should stage the equivalent of a funeral ceremony, an immediate vote which would serve to cast the already deceased king into eternal oblivion. Medically speaking, of course, Louis was still alive in 1792, but in the eyes of the Jacobins, the insurrection of 10 August had marked the end of his life.[34] On that fateful day, he had been sentenced to death by the highest tribunal in France, the people, leading Robespierre to ask, 'Quand un roi a été anéanti par le peuple, qui a le droit de le ressusciter pour en faire un nouveau prétexte de trouble et de rébellion?'[35] Likewise, his brother

---

33. *Le Pour et le contre: recueil complet des opinions prononcées à l'Assemblée Conventionnelle dans le procès de Louis XVI*, 7 vols (Paris, Buisson, An I), vol.1, p.120.
34. For more information on the insurrection of 10 August and its representation in the novels of the Revolution, see Catriona Seth's chapter 'The "dix août" (10 August 1792) in literary texts', p.75-92.
35. *Le Pour et le contre*, vol.3, p.390.

Augustin labelled Louis 'un cadavre',[36] and Pierre Philippeaux dubbed the former king a 'fantôme politique', as well as a rotting corpse responsible for the 'émanations mortifères' poisoning the minds and bodies of the deputies.[37] Clearly, a proper burial was urgently needed, starting with a ceremony conducted with 'une sorte de solennité funèbre', to quote Barère,[38] and ending with the king's summary execution. Only this final act could bring to an end Louis's existence as a ghost, at once dead and yet disturbingly alive.

By contrast, according to Robespierre, trying the king amounted to nothing less than resurrecting him ('le ressusciter'), particularly if the Convention observed the legal forms established in 1791, as the Girondins wanted. There are many reasons why the Jacobins opposed this resurrection, starting with the fact that a trial in due form would presuppose that the king might be innocent.[39] In their eyes, Louis was guilty of having been king (to quote Saint-Just, 'on ne peut point régner innocemment');[40] his culpability preceded not only the trial, but also any specific crimes. The 10 August had thus marked a decisive victory of good over evil, and as such could not be re-enacted in a trial, which is designed to stage, at least at the outset, a conflict between two morally neutral parties. As a result, they argued, a legal re-enactment could not offer an accurate repetition of the conflict, insofar as it rested upon the erasure of precisely that which it was intended to reveal – guilt. Far from confirming the accused's culpability, a trial only threatened to obscure it or, worse, to assign it, however briefly, to the accuser. In the words of Robespierre, 'proposer de faire le procès à Louis XVI [...] c'est mettre la révolution elle-même en litige',[41] for it amounted to the

---

36. *Le Pour et le contre*, vol.3, p.380.
37. *Le Pour et le contre*, vol.4, p.3. Even the moderate Kersaint admitted, albeit for different reasons, that 'aux yeux du philosophe, cet homme [Louis] est mort le 10 août'. *Le Pour et le contre*, vol.6, p.313.
38. 'Je rappelle aux citoyens que c'est ici une sorte de solennité funèbre. Les applaudissements et les murmures sont défendus.' *Archives parlementaires*, 100 vols (Paris, 1867-), vol.55, p.710.
39. *Le Pour et le contre*, vol.3, p.384.
40. *Le Pour et le contre*, vol.1, p.185.
41. *Le Pour et le contre*, vol.3, p.384.

blasphemous implication that innocence and the people, guilt and the monarchy, might not be at all times, and for all time, synonymous.

The Jacobins also showed great concern about the ease with which a re-enactment could be manipulated. They accused Girondins and royalists alike of seeking, through songs, plays and newspaper reports, to deflect attention from Louis's crimes onto the suffering which his imprisonment was causing him, and onto the love with which he cared for his son and for a sickly servant, even in the midst of his ordeal.[42] Concerned that Louis was being resurrected less as a tragic tyrant than as a character in a *drame bourgeois*, Hébert even demanded that the king's private life be 'ensevelie dans le plus profond oubli'.[43] Such fears may not have been unfounded, for some of Louis's jailers supposedly became convinced of his innocence, as in Chénier's *Jean Calas*, simply from witnessing the serenity of his sleep.[44] A public trial, the Jacobins worried, would only give the king's partisans further opportunities to promote the image of Louis as a domestic everyman, the stoic victim of a pitiless legal system – that is, of Louis Capet as a reincarnated Calas.

Furthermore, the Jacobins clashed with the Girondins because they had little faith in the cathartic value of a legal re-enactment. Their desire to simply bury the still-living Louis irritated Condorcet, who alleged that 'les partisans secrets du trône n'attendent que le moment de pouvoir *ensevelir* dans le jugement

---

42. These examples are taken from Jules Michelet, *Histoire de la révolution française*, 9 vols (Paris, 1888), vol.6, p.162. Interestingly, in his account of the trial, Michelet largely agrees with the Jacobins. The great historian blames the members of the Convention for having conducted a sensational trial, which reintroduced Louis to the general population as a suffering, family man. From a king, Michelet states, 'le procès en [fit] un homme' (*Histoire de la révolution française*, vol.6, p.304). As a result, pity supplanted justice, and the monarchy, if not the monarch, rose from its own ashes. Michelet differs from the Jacobins, however, in his belief that the king's execution, as much as his trial, was responsible for this resurrection: 'la royauté [...] venait de ressusciter par la force de la pitié et par la vertu du sang' (*Histoire de la révolution française*, vol.6, p.301).
43. Cited in Paul and Pierrette Girault de Coursac, *Enquête sur le procès du roi Louis XVI* (Paris, 1992), p.674.
44. Michelet, *Histoire de la révolution française*, vol.6, p.162.

précipité d'un roi, les crimes de la royauté'.[45] To the Girondins, too expeditious a trial amounted to the burial not only of Louis, but also of his crimes. By contrast, they argued, a meticulous prosecution of the king, conducted in accordance with the due process of law, would *unearth* his misdeeds and expose them in such a light as to win over the remaining doubters of Louis's guilt, foremost among them the European nations then at war with France. Without a ceremonial re-enactment of the crimes of the monarchy, there could be no catharsis for those already convinced of Louis's culpability, as well as no prospect of conversion for the others. In short, for the Girondins, unity depended upon repetition, whereas for the Jacobins, a trial's reproducibility meant an unsettled Republic, one eternally 'on trial'.[46] In the words of Robespierre, 'En ouvrant une arène aux champions de Louis XVI, vous renouvelez les querelles du despotisme contre la liberté'.[47] According to the Jacobins, the people's triumph on 10 August had inaugurated a new age of social and political homogeneity. As a result, to re-enact the conflicts that had preceded it would not, as the Girondins claimed, resolve residual tensions, but would, on the contrary, renew the quarrels of the pre-republican era. Tribunals should not function as public arenas, they argued, but as altogether different sites, in which could be conducted the ceremonial elimination of those no longer members of society.

To be sure, an intense fear of the past's possible resurrection seems to have haunted the Jacobins. As early as 1792, they set out to eradicate the *ancien régime* from living memory by destroying the symbols through which it had reproduced itself into a kind of immortality. Statues were torn down and converted into cannons; royal emblems were chiselled off or painted over; and all signs of the monarchy and of the nobility were strictly forbidden, in real

45. *Le Pour et le contre*, vol.2, p.37. Emphasis added.
46. This fear of repetition is omnipresent in Robespierre's famous speech, notably when he states: 'Quoi de plus légitime, quoi de plus naturel que de répéter partout les maximes que ses défenseurs pourront professer hautement à votre barre et dans votre tribune même! Quelle république que celle dont les fondateurs lui suscitent de toutes parts des adversaires pour l'attaquer dans son berceau!' *Le Pour et le contre*, vol.3, p.390-91.
47. *Le Pour et le contre*, vol.3, p.390.

life as on the stage.[48] The Jacobins expressed particular irritation at the multitude of plays ridiculing priests, noblemen and kings on stage. While these plays were filled with republican sentiments, they gave a theatrical afterlife to defeated foes. As a Jacobin newspaper, *La Feuille du salut public*, remarked, 'cette caste ennemie du peuple a été anéantie: pourquoi leurs caractères survivraient-ils sur la scène?'[49] Starting with the King's trial, however, this policy of erasure and forgetting took on a new, macabre, dimension, as the Jacobins' fear of resurrection led them to target the very bodies – not just the replicas – of the monarchy. Whereas, up until the Revolution, the remains of deceased kings and queens had been embalmed so as to preserve them after death, the corpses of Louis, Marie-Antoinette and their son were covered with quicklime in order to hasten their disintegration.

More tellingly yet, on 31 July 1793, the Convention sanctioned Barère's proposal that the insurrection of 10 August be commemorated by digging up the monarchs of France, dousing their remains with quicklime and discarding them in unmarked graves.[50] Such a ceremony meant the corpses of the monarchy were treated much as the Jacobins had wished that Louis himself be handled – as cadavers that had not been properly disposed of, that retained a strange power over the living and, as such, needed to be buried once more, but this time in such a way as to ensure their utter oblivion. Indeed, the fears of the Jacobins that the monarchs were not quite dead, that they could, like ghosts, rise from the grave, were confirmed by the remarkably good state of preservation in which many of the bodies were found, notably that of Henri IV, who was displayed to passers-by for several days, as well as reportedly struck by a woman for 'having borne the sceptre',[51] and that of Louis XIV, whose features were unchanged,

---

48. See Serge Bianchi, *La Révolution culturelle de l'An II: élites et peuple (1789-1799)* (Paris, 1982), p.159.
49. *La Feuille du salut public*, 31 August 1793.
50. For more details, see Jules-Julien-Gabriel Berthevin, *Recherches historiques sur les derniers jours des rois de France, leurs funérailles, leurs tombeaux* (Paris, 1825). See also Sophia Beale, *The Churches of Paris* (London, 1893). For a modern account of the exhumations, see Suzanne Lindsay, 'Mummies and tombs: Turenne, Napoleon, and death ritual', *The Art bulletin* 82 (Sep. 2000), p.476-502.
51. Lindsay, 'Mummies and tombs', p.3.

but whose face had turned pitch black, a reflection of his soul, if not of his moniker (the Sun King). The destruction of these undead monarchs consisted of a fitting commemoration of 10 August because, unlike the trial of Louis XVI, it served not as a re-enactment of the insurrection, but rather as its finale – a burial ceremony, in which the dead were not remembered but, on the contrary, obliterated once and for all.

The Calas plays and the king's trial illustrate therefore two very different ways of dealing with trauma, be it linked to a specific crime or, more generally, to the *ancien régime*. In the theatre as in the tribunal, the early years of the Revolution saw the rise of a conception of re-enactment as a means of resurrecting the past, in the hope of gaining mastery over it and relegating it once and for all to history. With time, however, the Jacobins grew increasingly concerned that re-enactments, far from closing the wounds left by the *ancien régime*, were actually fostering disunity and disagreement, by keeping alive and giving a voice to social categories that had been obliterated by the institution of the Republic. To counter this threat, the Jacobins reintroduced dramatic censorship, with a view towards banishing from the stage, to quote Latour-Lamontagne, 'tout ce qui peut nous rappeler nos anciennes erreurs'.[52] Likewise, they famously passed a series of laws that struck down many of the reforms introduced by the legal Code of 1791, reforms that had been expressly intended to create a more theatrical and agonistic mode of justice. Indeed, if the Revolutionaries' predominant desire was, in the early years, to work through past conflicts by means of public re-enactments, following the execution of Louis XVI, it shifted to the other extreme, developing into an irresistible urge to bury, not only figuratively, but also literally, as the rise and fall of the guillotine's blade came to be one of the only acts to be re-enacted without fail.

52. Cited in Pierre Caron, *Paris pendant la Terreur: rapports des agents secrets du ministre de l'intérieur*, 2 vols (Paris, 1910), vol.1, p.69. Latour-Lamontagne's report is dated 11 September 1793. A few days earlier, Aristide Valcour had made a nearly identical proposal, noting that 'les seuls comédiens jouissaient du privilège étonnant d'être monarchiens parfaits au sein de la République, de rappeler tous les abus, pour en faire l'éloge, à l'instant où la loi venait de les anéantir' (*Le Journal de la Montagne*, 7 September 1793).

Violence in the theatre of the Revolution[1]

PIERRE FRANTZ

Violence is so intrinsically linked to the memory and the representations of the Revolution as to have definitively skewed their meaning. Whereas the most recent revolutions in Portugal and Tunisia have been garlanded, as it were, with carnations and jasmines respectively, no such sweet-smelling flowers adorn the French Revolution. The period's theatre could not escape that violence with which nineteenth-century (indeed twentieth-century) historical accounts were obsessed; Charles Etienne and Alphonse Martainville (an *ultra* journalist and founder of the *Drapeau blanc*, and whose links with the Restoration are well known) established this historiography's particularly heinous ideology by stressing the performances that took place during the Terror.[2] Their book, along with the anecdotes it contains, has served as an unchallenged source for historians from Henri Welschinger to Marvin Carlson; yet Etienne and Martainville's study, replete with often unverifiable incidents, is so utterly dominated by a counter-revolutionary ideology that it should be treated with caution by any serious scholar.

Our first subject to consider is the theatre not of the Terror, but rather of the Directoire. It is a topic raised by Nodier in his magnificent preface to Pixerécourt's selected dramatic works:

> Ce qu'il y a de certain, c'est que dans les circonstances où il apparut, le mélodrame était une nécessité. Le peuple tout entier venait de jouer dans les rues et sur les places publiques le plus grand drame de l'histoire. Tout le monde avait été acteur dans cette pièce sanglante, tout le monde avait été ou soldat ou

---

1. Translated by Thomas Wynn.
2. *Histoire du théâtre français, depuis le commencement de la révolution jusqu'à la réunion générale*, 4 vols (Paris, Barba, 1802). For another account of violence and the theatrical stage, see Yann Robert's chapter, 'The everlasting trials of Jean Calas: justice, theatre and trauma in the early years of the Revolution', p.103-19.

révolutionnaire, ou proscrit. A ces spectateurs solennels qui sentaient la poudre et le sang, il fallait des émotions analogues à celles dont le retour à l'ordre les avait sevrés. Il leur fallait des conspirations, des cachots, des échafauds, des champs de bataille, de la poudre et du sang; les malheurs non mérités de la grandeur et de la gloire, les manœuvres insidieuses des traîtres, le dévouement périlleux des gens de bien. Il fallait leur rappeler dans un thème toujours nouveau de contexture, toujours uniforme de résultats, cette grande leçon dans laquelle se résument toutes les philosophies, appuyées sur toutes les religions: que même ici-bas, la vertu n'est jamais sans récompense, le crime n'est jamais sans châtiment. Et que l'on n'aille pas s'y tromper! ce n'était pas peu de chose que le mélodrame! C'était la moralité de la révolution.[3]

Reading Nodier, it appears that the performance of melodrama operates as much according to the perlocutionary conditions of morality and political propaganda, as to a process akin to that which Aristotle evokes in the *Politics* when he writes of musical catharsis. Theatre treats the illness of violence. It stages violence for the greatest benefit of order and orderliness. But it remains to be seen how that conversion takes place. Does melodrama function in a specific manner? Is the notion of catharsis or the cathartic process a reasonable and viable idea when one is dealing with revolutionary theatre? One might furthermore ask if Nodier's idea, born from his reflections on the theatre of Thermidor, the Directoire and the Empire, is also relevant to the theatre of the Terror? In other words, periodisation is a problem.

It is not simply a matter of the revolutionary repertoire, but also of the relationship with the audience. One cannot question aesthetics, history and the audience without accepting that these are all fundamentally linked. In Nodier's eyes, melodrama is a theatre that comes *after* the main event, it is a 'treatment' that aids in convalescence. But how then did this theatre function *during* the crisis itself? To answer this question, let us turn to some examples, which we hope will serve to evoke the wider panorama.

Contemporary evidence points overwhelmingly to the invasion of theatres – especially frequent during the Terror – by highly

3. Charles Nodier, 'Préface', in *Théâtre choisi de G. de Pixerécourt*, 4 vols (Nancy, 1841), vol.1, p.vii-viii.

politicised spectators, who would violently interrupt the performances. One should at once remark that that while violence did indeed erupt in the auditorium, it was not a phenomenon particular to this period. Well before the Revolution, eighteenth-century theatrical performances had been marked by intense audience interaction; spectators would directly intervene to impose the performance of such and such a play, to ban another, or to demand that a play's run be extended. The newspapers and journals of the period give many examples of unruly behaviour in Parisian as well as provincial theatres. However, although the introduction of seating in the *parterre* resulted in the 'cooling' of the audience (as numerous contemporaries attested), the rowdiness started up with renewed vigour from the start of the revolutionary events. Serious incidents marked the performances of *Charles IX* in 1789, *L'Ami des lois* in January 1793, and *Caïus Gracchus* in October 1793. But the troubles continued under the Directoire and the Consulat and even into the Empire: for example, the boisterousness of the club-wielding Muscadins in 1795, and the quarrels at performances of Lemierre's *Christophe Colomb*, which saw one man killed in 1809. One should also note the violence to which the actors were subjected, as much under the Terror as during the Thermidorian Reaction, and at the hands of the public and the authorities alike: Jean Bon Saint-André tasked an itinerant troupe of actors, surrounded by soldiers, with performing plays 'par et pour le peuple'; the actor Bordier was hanged; Dugazon was threatened, humiliated and forced by the sans-culottes to pay an 'amende honorable' for having mocked Marat. Yet, conversely, this same violence serves as a yardstick by which to measure the audience's fieriness, and the force of its enthusiasm: stories abound which foreground the audience's enthusiasm in Year II, and – although I will not dwell on such stories – it is important to keep in mind the theatre audience's astonishing reactivity. Greatly enhanced by the revolutionary context, this responsiveness is in fact a way into thinking more carefully and clearly about theatre as a lived experience (or the 'sens vécu'), that is to say, to pose more acutely the question of the audience's role and function. In other words, the representation or performance of violence through revolutionary theatre must be understood in its relation with the theatrical event in its entirety.

It is possible to distinguish a number of different cases or categories. Far from all the conventions imposed on the official theatres under the *ancien régime* (and which still weighed heavily in 1789, even though their impact had certainly grown weaker), the theatre of the Revolution was no longer burdened by *bienséances* when it came to the staging of murder or suicide. In the case of political murder, it was often a classical subject that served as the motivation or indeed justification of this violent act. This subject was explicitly correlated with clearly valorised behaviour. At the start of the Terror, Jean-François Delacroix (also called d'Eure-et-Loir) declared: 'Il n'est personne qui, en sortant de la représentation de *Brutus* ou de *La Mort de César*, ne soit disposé à poignarder le scélérat qui tenterait d'asservir son pays.'[4] It is most unlikely that the majority of Voltaire's audience in the 1730s and 1740s would ever have understood the play in these terms, even though some critics of *Brutus* did suggest it in 1730. But in August 1793, ten days after the Convention voted a decree in favour of performances 'par et pour le peuple' of these two plays in particular, that body's intention was clearer in the light of such declarations. Even if one accepts a certain amount of 'posturing', it must be acknowledged that this style of declaration is part of the Terrorist project. Furthermore Marie-Joseph Chénier had proposed this kind of slogan from February 1792 onwards. Clearly one can read in these famous lines from *Caïus Gracchus* (first performed 9 February 1792) a reaction against the violence of the Revolution's first years; in Act I, scene iv the eponymous hero urges the people not to take it upon themselves to punish the senators: 'Rome sait à quel point mon cœur doit les haïr, / Mais c'est avec la loi que je veux les punir.'[5] When the play was revived in October 1793, the hemistich 'Des lois et non du sang' (Act II, scene ii) was applauded while the Montagnard deputy Albitte vainly tried to stop the performance, only to be booed out of the auditorium. Chénier's reputation for 'modérantisme' and 'feuillantisme' was established from that point on, although he appears rather more ambiguous in *Timoléon* (1794); while Timoléon does not directly tarnish himself by killing his own

4. *Le Moniteur*, 15 August 1793.
5. Marie-Joseph Chénier, *Caïus Gracchus* (Paris, 1793), p.16.

brother Timophane, he does approve the murderer Ortagoras's actions, letting him proceed by veiling himself with his cloak:

ORTAGORAS (*frappant Timophane*)

Meurs, tyran.

TIMOPHANE

Ciel!
(*Il tombe auprès du tombeau de son père.*)[6]

The chorus ('du peuple et des guerriers') then justifies the murderer in the final scene (p.68): 'Les lois étaient sans force, et son trépas est juste: / Ton poignard a sauvé l'état.' Violence is external to the law: it is that of a citizen, a respectable *prytanis*, who acts in the name of republican principles but outside of all judgement. He comes to the aid of the republic, substituting his own violence for the law that is presented as powerless. It would be excessive, however, to interpret this episode as a call to political murder; from the winter of 1793 Chénier's situation was perilous, his brothers André and Louis-Sauveur were each to be imprisoned from spring 1794 on, he himself felt threatened, and he pledged obedience to the Montagnards. Nevertheless, a fundamental ambiguity must not be concealed here; it is undeniable that Chénier was haunted by a fratricidal fantasy, concealed as it was under the guise of fantasy of tyrannicide. Resonant with personal implications,[7] fratricide was exorcised by the play. Here, the interpretation of catharsis is unavoidable; Timoléon's brother Timophane strives for absolute power. He embodies the Terror whose political agenda he defends. Chénier therefore *authorises* tyrannicide and, along with it, fratricide, thereby repeating the accusation laid against Robespierre's supporters.

The subject of Brutus enjoyed marked success during the Terror. The Terror's violence never appeared so clearly as when mythology, conveyed not only in propaganda but also by

---

6. Marie-Joseph Chénier, *Timoléon, tragédie en trois actes avec des chœurs* (Paris, An III) p.65.
7. Marie-Joseph was slanderously accused of letting his brother be guillotined, whereas we know today that it was a reckless mistake on the part of the brothers' father which led to André's execution.

the theatre and all forms of representation, personified that violence in family relations: the Revolution demanded that one kill one's son, wife, brother and parents, as and when necessary. The successive elimination of Monarchiens, Feuillants, Girondins, Hébertistes and Dantonistes is clearly fratricide; and tragedy, which of course had long treated this theme, gives it a certain grandeur without one ever being able to assert (despite all the cant and all the censure, despite all the revolutionary *postures*) that it had played even the least direct part in any tyrannicide. The theme is taken to its extreme when it is, in a sense, 'de-aestheticised'. One might thus compare the performances of Voltaire's *Brutus* (sometimes followed, in 1791, by a *tableau vivant* representing David's famous painting) with a play like Pompigny's *L'Epoux républicain*. When *Brutus* was revived during the Revolution, the hero no doubt embodied republican values in the eyes of some of the audience. Since the play was written, however, there has been a debate over this austere *virtu*. David had endeavoured to tone down his hero's severe violence, emphasising not the violent act of his sons' execution, but rather the father's mourning; evidence of David's intention can be found in his preparatory sketches, which demonstrate how his treatment of the subject evolved. The Comédiens-Français had also emphasised the paternal tragedy, but while the aesthetic of the classical painting suspends violence, Pompigny's *drame* proposes a fully realised 'patriotic' model. The action takes place after the Law of Suspects was voted in (on 17 September 1793): a father, who has taken the name of Franklin, unhesitatingly denounces his son and wife; only the latter is guilty and, in this context, he knows that he is sending her to the guillotine. The contemporary context of the action, and the date of the performance (the play was staged on 8 February 1794) endow this praise of familial denouncement with direct resonance; a model of behaviour is here recommended to the citizen-spectators. In terms of intentions, values and aesthetics, Voltaire's tragedy and Pompigny's *drame* are utterly opposed.

The particularity of violence in revolutionary theatre is at its most acute in its representation and that of the forms with which it is associated. One might contrast, for instance, representation *through gesture* ['geste'] with that *in action* ['acte']. If one turns to those plays that stage scenes of collective violence, analogous to those occurring in what one might call 'revolutionary reality' (uprisings, revolts, lynchings, massacres), one can identify several types of treatment. Accused by the colonial lobby of inciting the Antilles slaves to violence, Olympe de Gouges defended herself in the preface to *L'Esclavage des noirs, ou L'Heureux Naufrage* (first performed as *L'Esclavage des nègres* at the Comédie-Française in December 1789) by highlighting the aim she was pursuing: 'Cette production est-elle incendiaire? Non. Présente-t-elle un caractère d'insurrection? Non. A-t-elle un but moral? Oui sans doute. Que me veulent donc ces colons avec des termes si peu ménagers?'[8] She then addressed the slaves, blaming their 'férocité' (p.4), and called for harmony far removed from 'le poison, le fer, les poignards, [les] supplices les plus barbares' (p.5). Revolt is simultaneously just and reprehensible. The slaves revolted in support of one of their fellows who was unfairly accused, and they were going to be executed but were finally pardoned by a decent soldier who declares in Act III, scene v: 'Je ne suis point envoyé ici pour ordonner le carnage et pour répandre du sang, mais pour ramener l'ordre' (p.73). With his refusal to use force, the representation of violence is now integrated into a moral lesson addressed to the slaves, as well as in an appeal to clemency. Insurrectional violence is explained, condemned, pardoned. Violence is suspended, as witnessed so often in the *drames bourgeois* and melodramas. *Action* becomes *gesture*.

Another example of this transformation can be found in *La Discipline républicaine*, a 'fait historique' with words by Plancher ('Aristide') Valcour set to music by François Foignet; it was performed in Year II (1794) at the Opéra-Comique. A good and compassionate representative has been sent to the Vendée, where he is obliged to have a royalist spy guillotined or shot, and the latter does not want to be saved despite all the republican hero's goodwill (p.21-23):

LE REPRÉSENTANT

Homme incorrigible! Ignores-tu qu'après avoir tenté tous les moyens de te sauver, je serai forcé de t'envoyer au supplice?

---

8. Olympe de Gouges, *L'Esclavage des noirs, ou L'Heureux Naufrage* (Paris, 1792), p.3-4.

L'ESPION

O mon Dieu! Oui; je m'y attends bien: mais le paradis est au bout.

LE REPRÉSENTANT

Qu'on le conduise à la Commission militaire.[9]

The execution is, in a sense, conjured away, just as it was with the guillotine.[10] A second case arrives to be judged: the unfortunate Victor has stolen a loaf with three of his comrades – will they be executed?

LE REPRÉSENTANT

Républicain! (Car tu mérites ce nom) Il me serait bien doux d'adopter à ton égard le parti de la clémence: mais la loi s'y oppose, et la discipline républicaine exige un exemple terrible. [...] Que chaque compagnie nomme un citoyen pour faire les fonctions de juge dans l'affaire des quatre soldats, prévenus et convaincus du délit de leur propre aveu.
(*Roulement: chaque compagnie forme un cercle*)
[...]
(*Roulement; on rompt les cercles; chaque compagnie se remet en bataille. Les six soldats désignés pour juger, restent hors des rangs, s'approchent les uns des autres et forment un nouveau cercle. A l'instant du roulement, Cécile a poussé un cri douloureux et perdu l'usage de ses sens; on lui donne des soins.*)

At the very moment that the court is to pronounce the death sentence, the *représentant* cuts off the judge and pardons the four young thieves. And he is right to do so: Victor and his friends go on to fight heroically, but only he survives, dedicating himself to the republican – or rather, Montagnard – cause (p.32). Valcour, in short, advocates clemency in the armed forces in the name of efficacy. This substituting of the simulacrum is intended to have a curative effect. It is from this viewpoint that one can analyse the various 'brigand plays', such as La Martellière's *Robert chef des brigands* (first performed in 1793); plays on this theme were especially numerous under the Directoire, The question of the legitimacy of violence is central here, and it is most often resolved

9. *La Discipline républicaine, fait historique, en un acte, en prose, mêlé d'ariettes* (Paris, Cailleau, 1794), p.16.
10. On the guillotine's *unspectacular* quality, see Paul Friedland's recent book, *Seeing justice done: the age of spectacular capital punishment in France* (Oxford, 2012).

in gesture, in a choreographic resolution, one might say, such as occurred in the famous performances at the Beijing opera during the Maoist period. The suspension of violence ultimately relieves the spectator. But at the same time, gesture is meant to intimidate, to break the courage of the enemies of the fatherland, to threaten. The threat is thus inextricably linked to exorcism.

A very different case is provided by the spectacular work *La Journée du dix août 1792, ou La Chute du dernier tyran*, written by Saulnier and with music by Darrieux:

> *Le peuple brise le trône et tout ce qu'il rencontre. Un filou profite de la confusion, met un effet précieux dans sa poche; un sans-culotte s'en aperçoit et le saisit.*
>
> LE SANS-CULOTTE
>
> Apprends malheureux! Que le peuple est ici pour punir un tyran, venger ses droits opprimés; et non pour commettre des bassesses. *(Il lui brûle la cervelle.)*[11]

It is not clear if the work was performed under this title in October 1792, or in August 1794. On the hypothesis that this play was indeed performed a mere two months after the recent events it depicts, in a period when the revolutionary leaders were confronted head on by the political problems of violence (after the events of 10 August and the September Massacres), its meaning appears most ambiguous. In this case, murder, lynching and summary justice give one food for thought, as the staged performance 'doubles' them, repeats them, one might even say 'rehearses' them, without however condemning them. What should we one to make of this scene in which a traitor is attacked, just one month after the September Massacres (p.38)?

> CHŒUR
>
> Le scélérat! frappons, arrachons lui la vie:
> Perfide, expire sous nos coups.
>
> *(Il est immolé par le peuple; son cadavre est traîné sur la scène, et suivi d'un peloton de piquiers conduits par un sans-culotte armé d'une hache.)*

11. Guillaume Saulnier and the Citoyen Darrieux, *La Journée du dix août 1792 ou La Chute du dernier tyran* (Paris, An II), p.47. On the representation of these events, see Catriona Seth, 'The "dix août" (10 August 1792) in literary texts', p.75-92.

LE JACOBIN

Courage, Citoyens! D'un vil conspirateur
Vous venez de purger la terre;
Que son corps tout sanglant, traîné dans la poussière,
Jusqu'au fond du palais apporte la terreur.

This episode prompts several remarks, the first of which is that the attack is carried out not by an identifiable character, but rather by the chorus that represents the people. Next, there is an appeal to the diegetic citizens that seems to cross the fourth wall, addressing the extra-diegetic theatre audience. And there is an epic and literary echo, that of Hector's corpse dragged through the dust. With the establishment of the Revolutionary Tribunal on 17 August 1792 with the (unfulfilled) aim of averting further violence, such a justification of violence and such a call to violence in an operatic work can only be interpreted in view of the date at which that piece was performed; violence is (vainly) deployed in a homeopathic sense, a controlled dose of violence is exerted in the hope of preventing further outbreaks.

A series of plays in the same spirit also incite violence, albeit laughing innocently as they do so. This is the case with plays promoting dechristianisation and those works imbued with the festive and anticlerical mood of autumn 1793; one should also take into account those carnivalesque comedies that challenge the symbols of the Church and the monarchy. Consider for instance, Lebrun-Tossa's three-act prose comedy *La Folie de Georges* (first performed at the Théâtre de la Cité on 4 pluviôse An II); in his madness, King George III takes himself for a young girl, thereby recalling the gender-inversion that is present in the most traditional of carnival rituals; he sobs 'Je suis la plus malheureuse des femmes';[12] and he confuses Burke with Alexander the Great's steed Bucephalus – whom he wants to mount and spur on – and then with Don Quixote's nag Rocinante. At the end of *La Folie de Georges* a procession appears that leads the mad king to his secure asylum. The procession is led by Grey, Fox

---

12. Jean-Antoine Lebrun-Tossa, *La Folie de Georges, ou L'Ouverture du parlement d'Angleterre* (Paris, Barba, An II), p.16.

and Sheridan 'en bonnet rouge', who cry out 'Vive la Nation!' The stage directions read (p.45-46):

> Calonne [...] conduit ensuite par le licou un âne couvert du manteau royal, portant le sceptre et la couronne entre les deux oreilles; lui, il porte écriteau devant et derrière avec ces inscriptions: Faux monnayeur, voleur public. La cage, dans laquelle est le roi, sur un char, suit l'âne. Burke, Greenville, Chesfield, Lansdown, tirent le char; d'autres lords enchaînés les suivent.

In Sylvain Maréchal's famous *Le Jugement dernier des rois*, comic acts of violence are inflicted on the sovereigns of Europe before a volcano erupts, killing them all. The theatre audience's laughter, shared with the sans-culottes, welcomed these violent scenes, as contemporary accounts attest, and this laughter can be analysed in two distinct and opposed ways. Firstly, one perceives therein a symbolic violence, as derision comes to the service of violence by making it in some way *innocent*, child-like. Consider, for instance, that *Le Jugement dernier des rois* was performed just two days after Marie-Antoinette's execution; one might treat this performance as a kind of joyous repetition in which nature takes on the role of the executioner Sanson, and in which case theatre functions as a euphoric liberation through violence. Theatre saps violence of the anxiety that is germane to the Terror. Secondly, a different interpretation suggests a shrinking from violence; the sans-culottes refrain from killing the monarchs themselves and the carnivalesque ritual derives from a saturnalian economy, in which case this is a festive outlet, a brief moment of catharsis, wherein violence is represented by means of gesture.

One might mention yet another type of representation of violence, one which is embedded in mythology and in the rhetoric of sacrifice. There is a vast repertoire of plays dedicated to the martyrs of the Revolution including Marat, Lepeletier de Saint-Fargeau, Beaurepaire, Viala and Bara. Let us consider for example those plays that stage the spectacle of the heroic deaths of the Viala and Bara children. In *Agricol Viala, ou Le Jeune héros de la Durance* (first performed at the Théâtre des Amis de la patrie on 13 Messidor An II), the eponymous hero is eager to fight the federalists who wish to cross the Durance river, and his mother Pauline tells him: 'Ne nous occupons que de la République, mon cher Agricol; voilà ta véritable mère: et, si l'ennemi vient, ne songe qu'à elle; oublie ton âge; sois un homme! Il faut qu'aujourd'hui le laurier de la victoire ceigne ton front, ou que la palme civique orne ton cercueil.'[13] He charges off to cut the cable of the pontoon seized by his enemies when he was distracted: 'Agricol, en chemise, en caleçon, nus pieds, les manches de sa chemise retroussées, une petite hache à la main' (p.24). The martyr's heroism and the enemies' violence lead to a violent but justified reaction. Shots are fired, but the boy's mission is successful. He has been shot, and, laid out, utters his final words: 'Je meurs; cela m'est égal: c'est pour la liberté!' (p.25). Martial songs, taken up in chorus by the audience, popularised this military enthusiasm, which is entirely in the spirit of mass conscription.

In Briois's *La Mort du jeune Bar[r]a* (first performed at the Théâtre Républicain on 15 floréal An II), the eponymous youth, pursued by his enemies, draws them towards him:

> Nul danger n'est certain, et je ne dois pas souffrir que ces êtres-là respirent: j'en détruis deux, quatre; j'en effraie cent, et la terreur est la mort des traîtres. Ne m'ont-ils pas tué mes trois camarades; ils m'ont vu seul; ils avaient d'un coup de carabine brisé mon pistolet dans ma main; ils me tenaient, si je n'avais eu bonnes jambes: un seul m'a poursuivi ici, et je l'y ai attiré pour le payer.[14]

Courage prevails, and he is ready to kill them face to face: 'Terrassons, portons partout la mort, mais en face. Point de moyens sourds, ils sont faits pour les Pitt, les Cobourg, les Guillaume' (p.12). The boy fights like a soldier, joyously and in song: 'nous secondons les efforts de ces braves Montagnards en tuant le plus de brigands que nous pouvons, et nous ne chantons que *ça ira* en nous précipitant sur leurs pas, ou *La Carmagnole* en frappant du sabre et de la bayonnette' (p.20). His mother joins in the party, and shoots down some enemies who have forced open her door. Bara is killed, and instead of crying 'Vive le roi', he shouts 'Vive la république'. The play ends with a tableau (p.37):

---

13. *Agricol Viala, ou Le Jeune héros de la Durance, fait historique et patriotique [...] paroles du Citoyen Philipon [de la Madeleine], musique du Citoyen L. Jadin* (Paris, Duchesne An VII), p.22.
14. Citoyen Briois, *La Mort du jeune Bar[r]a, ou Une journée de la Vendée, drame historique en un acte* (Paris, Barba, An II), p.10.

Quand on apporte Barra, les deux Hussards le soutiennent sur leurs bras; quelques volontaires suivent derrière, et font groupe. On le place sur une chaise vers un côté de la scène. Sa veste doit avoir une manche déchirée au-dessus de l'avant-bras, et on voit la chemise teinte de sang en abondance; des serviettes qui lui ceignent le corps en sont toutes imbibées; il en coule de sa tête, et il n'a ni bonnet ni manteau.

The staging of the hero's death and the final words are the result of a relatively sophisticated aesthetic treatment, whereby the *pathétique* is held in tension with epic exaltation. The hero's joy, his death-defying enthusiasm, the elements of comedy mixed with emotion, the prosaic simplicity of the spectacle and the characters' speech give this representation an Eisensteinian dimension. The ritual representation of mourning, which swept through the period's serious theatre, allowed sacredness to be transferred to the stage, and thereby truly transformed the spectacle of violence.

The staging of the spectacle of mass violence in such *faits historiques et patriotiques* is typical of the theatre in the second year of the new republic. Violent actions or gestures were imitated in the playhouses. The stages were overrun by bellicose spectacles, and the majority of the Revolution's great military episodes were represented in dramatic form soon after they occurred in reality. This is the case for the various 'siege-plays' (*Le Siège de Lille, de Toulon, de Thionville, de Verdun...*); and the same is true of the great revolutionary *journées* (storming of the Bastille; 10 August), as well as of the war in the Vendée, and the war against the federalist insurgency. These were occasions of military spectacle. Despite being in short supply, the Convention released large amounts of saltpetre for these performances which prompted, as Michel Noiray puts it, a 'tapage de chien'.[15] Authors collaborated with theatre troupe directors in creating spectacles that would take advantage of all the stage's possibilities, making particular use of the wings where the dramatic action would continue through sound; spatial and aural expansion thereby effectively extended the spectacle. As just one example of these

---

15. Michel Noiray, 'L'opéra de la Révolution (1790-1794): un "tapage de chien"?', in *La Carmagnole des muses: l'homme de lettres et l'artiste dans la Révolution*, ed. Jean-Claude Bonnet (Paris, 1988), p.359-79.

'superproductions', let us turn to Joigny's *Le Siège de Lille, ou Cécile et Julien* (first performed on 21 November 1792 at the Opéra-Comique):

> On bat la générale et le tocsin sonne dans toute la ville, une patrouille traverse le théâtre. Le canon se fait entendre avec force. L'on voit passer des bombes de tous côtés, et les cris au feu se font entendre.
>
> Le feu prend aux bâtiments du fond. Au même instant le factionnaire qu'on a posté sur le théâtre fait feu.[16]

No less than nine successive dialogue-free scenes show episodes from the siege, with typically violent scenes such as women fainting and mothers fleeing with their children: 'Les volets d'une croisée de cette maison se brisent, une femme échevelée, et tenant son enfant à la mamelle, paraît à cette croisée, en poussant des cris perçants. Elle jette son enfant après l'avoir embrassé à ceux qui sont en bas en dessous de cette croisée' (p.57). This realism cannot effacer la symbolic stylisation, which is so evident in the image of the child at his mother's breast. The playwright thereby gives spectacular form to typically journalistic topics, and such a form throws the horrors of war into stark contrast against republican order. Military parades, republican songs, heroic acts – these all conjure away violence in a spectacle that celebrates a return to order. Chaos is transformed into an order now dominated by the republic.

The omnipresence of violence in the republican repertory and in the spectacles of the Revolution invites us to reflect on the limits of art. The spectacle of violence is transformed through the combination of, on the one hand the *drame* and tragedy (which are necessarily mimetic), and on the other the *realia* of lived experience (which are inevitably made unreal by the very fact of being staged). But forms, intentions and the proximity to historical events can establish a (sometimes abject) contiguity with revolutionary violence.[17] The ambiguity of these performances indicates the need for further research towards an anthropology

---

16. Citoyen Joigny, *Le Siège de Lille, ou Cécile et Julie* (Paris, An II), p.55.
17. Judith Schlanger, 'Théâtre révolutionnaire et représentation du bien', *Poétique* 22 (1975) p.268-83.

of theatre, while encouraging us to gather more contemporary observations and to pursue our analysis of accounts and documents concerning such performances. There remains the powerful fascination exerted by the spectacle of revolutionary violence, a fascination and a horror epitomised in the guillotine, which was so often described by contemporaries as a 'fatal théâtre'. Dubos and then Burke suggestively evoked the scaffold's telling force when they described tragedy through this topical comparison; the reflections of Diderot and Rousseau, of Plutarch too, are of interest here. Without doubt, the representation of violence is at the heart of theatre, and it is this representation that is so central to the fascinating power that the image of the Revolution continues to exert today.

III

Violence and institutions

Violence, vulnerability and subjectivity in Sade

THOMAS WYNN

In the wake of Apollinaire's celebrated description of the marquis de Sade as 'cet esprit le plus libre qui ait encore existé',[1] a critical focus on the extreme Sadean self has served to bring an otherwise marginalised writer into the canon.[2] The assumption that the Sadean subject (as found in the marquis's fiction and biography alike) is sovereign, isolated and immutable has proved to be remarkably tenacious. Simone de Beauvoir's account, for example, of the tensions in Sade's thought between the individual and the collective is founded on three assumptions about the Sadean subject; it is pre-constituted and bears no trace of its genesis ('Quand nous commençons à découvrir Sade, il est fait déjà et nous ne savons pas comment il est devenu ce qu'il est'); it is immutable (Sade is 'entêté dans ses singularités'); and its obstinate isolation is founded on the refusal of ethical intersubjectivity ('Sade conteste [...] l'existence *a priori* d'une relation donnée entre moi et l'autre sur laquelle ma conduite devrait abstraitement se régler').[3] In a similar vein, Adorno and Horkheimer anchored their critique of the Enlightenment in an analysis of Juliette's extreme independence;[4] and Jean Deprun, Alice Laborde and Pierre Hartmann have argued that 'isolisme' and a radical critique of intersubjectivity lie at the heart of Sade's thought.[5]

1. Guillaume Apollinaire, *L'Œuvre du marquis de Sade* (Paris, 1909), p.17.
2. On Sade's reception, see Françoise Laugaa-Traut, *Lectures de Sade* (Paris, 1973); and Eric Marty, *Pourquoi le XXᵉ siècle a-t-il pris Sade au sérieux?* (Paris, 2011). I will use the words 'subject' and 'self' interchangeably to indicate a model for intelligibility and agency.
3. Simone de Beauvoir, *Faut-il brûler Sade?* (Paris, 1955), p.15, 13, 76.
4. Theodor W. Adorno and Max Horkheimer, *Dialectic of Enlightenment* (London, 1997).
5. Jean Deprun, 'Sade philosophe', in Sade, *Œuvres*, ed. Michel Delon, 3 vols (Paris, 1990-1997), vol.1, p.lix-lxix; Alice M. Laborde, 'La notion d'isolisme et ses implications lyriques dans l'œuvre du marquis de Sade', *SVEC* 88 (1972),

More recently Norbert Sclippa has analysed the absolute liberty and immunity enjoyed by Sade's fictional heroes,[6] and Susan Searls Giroux has seen in the 'relentless social fragmentation and violent isolation' that characterises Sade's work, the 'unerring prophesy of our time', a period which follows Sade in its 'exaltation of the solitary Survivor whose success is predicated on the elimination of a world with others'.[7]

A passage from *Les Cent vingt journées de Sodome* presents in acute form the stereotypically Sadean relation between the subject and the object of violence. On 20 February, at the château de Silling, Desgranges recounts the following *passion meurtrière*:

> Celui du 29 décembre, de Champville, qui aimait à fouetter des femmes grosses, veut la mère et la fille toutes deux grosses; il les lie chacune sur une plaque de fer, l'une au-dessus de l'autre; un ressort part, les deux plaques se rejoignent étroitement, et avec une telle violence, que les deux femmes sont réduites en poudre, elles et leurs fruits.[8]

The libertine agent is singular and pre-constituted, having already appeared in the narrative of Champville, another *historienne* at Silling. Recognisable despite his anonymity, this subject is not threatened by the brutality he has engineered, and he remains pristine, emerging intact from the violent scenario. The objects, on the other hand, are multiple; the women are pregnant so as to increase the number of victims whilst simultaneously denying recognition or individuation to those invisible foetuses. Desgranges's story crystallises the libertine search for pleasure which, as Thomas DiPiero tells us, 'can properly be described as inscription or writing of violence performed not just on the victim's body but on her entire subjectivity'.[9] Here, in that

---

p.871-80; Pierre Hartmann, *Le Contrat et la séduction: essai sur la subjectivité amoureuse dans le roman des Lumières* (Paris, 1998), p.305-54.

6. Norbert Sclippa, *Pour Sade* (Paris, 2006), p.31-42.
7. Susan Searls Giroux, 'Sade's revenge: racial neoliberalism and the sovereignty of negation', *Symposium* 44:1 (2010), p.1-26 (19).
8. D. A. F. de Sade, *Les Cent vingt journées de Sodome*, in *Œuvres*, vol.1, p.366. For other accounts of violence in Sade, see this volume's chapters by Michèle Vallenthini (p.93-102), Jean-Christophe Abramovici (p.221-28) and Will McMorran (p.229-49).
9. Thomas DiPiero, 'Disfiguring the victim's body in Sade's *Justine*', in Veronica

dual process's extreme form, the annihilation of the body is concurrent with that of the self, as the already insignificant victims are literally pulverised.

This chapter aims to decentre and destabilise this enduring narrative that has proved so seductive to writers and scholars. Analysis may hitherto have focused on an individualism founded on the brutalisation and destruction of others, but an examination of vulnerability to violence reveals a different ethical valence in Sade's thought. Claims that Sadean subjectivity is resolute and absolute have been overstated.[10] Consider, for instance, how Sade starts his *grande lettre* of 20 February 1781: 'Le malheur ne m'avilira jamais; / Je n'ai point dans les fers pris le cœur d'un esclave (*Les Arsacides*) / et je ne l'y prendrai jamais.'[11] What appears to be a forceful statement of independence is nothing of the sort. By citing Peyraud de Beaussol's tragedy, Sade does not confirm his integral self so much as decentre and diminish it through comparison ('I am as unique and as strong as this fictional hero...'). Consider, too, the episode in *Aline et Valcour* when the infant Valcour is expelled from the royal palace having thumped the 'prince illustre'.[12] Although one might be tempted to treat this outburst as the precocious violence of a fully constituted and singular brute ('il semblait que tout dût me céder,

---

Kelly and Dorothea Von Mücke (eds), *Body and text in the eighteenth century* (Stanford, CA, 1994), p.247-65 (255).

10. Some critics have, nonetheless, questioned the fixity of the Sadean self, stressing instead its fragility, contingency and volatility; Julie Candler Hayes, *Identity and ideology: Diderot, Sade, and the serious genre* (Amsterdam and Philadelphia, PA, 1991), especially p.105-108; DiPiero, 'Disfiguring the victim's body in Sade's *Justine*'; Michel Delon, 'Le tremblement de l'identité', in *Sade en toutes lettres: autour d'Aline et Valcour*, ed. Michel Delon and Catriona Seth (Paris, 2004), p.60-69; Thomas Wynn, *Sade's theatre: pleasure, vision, masochism*, SVEC 2007:02.

11. *Correspondance du marquis de Sade et de ses proches enrichies de documents, notes et commentaires*, ed. Alice Laborde, 20 vols (Geneva, 1999-), vol.16, p.41-42. Unless indicated otherwise, the recipient of all Sade's letters quoted here is his wife.

12. Sade, *Aline et Valcour, Œuvres*, vol.1, p.403. Delon cautions against the conventional reading of this passage as transparently biographical; see 'Sade autobiographe: les personnages de Valcour et de Rodin', in *Autobiography, historiography, rhetoric*, ed. Mary Donaldson-Evans, Lucienne Frappier-Mazur and Gerald Prince (Amsterdam, 1994), p.75-86.

que l'univers entier dût flatter mes caprices, et qu'il n'appartenait qu'à moi seul et d'en former et de les satisfaire'), the violence in this sequence in fact continues to constitute the impressionable[13] Valcour as a subject, for whereas the prince and Valcour had previously been somewhat of a unit ('on s'empressait de me *réunir à lui*', emphasis added), it is through bearing the violence of others that the latter achieves greater distinction: 'je me vengeai de ses résistances par des coups très multipliés, sans qu'aucune considération m'arrêtât, et sans qu'autre chose que la force et la *violence* pussent parvenir à me *séparer* de mon adversaire' (emphasis added). Valcour is recognised as a distinct individual less on account of his acts of violence, but crucially because he is subjected to the violence committed by nameless others. The Valcour episode demonstrates that violence exerts a creative as well as a destructive force upon its object, in that it brings the recognisable subject into being. If the self is indeed constituted at least in part by others, then the role violence plays in subjectivity cannot be limited to the expression of an already autonomous self.[14]

To explore further violence's role in subjection we might turn to a series of texts in which Sade returns repeatedly to brutality, vulnerability and selfhood, namely his prison correspondence.[15] Having already been incarcerated at Saumur, Miolans and Pierre-Encise, he was imprisoned at Vincennes in 1777 and then at the Bastille in 1784, before being hastily transferred to Charenton during the unrest of July 1789; after a period of liberty, he was returned to the asylum in 1803. Much of his extant correspondence dates from his incarceration at Vincennes and the Bastille, during which time he frequently evokes the 'nouvelles horreurs

13. 'Je crus, dès que je pus raisonner, que la nature et la fortune se réunissaient pour me combler de leurs dons; je le crus, parce qu'on avait la sottise de me le dire, et ce préjugé ridicule me rendit hautain, despote et colère.' Sade, *Aline et Valcour, Œuvres*, vol.1, p.403.
14. John Dunkley examines the moral ambiguity of the agent of violence in 'Gambling and violence; Loaisel de Tréogate as a neuroscientist?', p.17-33.
15. Odile Jaffré-Cook's chapter in this current volume also analyses prison correspondence, that of Dutailli de Saint-Pierre; see p.161-75. On the status of Sade's correspondence as literature, see Philippe Roger, 'Note conjointe sur Sade épistolier', in *La Fin de l'ancien régime: Sade, Rétif, Beaumarchais, Laclos*, ed. Béatrice Didier and Jacques Neef (Saint-Denis, 1991), p.45-53.

dont on [le] rend victime'.[16] Sade's letters will be analysed not as documentary evidence of his 'true' feelings, but rather as texts in which ideas, problems and fantasies are explored, often in a way at odds with the historical 'reality' of his biography. Examining these letters will enable us to perceive a less familiar Sade, given that scholars tend to analyse a fairly limited set of familiar texts, namely *Justine*, *La Philosophie dans le boudoir* and the *Histoire de Juliette*. By contextualising Sade within his own period and by returning to his own work, this chapter attempts to shed new light upon Sadean subjectivity, misrepresentations of which persist given scholars' tendency to treat Sade at one remove, that is to say as he has been presented (one might say 'produced') by Barthes or Lacan, for example.[17]

Rather than treat violence as the expression of a preconstituted and autonomous self, one may distinguish a kind of subjection (which might also be called subjectification) in which violence plays a creative or generative function. As Judith Butler puts it, '"Subjection" signifies the process of becoming subordinated by power as well as the process of becoming a subject.'[18] Butler's attention to the constitutive effect of violence on the victim may be contrasted with Michel Wieviorka's focus on the developing subjectivity of the violent act's author. There is in Wievorka's account a curious blind spot regarding the victim's experience: 'The actual experience of violence cannot be discussed here; let us simply say that trying to recover from the trauma sometimes allows the victims to become subject.'[19] Butler helps us to illuminate that blind spot, observing that 'each of us is constituted politically in part by virtue of the social vulnerability of our bodies'.[20] She provides us with a model of subjection

16. Letter to M. Lenoir, governor of Vincennes, 22 October 1782; *Correspondance du marquis de Sade*, vol.17, p.160.
17. That is not so say that it is impossible to produce compelling work on such writers' deployment of Sade; see, for instance, Viola Brisolin, *Power and subjectivity in the late work of Roland Barthes and Pier Paolo Pasolini* (Bern, 2011), p.88-135.
18. Judith Butler, *The Psychic life of power* (Stanford, CA, 1997), p.2.
19. Michel Wieviorka, *Violence: a new approach*, trans. David Macey (London, 2009). p.161.
20. Judith Butler, *Precarious life: the powers of mourning and violence* (London, 2004), p.20.

whereby the subject has no intelligibility or agency prior to the instantiating violence that it endures. Butler's analysis of violence and the self is particularly appropriate to illuminating Sade's correspondence, in that both writers maintain the distinction between subject and object positions: this approach may be contrasted with, for instance, Gilles Deleuze's account of masochist violence whereby violence tests rather than constitutes the self;[21] the masochistic model may be apt for Sade's theatre,[22] but it is less appropriate for the marquis's correspondence. Although this chapter will draw principally on Butler's insights into violence and vulnerability as explored in *The Psychic life of power* and developed in *Precarious life* (which sees an explicit turn towards political actuality), her analysis of subjection has long been attentive both to the social conditions of our formation, and to the vulnerability inherent in that process. Following Louis Althusser, she insists that the speech act initiates the subject through a submission to power, but she differs from him in arguing that it is 'not simply that one requires the recognition of the other and that a form of recognition is conferred though subordination, but rather that one is dependent on power for one's very formation, and that formation is impossible without dependency'.[23] In this mode of subjection exposure to violence is unavoidable, as evidenced in the case of hate speech which may be considered as linguistic violence. Butler contends in *Excitable speech* that the very forms of address that threaten us are those that sustain us: 'We sometimes cling to the terms that pain us because, at a minimum, they offer us some form of social and discursive existence. The address that inaugurates the possibility of agency, in a single stroke, forecloses the possibility of radical autonomy.'[24] Violence's role in subjection is increasingly pronounced in Butler's more recent work when she considers the essential sociality of embodied life: 'we are, from the start,

---

21. Gilles Deleuze, *Présentation de Sacher-Masoch: le froid et le cruel* (Paris, 1967).
22. Thomas Wynn, 'Masochisme et le tableau sadien', in *Lire Sade*, ed. Norbert Sclippa (Paris, 2004), p.245-57.
23. Butler, *The Psychic life of power*, p.9.
24. Judith Butler, *Excitable speech: a politics of the performative* (New York and London, 1997), p.26.

even prior to individuation itself, and by virtue of our bodily requirements, given over to some set of primary others: this conception means that we are vulnerable to those we are too young to know and to judge and, hence, vulnerable to violence'.[25] The subject cannot protect or institute against this primary vulnerability, for, given the social terms of our embodiment, it is precisely in the state of painful vulnerability that subjection occurs. Physical and emotional violence reminds us that we are constituted as subjects in a distinctly social manner: 'the wound testifies to the fact that I am impressionable, given over to the Other in ways that I cannot fully predict or control'.[26] Just as there is no single founding moment of the subject, so the process of subjection is never complete given that the conditions of power must be reiterated if they are to persist.[27] Given the ongoing 'vulnerability to the other that is part of bodily life', the new wounds to which we are exposed, and which continue to instantiate us as subjects, remind us that 'violence is, always, an exploitation of that primary tie, that primary way in which we are, as bodies, outside ourselves and for one another'.[28]

Maurice Blanchot has posited most clearly the argument that the agent of violence in Sade's work is a forceful, unitary and pristine subject. He proposed in 'La raison de Sade' (1963) that the violence exercised by the Sadean libertine serves as an affirmation of that subject's sovereignty:

> Dans la mesure où l'homme sadique paraît étonnamment libre à l'égard de ses victimes, dont pourtant ses plaisirs dépendent, c'est que la violence, en elles, vise autre chose qu'elles, va bien au-delà d'elles et ne fait que vérifier, frénétiquement, à l'infini, sur chaque cas particulier, l'acte général de destruction par lequel il a réduit Dieu et le monde à rien.

As with the *passion meurtrière* described by Desgranges, the agent pre-exists the immense negation that he wreaks upon the numerous (indeed numberless) victims who are 'déjà,

---

25. Butler, *Precarious life*, p.31.
26. Butler, *Precarious life*, p.46.
27. Butler, *The Psychic life of power*, p.16.
28. Butler, *Precarious life*, p.29 and p.27.

antérieurement, tenus pour nuls'.[29] Such is the victim's essential nullity that the libertine does not even require a real individual on whose corpse to found his/her sovereignty, as Juliette's education in violence shows:

> Persuadez-vous bien que toute la terre est à vous... que vous avez bien le droit de changer, mutiler, détruire, bouleverser tous les êtres que bon vous semblera; vous n'avez rien à craindre là; choisissez ce qui vous fait plaisir, mais plus d'exception, ne supprimez rien; nul égard pour qui que ce soit; qu'aucun lien ne vous captive; qu'aucun frein ne vous retienne.[30]

It is in the most autonomous of realms, that of the private imagination, that the libertines assert their status as independent subjects; there they have sole access to unlimited energy and power, an authority that sets them apart as self-determined subjects from the slaughtered mass. Yet if Blanchot argues that violence is the affirmation of an already established independence, his acknowledgement of 'la prétention extrêmement ferme [chez Sade] de fonder la souveraineté de l'homme sur un pouvoir transcendant de négation' implies that the libertine's sovereignty might be predicated on negation,[31] and therefore that sovereignty follows rather than precedes negation. In other words, the Sadean self is bolstered, perhaps even constituted, through the exercise of extreme violence. Svein-Eirik Fauskevåg's account of Sadean subjectivity similarly links violence, solitude and sovereignty: 'L'isolement répond donc à la volonté démesurée qui le pousse à se constituer en sujet absolu. Car l'isolement est ce qui permet au fort de concentrer en lui-même une énergie dont le dosage est coextensif au régime de *désolation* qu'il impose brutalement aux autres.'[32] Here the rejection of

---

29. Maurice Blanchot, *Sade et Restif de la Bretonne* (Brussels, 1986), p.41 and p.43.
30. Sade, *Histoire de Juliette*, in *Œuvres*, vol.3, p.752-53.
31. Blanchot, *Sade et Restif de la Bretonne*, p.43. Georges Bataille observes that the extreme negation of the other entails the negation of the sovereign agent: 'la jouissance personnelle ne compte plus, seul compte le crime et il n'importe pas d'en être la victime: il importe seulement que le crime atteigne le sommet du crime'; see *L'Erotisme* (Paris, 1958), p.195.
32. *Sade ou la tentation solitaire: étude sur l'anthropologie littéraire dans La Nouvelle Justine et l'Histoire de Juliette* (Paris 2001), p.114. See also Godelieve Mercken-Spaas,

intersubjective relations is a condition of the elaboration of an autonomous self, which in turn allows for the destruction of others.[33] But this retreat from sociability does not entirely do away with the problem of relationality; the libertine might still owe a debt to those spurned individuals who are occluded in the process of (ostensibly) self-referential subjection.

The problem of relationality is repeatedly and resentfully treated in Sade's prison correspondence. Sade's imprisonment serves, according to many critics, to permit an already constituted self to be displayed. Gilbert Lely, for instance, admires 'la haute leçon de fermeté' offered by the correspondence, whose author humorously and heroically defends 'l'être humain contre les agressions de la réalité extérieure';[34] Béatrice Didier states that the humiliation of his detention served as a stimulus to revolt and to self-affirmation;[35] and, for Maurice Lever, Sade's prison correspondence represents the 'nouvelle revendication de sa singularité à la face du monde, fière et belle comme un défi'.[36] Most recently, Jean-Luc Peurot has characterised the correspondence as a place in which autonomous Sadean subjectivity is expressed most forcefully: 'La correspondance – sans retenue: un espace vertigineux de totale liberté. Le lieu et le moment où s'épanouit, où triomphe sa subjectivité.'[37] This extreme, unique and immutable self has been identified not only by Sade's supporters, but also by his critics, including notably his mother-in-law Mme de Montreuil who told his lawyer Gaufridy 'que l'effervescence du caractère ne change point et qu'on craindrait que les mêmes effets qu'elle a produit jusqu'ici ne suivissent la liberté'.[38]

'Some aspects of the Self and the Other in Rousseau and Sade', *SubStance*, 20 (1978), p.71-77.

33. Also relevant here is Wieviorka's figure of the 'anti-subject' who denies his victim elementary rights, who cannot enter into intersubjective relationships, and who uses violence to trigger a logic by which he emerges as subject; see *Violence*, p.149-61.
34. Sade, *L'Aigle, Mademoiselle....* ed. Gilbert Lely (Paris, 1949), p.xxxiii.
35. Béatrice Didier, 'Sade dramaturge de ses *carceri*', *La Nouvelle Revue française* 216 (1970), p.72-80 (79).
36. Maurice Lever, *Donatien Alphonse François, marquis de Sade* (Paris, 1991), p.347.
37. Jean-Luc Peurot, *Tombeau du marquis de Sade* (Paris, 2012), p.55.
38. *Correspondance du marquis de Sade*, vol.19, p.136.

Evidence in the correspondence undoubtedly supports this reading of an unbending Sade who is resistant to carceral violence: 'Dussent-ils, ces fers malheureux, oui, dussent-ils me conduire au tombeau, vous me verrez toujours le même. J'ai le malheur d'avoir reçu une âme ferme qui n'a jamais su plier et qui ne pliera jamais.'[39] He makes similar claims in November 1783: 'impérieux, colère, emporté, extrême en tout, d'un dérèglement d'imagination sur les mœurs qui de la vie n'a eu son pareil, athée jusqu'au fanatisme, en deux mots me voilà et encore un coup tuez-moi ou prenez-moi comme cela, car je ne changerai pas.'[40] Sade offers a materialist account for his apparent immutability, arguing that the self springs from one's physiological constitution. He tells his wife that 'les mœurs ne dépendent pas de nous, elles tiennent à notre construction, à notre organisation',[41] and in November 1783 that: 'Ma façon de penser est le fruit de mes réflexions; elle tient à mon existence, à mon organisation. Je ne suis pas le maître de la changer.'[42] Sade deploys materialism in his claim of noble superiority, stating that 'nous tenons toujours à la pureté de notre origine et le sang ne se trahit jamais'.[43] His enemies are marked as morally suspect by their murky genealogy; thus the governor of Vincennes, Charles de Rougement, is described as a 'petit bâtard', and the *lieutenant de police*, Antoine de Sartine, is supposed to have been found 'un beau matin à Paris sans qu'on sache ni d'où il venait ni d'où il arrivait, à peu près comme ces champignons empoisonnés qu'on trouve éclos tout à coup au coin d'un bois'.[44] Sade, however, can identify his own origin in a noble lineage that precedes his appearance in the world, and it is with reference to this noble status that he lays claim to an independence of sorts: on 28 June 1780 he states that he prefers death to the state of ignominy; on 20 February 1781, and 10 May 1782, he declares that he owes fealty to one man alone: 'Je ne dépends que du roi, ne connais de maître que le roi,

---

39. 20 February 1781; *Correspondance du marquis de Sade*, vol.16, p.42.
40. *Correspondance du marquis de Sade*, vol.18 p.190.
41. The letter possibly dates from the end of August 1782; *Correspondance du marquis de Sade*, vol.17, p.159.
42. *Correspondance du marquis de Sade*, vol.18, p.166.
43. 1 April 1781; *Correspondance du marquis de Sade*, vol.16, p.94.
44. 1 May 1781; *Correspondance du marquis de Sade*, vol.16, p.165-66.

suis prêt à lui donner mille vies et mille fois mon sang, s'il les veut, mais au-dessous de lui, je ne connais aucune dépendance, parce que entre lui, ses princes et moi, je ne vois que des inférieurs, et que je ne dois rien à mes inférieurs.'[45] Although effectively deprived of all agency, this prisoner is willing to be an object of violence only within a strictly aristocratic perspective that serves to confirm his own autonomy.

Sade thus appears to subscribe to a pristine notion of the subject. He suggests that the self is constituted without primary social interaction and, in rejecting further social relations and duties except those to the highest authority in the land, he thereby creates a fantasy of self-sufficiency and unbridled sovereignty in which the self remains immune to almost all external forces. Unlike Laclos's Mme de Merteuil, who claims to be her 'propre ouvrage', or Diderot, for whom the self is integrated in a system of relationships and which in turn (partially) constitute that self, Sade would resemble Athena, emerging from Zeus's head fully formed into existence. And, like that goddess in her bellicose guise as Athena Promachos, Sade is the subject and not an object of violence. An incident that occurred at Vincennes in June 1780 exemplifies this conventional account of imprisonment, violence and subjectivity in Sade's correspondence.

> Le 26 au matin, l'homme qui me sert manqua envers moi essentiellement à son service; je lui en fis des reproches. Il me répondit des insolences. J'eus la patience de lui répéter bien doucement par trois fois de se taire. Il redoubla toujours. A la fin, le sang me monta à la tête, mais pas au point pourtant de n'être pas bien maître de moi. Je fis mine de le vouloir frapper pour le punir de ses insolences. Il courut dire que je l'avais frappé. [...] Je donne ma parole d'honneur que le fait est faux et qu'il n'a même pas été touché.[46]

---

45. *Correspondance du marquis de Sade*, vol.15, p.94; vol.16, p.42; and vol.17, p.86. If one were tempted to dismiss Sade's praise for the king as little more than an astute gesture by a prisoner whose correspondence is subject to censorship, one must nonetheless recognise that his commitment to a caste-based society is coherent with his view of the self as hitherto described.
46. 28 June 1780; *Correspondance du marquis de Sade*, vol.15, p.92-93.

This episode features all the essential elements that we might expect of a violent scenario in Sade (albeit one in which violence is postponed). As in the *passion meurtrière* recounted by Desgranges, the subject and the object of the violent act are clearly distinct, and that separation is based on previously constituted identities; Sade considers that his subordinate is lacking in respect, and it is the *grand seigneur*'s birthright to punish the valet. Furthermore, violence (or the threat of it) ensues without the integrity of the subject's self being in any way compromised ('mais pas au point pourtant de n'être pas bien maître de moi'). Finally that integrity is confirmed in a somewhat circular manner, by referring to his 'parole d'honneur', the mark of a gentleman. In short, violence is an expression of a pre-constituted self, a belief Sade summarises in a terse statement in a letter dated 4 October 1778: 'Je n'ai jamais de ma vie été embarrassé de punir des insolents de cette classe-là.'[47] The 'I' is sovereign and immutable; it is distant from and unconcerned by those other individuals upon whom it exacts violence.

Yet no violent act of sovereignty can foreclose each individual's fundamental dependency on others.[48] No carapace can protect against the subordinating effects of violence, for these effects are the conditions by which agency may be achieved. One should not be misled by the elaborate lists of foodstuffs, books and other apparent necessities that the imprisoned Sade sends to his wife, as on 18 March 1783 when he demands items including two dozen meringues, two dozen lemon biscuits, two fine sponges, chocolate, a dark green jacket embroidered with silk but no gold or silver, and a pet dog but only if it is a spaniel or a setter.[49] Suggesting that all these items seem to be an attempt to protect the inmate's fragile body from the violence of the prison, Michel Delon rightly sees in such demands 'un *souci* de soi qui perdure à travers le malheur et la persécution',[50] but these demands arguably betray

---

47. *Correspondance du marquis de Sade*, vol.13, p.53.
48. Butler, *Precarious life*, p.xii.
49. *Correspondance du marquis de Sade*, vol.18, p.47-48. Sade had two setters when imprisoned at Miolans (Lever, *Sade*, p.241).
50. Michel Delon, 'Voltaire et Sade, deux philosophes emblématiques à la Bastille', in *La Bastille ou l'enfer des vivants*, ed. Elise Dutray-Lecoin and Danielle Muzerelle (Paris, 2010), p.124-29 (126, emphasis added).

not just *displeasure* that his rank is being ignored, but a more profound *anxiety* that his self is disintegrating under the coercive effects of power. Thus instead of repeating the tired critical consensus that Sade is the subject of violence or that he resists violence, we might consider instead how Sade responds as the object of carceral violence.

One might counter that violence is not especially germane to the early modern prison, given that, following the *Ordonnance criminelle* of 1670, prisons were not considered to be a punishment; contemporary sources state that 'la prison n'est pas donnée comme peine mais pour la garde des criminels',[51] and 'les prisons ne sont établies que pour garder les criminels, et non pas pour les punir'.[52] A prison was a kind of holding house where the criminal was kept before other punishments were inflicted,[53] but that purpose did not preclude violence, whether of a physical or a psychic nature. The contemporary jurist Daniel Jousse described incarceration as 'une espèce de torture' and noted that prison exposes the convict to (unspecified) 'horreurs'.[54] Other critiques of prisons also emphasised the violence endured by the inmates; for example, the *Remarques historiques et anecdotes sur la Bastille* begin by attacking the mental and physical brutality of prisons in general:

> De tous les supplices imaginés par les hommes pour tourmenter leurs semblables, la prison, surtout quand elle est prolongée, est peut-être le plus rigoureux et le plus insupportable. La perte de la liberté, l'incertitude de son sort, la vue continuelle d'objets hideux, et les mauvais traitements multipliés d'êtres féroces qui se font un jeu barbare d'aggraver les peines des malheureux, sont des tourments beaucoup plus sensibles qu'on ne le peut croire [...].[55]

---

51. Daniel Jousse, *Traité de la justice criminelle de France*, 4 vols (Paris, Debure père, 1771), vol.2, p.223.
52. Claude-Joseph de Ferrière, *Dictionnaire de droit et de pratique, nouvelle édition*, 2 vols (Toulouse, Rayet, 1787), vol.2, p.384.
53. Christian Carlier, *Histoire du personnel des prisons françaises du XVIIIe siècle à nos jours* (Paris, 1997), p.17.
54. Jousse, *Traité*, vol.2, p.223.
55. *Remarques historiques sur la Bastille: nouvelle édition, augmentée d'un grand nombre d'anecdotes intéressantes et peu connues* (London, 1783), p.10.

Mirabeau, imprisoned for a time alongside Sade at Vincennes, makes clear that the psychic torment of indefinite (not to be confused with permanent) detention equals, indeed surpasses any physical violence inflicted upon the prisoner: 'Le supplice de la solitude, de l'incertitude profonde de l'avenir et même du présent de la privation absolue de toute espèce de société, souvent même de toute distraction, puisque les moyens de lire, d'écrire sont ordinairement ôtés et toujours très gênés, ce supplice, dis-je, pour être plus lent que la torture, est-il moins cruel?'[56] Simon-Nicolas-Henri Linguet, imprisoned in the Bastille between 27 September 1780 and 19 May 1782, describes in his memoires 'ces convulsions prolongées, cette agonie perpétuelle qui éternise [sic] les douleurs de la mort' and 'tout ce que les geôliers de la Bastille peuvent faire souffrir'. He makes explicit the violence suffered by the prisoners when he writes that the motto of the gaolers is 'le mot qu'adressait à ses bourreaux Caligula, quand il leur commandait un assassinat: *Frappe de façon qu'il se sente mourir*'.[57]

Thus it is precisely because incarceration was envisaged as a preventive rather than a repressive measure, that prison might be viewed as a violent punishment in itself: 'Ce que nous venons de dire, que la prison est plutôt considérée comme un lieu de sûreté, que comme une peine, ne doit point s'appliquer à la prison perpétuelle pour un temps, à laquelle un criminelle serait condamné *in pœnam deliciti*, pour des considérations particulières, comme s'il y avait été condamné pour sauver l'honneur de sa famille [...].'[58] It was on these very grounds that Sade was imprisoned. His conviction for 'crimes prétendus de poison et de pédérastie'[59] against prostitutes in Marseille on 27 June 1772 may have been overturned by the Aix *parlement* on 30 June 1778

56. Honoré-Gabriel Riquetti, comte de Mirabeau, *Des lettres de cachet et des prisons d'état*, 2 vols (Hamburg, 1782), vol.1, p.93. The *procès-verbal* which Mirabeau signed upon leaving Vincennes on 13 December 1780 appears on the reverse of the document noting Sade's imprisonment on 13 February 1777.
57. *Mémoires de Linguet sur la Bastille, et de Dusaulx, sur le 14 juillet* (Paris, 1821), p.47-48, 70.
58. Ferrière, *Dictionnaire de droit et de pratique* vol.2, p.328. See also Catherine Frade, 'Les prisons de Paris', in Dutray-Lecoin and Muzerelle, *La Bastille ou l'enfer des vivants'*, p.25-28.
59. These are the terms used by the Aix *parlement*; see *Correspondance du marquis de Sade*, vol.7, p.218.

(the *cassation* was formalised on 14 July), but on 15 July he was arrested on a *lettre de cachet* originally dated 13 February, and renewed following Mme de Montreuil's efforts. She reveals her objective in a letter to Gaufridy: 'J'attends avec impatience la fin de tout. Non sans un peu d'inquiétude, non pour la personne [that is, Sade] car on m'a accordé toute sûreté pour elle au cas d'opinions ou informations dangereuses, mais je voudrais bien qu'il ne restât nulle tâche.'[60] Sade was imprisoned in order to prevent the family name being stained anew, as his wife wrote to Gaufridy on 27 July: '[Mme de Montreuil] me disait que jamais les *familles* (elle est bien forte avec ce mot-là) ne souffriraient qu'il sorte.'[61] Sade constantly presents his ignorance of his prison term in violent imagery, as in the letter to his wife dated 17 February 1779, in which he complains that he has been led to believe that he might be freed in a year: 'Voilà en deux mots quel a été et quel est encore l'ouvrage de mes bourreaux, car quel nom donner à ceux de qui j'ai reçu des coups de poignard les plus violents? Dès que vous me disiez: trois ans, dès que je m'y attendais, pourquoi détruire mon illusion?'[62] For Sade, prison is nothing less than the site of inevitable vulnerability, exposed as he is to the 'bourreaux de l'enfer qui, dit-on, renouvelleront sans cesse blessure sur blessure et s'attacheront plus fortement encore à la partie déjà déchirée qu'à d'autres'.[63]

Sade is, of course, hardly unique in describing the hardship of imprisonment. Hans-Jürgen Lüsebrink and Rolf Reichardt have identified common narrative sequences across seven biographical accounts of imprisonment in the Bastille; all stress not only physical suffering, but also – and at least as much – humiliations and mental agonies.[64] But whereas other writers describe their suffering so as to proclaim more forcefully their innocence, Sade

---

60. 14 July 1778; *Correspondance du marquis de Sade*, vol.7, p.236. Despite Mme de Montreuil's confidence, Sade managed to escape from Aix, but was captured and returned to Vincennes; see Lever, *Sade*, 316-28.
61. *Correspondance du marquis de Sade*, vol.7, p.254.
62. *Correspondance du marquis de Sade*, vol.14, p.58.
63. 20 February 1781; *Correspondance du marquis de Sade*, vol.16, p.43.
64. *The Bastille: a history of a symbol of despotism and freedom*, trans. Norbert Schürer (London, 1997), p.7-9. See also Monique Cottret, *La Bastille à prendre: histoire et mythe de la forteresse royale* (Paris, 1986).

does not attempt to exculpate himself for having insufficiently respected 'le cul d'une putain' and other insignificant misdemeanours.[65] According to Marcia Cavell, one becomes a subject or self-reflexive agent 'through those very understandings that allow [one] to speak for [oneself]',[66] by which I understand that subjectivity is achieved only when one acknowledges the relational and contextual nature of subjection. In light of Cavell's proposition, one might argue that Sade emphasises his wretched living conditions ('l'ordure et la malpropreté jusqu'au col, mangé de punaises, de puces, de souris et d'araignées')[67] to flag up the circumstances in which his own (re)constitution as a subject occurs. Indeed, for all his apparent belief in a pristine and inalterable self, one finds in his correspondence significant evidence of another view of subjectivity, one that is more attentive to the social and moral conditions of subjection.

In his history of Vincennes, Pierre-Jean-Baptiste Nougaret gives a colourful account of the Marseille affair (which resulted in Sade being burnt in effigy) and concludes that its protagonist undoubtedly deserved to be sequestered from society.[68] Some contemporaries considered that isolation might have a beneficial effect upon inmates; for instance, the architect and commissioner M. Jaillier suggested in his report on Vincennes that the prisoner, cut off from wicked company, would turn in upon himself, repent and signal 'un prochain retour à des sentiments de vertu'.[69] Sade rejects such arguments outright. He told his wife on 30 April 1781 that he was at work on a 'petite dissertation [...] *Sur les dangers de la solitude et les funestes effets des prisons où elle s'exige.* [...] C'est peut-être le seul ouvrage pour la composition duquel je n'avais besoin

---

65. The first letter is dated to roughly 1781, the second 20 February 1781; *Correspondance du marquis de Sade*, vol.16, p.252 and p.45.
66. Marcia Cavell, *Becoming a Subject: reflections in philosophy and psychoanalysis* (Oxford, 2006), p.85.
67. 27 July 1780; *Correspondance du marquis de Sade*, vol.15, p.132.
68. *Histoire du donjon et du château de Vincennes, depuis leur origine jusqu'à l'époque de la révolution*, 3 vols (Paris, 1807), vol.3, p.258.
69. 'Rapport sur le donjon de Vincennes, fait au Conseil Municipal, en la séance du lundi 15 novembre 1790, par M. Jallier, architecte, officier municipal, l'un des commissaires nommés pour en faire la visite', in Nougaret, *Histoire du donjon et du château de Vincennes*, vol.3, p.275-81 (281).

d'aucun livre.'[70] In the event this manuscript seems not to have survived or even to have been written, but other texts confirm his belief that rehabilitation can only occur in society. Included in a notebook of reflections composed at Vincennes between 12 June and 21 August 1780 is a manuscript 'Sur la punition', in which Sade states that 'La véritable façon de ramener à la vertu est d'en faire connaître tout le charme et, plus que tout la nécessité dont elle est, dans le commerce de la vie. Si vous voulez qu'on respecte les liens de la société, faites en bien sentir la puissance et la réalité, mais n'imaginez pas réussir en les brisant.'[71] The beneficial effects of society and socialisation are repeated in *Aline et Valcour*, when Zamé explains that 'ce n'est pas en isolant un malfaiteur qu'on le corrige, c'est en le livrant à la société qu'il a outragée; c'est d'elle qu'il doit recevoir journellement sa punition, et ce n'est qu'à cette école qu'il peut redevenir meilleur; réduit à une solitude funeste, ses vices germent, son sang bouillonne, sa tête fermente'.[72] Clearly part of Sade's argument that carceral isolation can only ever be pernicious – 'le remède, en un mot, peut bien servir à rendre pis, mais sûrement jamais à rendre meilleur'[73] – is that one's somatically founded character is ineradicable,[74] but nonetheless inmates are susceptible to external influences: 'C'est précisément cette privation de la liberté qui les rendrait mille fois plus sensibles aux moindres petites attentions.'[75]

The ostensibly immutable Sadean self is susceptible to change, as the marquis tells his wife in late August 1781: 'Le caractère naturel de l'homme est d'imiter; celui de l'homme sensible est de ressembler à celui qu'il aime. Ce n'est qu'à l'exemple des vices que j'ai toujours dû mes malheurs: ne les éternisez pas par le plus

---

70. *Correspondance du marquis de Sade*, vol.16, p.141.
71. *Correspondance du marquis de Sade*, vol.15, p.113.
72. Sade, *Aline et Valcour, Œuvres*, vol.1, p.658. See also Sade's letter to the marquise from the end of 1784; *Correspondance du marquis de Sade*, vol.19, p.91.
73. *Correspondance du marquis de Sade*, vol.15, p.80.
74. Edme de La Poix de Freminville similarly posits that 'Il semblerait que la captivité de la prison devrait rendre plus traitables ceux qui ont le malheur d'y être détenus. Cependant il y en a à qui cela ne fait point perdre la férocité de leur caractère, malgré qu'ils devraient sentir qu'ils ne peuvent échapper la punition de leurs violences'; see *Dictionnaire ou traité de la police générale des villes, bourgs, paroisses et seigneuries de la campagne* (Paris, Gissey, 1758), p.483.
75. *Correspondance du marquis de Sade*, vol.14, p.24.

affreux qui puisse m'être offert.'[76] Undoubtedly such an opportunistic statement is intended to mitigate Sade's own criminal responsibility, but it does presuppose that the vulnerable self is never immune to external forces. Claiming, in the face of historical fact, that he was a well-behaved youth,[77] Sade contends that prison has only served 'perdre l'esprit, l'humeur, le caractère et tout ce qui constitue un homme'.[78] In short, imprisonment dismantles and reduces the apparently autonomous self: 'Qu'importe mon existence! [...] je n'ai plus qu'à mourir de chagrin.'[79] Incarceration results in the prisoner being reconstituted within the inescapable terms of the dominant and coercive power which, argues Sade in November 1781, is corrupt and corrupting: 'Ah! quel regret vous devriez avoir, si vous aviez un peu d'âme, de n'avoir fait servir tant d'années qu'à gâter mon cœur et mon esprit, tandis qu'avec des procédés différents il eût été si aisé de me refondre totalement!'[80] Sade is explicit about this process of pernicious subjection, about imprisonment's poisonous effects upon his self, here described in bodily terms: 'Si l'on pouvait lire au fond de mon cœur, voir tout ce qu'elle y opère, cette conduite-là, je crois qu'on renoncerait à l'employer.'[81]

Michel Delon has proposed that prison assigned to Sade a single status, one of an unruly and punished *fils de famille*, and that the marquis responded with 'la multiplicité des visages et des masques'.[82] If Butler is correct in proposing that subjection is impossible outside the dominant frame of power,[83] then such

76. *Correspondance du marquis de Sade*, vol.16, p.212.
77. 20 February 1781; *Correspondance du marquis de Sade*, vol.16, p.57.
78. *Correspondance du marquis de Sade*, vol.15, p.192.
79. Dated to 7-28 September 1778; *Correspondance du marquis de Sade*, vol.13, p.31. Compare to Mirabeau's similar assertion that the prisoner is reduced to a non-entity: 'il ne vit que pour la douleur: nulle correspondance, nulle société, nul éclaircissement de son sort. Quelle mutilation de l'existence!' (*Des lettres de cachet*, vol.1, p.97). The argument that the prisoner is reduced to utter insignificance should be tempered by the fact that in the *ancien régime* an inmate retained the privileges pertaining to his caste: 'une personne d'une condition distinguée, doit être renfermée moins durement qu'une personne vile, ou qu'un vagabond' (Jousse, *Traité*, vol.2, p.224).
80. *Correspondance du marquis de Sade*, vol.16, p.262.
81. *Correspondance du marquis de Sade*, vol.15, p.136.
82. Michel Delon, *Les Vies de Sade*, 2 vols (Paris, 2007), vol.1, p.58.
83. Butler, *The Psychic life of power*, p.3.

faces and masks must bear the trace of the imprisoning forces. The Sadean self cannot reject wholesale the conditions of power, it can only pervert them; consequently, the subject's agency repeats in some form the power by which that subject was pressed into being. Sade's acute sense of revenge may be seen in this light. On 20 September 1780 he states that prison 'gâte le caractère, elle abrutit l'esprit, elle abîme la santé, et les seuls sentiments qu'on y forme sont ceux de la vengeance',[84] and in March 1784 he tells the governor of Vincennes:

> Ce n'est pas par des procédés pareils qu'on gagnera quelque chose sur mon âme. On l'aigrit, on la révolte, en accumulant les sentiments de haine et de vengeance dont cette âme malheureuse et tourmentée souffre sans cesse et tout ce que vous aurez gagné, soyez-en bien certainement sûr, [sera] de m'avoir rendu pis que je n'aurais été de ma vie.[85]

Sade constantly claims vengeance in part because he is in thrall to the violence that constitutes him, and to deny that violence would be 'to lose the condition of one's being and becoming'.[86] The agency to which he aspires is certainly spectacular and brutal, as evidenced in his imagined torture of Mme de Montreuil: 'Depuis que je ne puis plus lire ni écrire, voilà le cent onzième supplice que j'invente pour elle. Ce matin, en souffrant, je la voyais, la garce, je la voyais écorchée vive, traînée sur des chardons et jetée ensuite dans une cuve de vinaigre.'[87] But that agency springs not from some apparently immutable self, as other critics would argue, rather it derives from his status as a suffering subject, as an exemplary victim: 'Aucune des punitions infligées à tout ce que notre siècle nous offre de plus grands coupables n'est jamais approchée de la mienne. Il doit donc m'être permis de me plaindre et de me venger par tout ce que je peux.'[88] For all that its author sincerely wished for liberation, Sade's prison corre-

---

84. *Correspondance du marquis de Sade*, vol.15, p.153.
85. *Correspondance du marquis de Sade*, vol.19, p.36. See also his letter to the marquise dated 12 December 1784 (vol.19, p.95).
86. Butler, *Precarious life*, p.45.
87. 'Aux stupides scélérats qui me tourmentent', written around 10 February 1783; *Correspondance du marquis de Sade*, vol.18, p.38.
88. *Correspondance du marquis de Sade*, vol.16, p.243.

spondence shows us that 'to desire the conditions of one's subordination is [...] required to persist as oneself'.[89]

How, then, to resolve the contradiction between the two models of subjectivity – ontological and relational – that Sade's prison correspondence offers? One might, with some justification, argue that Sade is nothing more than an opportunist who blames others for his poor behaviour (realised or desired): 'vous avez échauffé ma tête, vous m'avez fait former des fantômes qu'il faudra que je realise'.[90] But that answer risks simply reifying the false distinction between the 'real' Sade (the singular and private individual behind *Les Cingt vingt journées de Sodome*, *Justine* and the *Histoire de Juliette*) and the 'false' Sade (public author of, for instance, *La Marquise de Gange* and the plays).[91] One might instead turn again to Butler's account of subjection, for she contends that the 'posture of the adult subject consists precisely in the denial and re-enactment of this dependency. The "I" emerges on the condition that it deny its formation in dependency, the conditions of its own possibility.'[92] The Sadean subject emerges precisely by recoiling from external power, by denying its own instantiating subordination, and by then claiming that the self is immune and immutable. As Butler puts it, 'I may wish to reconstitute my "self" as if it were there all along, a tacit ego with acumen from the start.'[93] With this comforting fiction of plenitude in place, the subject sustains itself by denying its own vulnerability and dependency, and by exploiting those same features in others, thereby making such features other to itself.[94]

---

89. Butler, *The Psychic life of power*, p.9.
90. July 1783; *Correspondance du marquis de Sade*, vol.18, p.117.
91. This distinction is expressed in clearest form by Gilbert Lely, who baulked at the publication of Sade's theatre as it was 'si capable de salir les lauriers de celui dont la gloire nous était chère'; see his *Vie du marquis de Sade* (Paris, 1982), p.393.
92. Butler, *The Psychic life of power*, p.8-9.
93. Butler, *Precarious life*, p.27.
94. Butler, *Precarious life*, p.41. James Dodd also recognises that violence offers the illusion of an unequivocal self, but he differs from Butler in his rather more optimistic recognition that such a questionable or illusory act may nonetheless provide 'a real opportunity for coming to a conclusion about oneself that would not have otherwise been possible'; see *Violence and phenomenology* (New York, 2009), p.139.

In short, the ontological self is a discursive effect of one's inevitable vulnerability to violence.

In conclusion, the mode of subjection traced here not only offers an alternative to the received account of Sadean subjectivity, it also subsumes that version, explaining away as it does the insistence upon the radical and preconstituted autonomy which has held such critical sway. Cavell contends that 'who we are is a complicated interaction between the contingent and the uncontingent, the given and the chosen, the not-I, or the not-yet-I, and the I';[95] the marquis's prison correspondence shows us that the Sadean subject may indeed have a history, but that it is reconstituted under repeated violence. The self becomes recognisable and finds its agency according to the terms of that violence. There are, of course, key aspects of Sade's prison correspondence for which Butler's theory of subjection cannot account. Above all there is the question of class; Butler is correct to attend to the history of the victim of violence, but she is less clear on the role of the agent, and in *ancien-régime* France the nuances of that agent's status cannot be ignored. It is clear that, for Sade, one's vulnerability is affected as much by the hierarchical position of the agent – whether noble (for instance, Mirabeau) or common (the prison guard) – as by one's position as object. Nonetheless, the argument that violence is creative does not excuse that violence, rather it urges an ethical reading of Sade;[96] when violence results not in the meaningless dust of an annihilated victim but in the bruised and still-living body of a vengeful agent (who demands recognition), then obligations and duties are required, if only for reasons of self-interest and self-protection. This account of violence and subjection in Sade's prison correspondence might help us not only to navigate more clearly through one of the thornier and most persistent ethical problems of Sade's thought, but also to think differently about other aspects of his writings, such as the status of the reader. If the correspondence does indeed indicate that the subject is pressed into being by violence, then it seems feasible that Sade's more brutal novels

95. Cavell, *Becoming a Subject*, p.92.
96. Will McMorran's chapter 'The sound of violence: listening to rape in Sade' is attentive to the ethical implications of reading Sade; see p.229-49.

and dialogues do not abide solely by a rhetoric of enticement ('C'est ici l'histoire d'un magnifique repas où six cents plats divers s'offrent à ton appétit'),[97] nor that only they preach to the converted ('Voluptueux de tous les âges et de tous les sexes, c'est à vous seuls que j'offre cet ouvrage'),[98] nor that they force the reader into submission. Instead, the reader might be repulsed (perhaps also excited) by the violent scenes, but is in that very recoil constituted within the frame of Sade's coercive power; my disgust retains Sade's imprint. The philosophical, ethical and aesthetic remain tightly linked in Sade's thought, but a different understanding of violence places them in a new configuration.

---

97. Sade, *Les Cingt vingt journées de Sodome*, *Œuvres*, vol.1, p.69. On Sade's rhetorical strategies in this novel, see Jean-Christophe Abramovici's contribution to this volume, p.221-28.
98. Sade, *La Philosophie dans le boudoir*, *Œuvres*, vol.3, p.3.

The Bastille or the 'Enfer de Dutailli de Saint-Pierre'[1]

ODILE JAFFRÉ-COOK

> C'était un épouvantail que cette Bastille redoutée, sur laquelle, en allant chaque soir dans la rue Saint-Gilles, je n'osais jeter les yeux
>
> Restif de La Bretonne, *Les Nuits de Paris*[2]

The exhibition *La Bastille, ou 'L'Enfer des vivants'*, held at the Bibliothèque de l'Arsenal from November 2010 to February 2011, was designed to re-evaluate the myth of the Bastille and, drawing on archival material, to give as exact an image as possible of the prisoners' everyday lives. According to the pedagogical material that accompanied the exhibition, 'à la prison d'état de la Bastille, on est mieux traité qu'ailleurs [...]. La plupart des cellules sont passablement éclairées, meublées et chauffées (tout aménagement est possible aux frais du prisonnier). On y mange très bien [...], des visites sont assez facilement autorisées.'[3] The exhibition was intended to demystify the prison, the 'lieu maudit qui illustre la rupture progressive et bientôt violente du consensus qui unit une société à son Etat' (p.1). While the Bastille may not have been the demonic 'insatiable dévoreur de chair humaine' (p.1) it has been portrayed, its history is nonetheless steeped in violence.

This violence could take various forms, from the storming of the fortress in 1789 to the violation of human rights (prisoners were incarcerated there before being judged). It was the latter type of violence that was suffered by Bernardin de Saint-Pierre's

---

1. Translated by Thomas Wynn.
2. Quoted in Frantz Funck-Brentano, *Légendes et archives de la Bastille*, 4th edn (Paris, 1898), p.2.
3. http://classes.bnf.fr/classes/pages/pdf/Bastille1.pdf, p.5.

brother, Joseph Du Taillis de Saint-Pierre.[4] Having gone to seek his fortune in the Antilles, he rallied to the cause of the American insurgents, but he was arrested in Saint-Domingue and accused by the island's governor of spying for the English. He had come up with a fanciful scheme to be deployed in case of capture by the English. He had elaborated a plan, it would seem, for the English to invade Georgia, and this plan would – at least in theory – prove that he was acting for them, and would thereby keep him from being thrown into an English prison. He was kept in a cell in Cap-Français (the capital of Saint-Domingue) for four months before being transferred to the Bastille, which, as a *prison d'état*, was used to hold inmates considered a danger to the state, such as those suspected of spying.[5] Four months after he was arrested, he arrived at the Bastille in the evening of 23 March 1779, and was imprisoned in cell three of the *tour de la Bertaudière*; he remained there until 2 January 1782, when he was transferred to the château de Ham.[6]

The correspondence between Bernardin de Saint-Pierre and his brother Dutailli during the latter's imprisonment sheds light not only on the two men's characters, but also on the carceral environment, whether viewed from inside or outside the prison walls.[7] We possess only two letters from Bernardin to Dutailli,[8] compared to seventeen from Dutailli to his brother (most of these are drafts or scraps held in the archives of the Arsenal). There are only two extant full letters from Dutailli to his brother (these are held in Kraków); this tally indicates that Dutailli's letters (or at least some of them) were authorised to leave the Bastille, and that Bernardin or his secretary Louis Aimé-Martin may have destroyed those they judged to be too embarrassing. There are, however, at least fifty letters from Bernardin concerning his

4. On violence in Bernardin de Saint-Pierre, see Malcolm Cook's chapter, p.191-202.
5. Christian Carlier, *Histoire du personnel des prisons françaises du XVIIIe siècle à nos jours* (Paris, 1997).
6. For a detailed account of the causes of his imprisonment, see Patrick Villiers,'Redécouvrir la justice d'ancien régime', in *Aventures et dossiers secrets de l'Histoire* 52 (2004).
7. For another analysis of violence and prison correspondence, see Thomas Wynn's chapter, 'Violence, vulnerability and subjectivity in Sade', p.139-60.
8. This is how each man signed his letters, and thus the form that I shall use.

brother; from the start he set out to defend Dutailli, writing a *mémoire*, soliciting the aid of important figures such as Sartine,[9] Lenoir,[10] the comte d'Estaing,[11] the marquis de Castries[12] and so on. He did not relent until Dutailli's death in 1791.

Life at the Bastille, as described by Dutailli

We have no surviving correspondence between the two brothers from the start of Dutailli's imprisonment at the Bastille. We know, nonetheless, that Dutailli was busy with his own defence, writing reports to different authorities, and that Bernardin was similarly engaged.[13] Dutailli was questioned in April, reports were written in May, and in June it was decided that he should remain locked up: 'Le Roy, a qui j'ai rendu compte de cette affaire a décidé que le Sr Dutailly restera provisoirement à la Bastille où il jouira de toutes les douceurs qu'on peut procurer au prisonnier.'[14] The word 'douceur' merits further attention. In *Surveiller et punir* Michel Foucault reminds us that in the eighteenth century 'le châtiment doit avoir l'"humanité" pour "mesure"', and that this movement was supported by figures as diverse as Voltaire, Brissot, Marat and even Servan and Dupaty.[15] One of the chapters of Beccaria's *Traité des délits et des peines* (1764) was entitled 'De la douceur des peines', and in which he maintains that 'l'âme s'endurcit par le spectacle renouvelé de la cruauté';[16] Voltaire

---

9. Antoine de Sartine, comte d'Alby (1729-1801), *secrétaire d'état à la marine* from 24 August 1774 until 13 October 1780.
10. Jean-Charles-Pierre Lenoir (1732-1807), Paris's *lieutenant général de la police* from 30 August 1774 until May 1775, and then again from 19 June 1776 until August 1785.
11. Charles Hector, comte d'Estaing (1729-1794), general and admiral.
12. Charles Eugène Gabriel de la Croix de Castries (1727-1801), *secrétaire d'état à la marine* from 13 October 1780 until 24 August 1787.
13. These reports are held at the Archives Nationales d'Outre-Mer (ANOM) in the dossier Col E. 363, and at the Bibliothèque du Havre, where the dossiers 58 and 100 contain most references to the Dutailli affair.
14. ANOM, Col E. 363, f.45-46 [Instrument de recherche en ligne (IREL): 463-64 & 465-66].
15. Michel Foucault, *Surveiller et punir, naissance de la prison* (Paris, 1975), p.89.
16. Cesare Beccaria, *Des délits et des peines*, in *Bibliothèque philosophique du législateur, du politique, du jurisconsulte*, ed. J. P. Brissot de Warville, 6 vols (Paris, Desauges, 1782), vol.1, p.110.

expressed the hope that 'cet ouvrage adoucirait ce qui reste de barbare dans la jurisprudence de tant de nations'.[17] No doubt echoing Beccaria's phrase, Foucault entitles one of his own chapters 'La douceur des peines', but casts it in a new light, arguing 'le corps, selon cette pénalité, est pris dans un système de contrainte et de privation, d'obligations et d'interdits',[18] and that, finally, deprivation of liberty, in and of itself constitutes punishment. There is thus a contradiction between the term 'douceur' (which implies treating the inmate in a manner far removed from violence), and the force that strikes against the individual's liberty (that is to say violence).

Frantz Funck-Brentano posits that under Louis XVI the Bastille was a prison much like any other, that its inmates received better treatment than elsewhere, and that 'les témoignages établissant que la Bastille était de beaucoup la plus douce du royaume sont innombrables'.[19] He adds that there was not in the eighteenth century 'un lieu de détention en Europe où les prisonniers fussent entourés d'autant d'égards et de confort'.[20] What then were the comforts, or the *douceurs* that Dutailli enjoyed? Food occupies an important place in his correspondence; this is the case with many other prisoners, left alone in a cell with few distractions. Although Claude Quétel has recently argued that 'à la différence des conditions d'hébergement presque toujours décriées, les prisonniers qui critiquent la nourriture sont rares et, au contraire, les témoignages de satisfaction abondent',[21] Dutailli's own testimony suggests that such satisfaction was far from universal. In November 1781, for instance, the meals he was served were his principal concerns:

> Je viens enfin, mon pauvre frere, de profiter d'un diné reglé pour les autres prisonniers d'Etat: cest une merveille; mais je le dois a la méprise heureuse faite dans une cuisine ou par un porte clef.
> Il faut en faire l'histoire. Dans les trois plats que l'on nous donnent en maigre, j'ai eu tout le tems d'appercevoir que l'on s'est

---

17. Voltaire, *Commentaire sur le Traité des délits et des peines*, in *Bibliothèque philosophique du législateur*, ed. Brissot de Warville, vol.1, p.201.
18. Foucault, *Surveiller et punir*, p.18.
19. Funck-Brentano, *Légendes et archives de la Bastille*, p.37.
20. Funck-Brentano, *Légendes et archives de la Bastille*, p.82.
21. Claude Quétel, *Histoire véritable de la Bastille* (Paris, 2006), p.293.

engagé *par le marché* a en donner un en poisson, un second aux œufs et le troisieme en Légumes. La méprise a donné lieu a servir sur ma table deux plats de poisson avec un autre en oeufs.

This meal, worthy of a fairy tale, confirms that a prisoner's culinary comforts depended on his status and purse: 'Quand un prisonnier est riche, il peut vivre à la Bastille d'une manière princière; quand il est pauvre, il y vit très misérablement.'[22] Dutailli, like his brother, was a man of limited means and thus had to make do with standard fare. In a draft of a letter dated December 1779 he writes:

> Il ma falu en venir encore, cher frere, a jetter pour la *cinquieme fois mon repas à la porte;* les peaux du roti d'hier au soir. Le second plat de poitrine de mouton Etique, (comme cette *charogne* que j'eus a jetter la premiere fois) méritoit bien de suivre le même chemin: mais le porte clef ma fait entendre que c'etoit un regal pour ses Enfants. Vous sentez si je n'en continue pas moins a faire la plupart de mes repas au pain sec, *& tres sec dans la Bastille*.[23]

The draft of a similar letter follows the next day:

> *Pour troisieme Lettre de suite.*
> C'est pour *la sixieme fois*, cher frere, qu'il ma falu encore en venir a jetter à ma porte une partie du souper. Cette fois on ne peut pas dire que ce fut *de la charogne*. C'etoit un morceau paroissant d'une bonne qualité de veau mais resté d'*un bouilli ou* &^{ca}. Et pour second plat *une rognure* de cotes de veau, dont la sausse pourtant mon fait manger. Il s'en est guere falu que je ne l'aye expedié aussi a la porte. Ne voyez vous pas, cher frere, que l'honnete Gouverneur trouve toujours son compte a continuer a faire manger des Restes des tables quil qualifient de *miroton, de saut du piquet*; &$^{ca;}$ *de la charogne* deguisé en ragout tantot aux navets, *tantot aux carottes,* ou les trippes *de beuf de la Bastille* deguisées *en point blanc* dans ses hachis, &^{ca}, &^{ca}. &^{ca} [24]

---

22. Funck-Brentano, *Légendes et archives de la Bastille*. p.49.
23. (Bernadin de Saint-Pierre) BSP_406. (18 December 1779). I have kept the original spelling and punctuation for all these letters. These letters have been collated by Malcolm Cook; for the inventory of Bernardin's correspondence, see http://163.1.150.210/fmi/iwp/res/iwp_home.html.
24. BSP_407. (19 December 1779). Compare Funck-Brentano, *Légendes et archives de la Bastille*, p.69-70.

The language used in these letters clearly expresses the author's frustration: the underlining of words, the repetition of terms such as 'charogne' (suggestive of rotting meat), the descriptions of violent behaviour (throwing one's food to the floor); the letter reveals a place saturated with violent words and gestures that come not from the guards but from the prisoner himself, who seems not to have received the comforts promised to him. One might assume that Dutailli is exaggerating the harshness of his treatment, but consider a letter dated 14 December 1781 that Dutailli addressed to the *lieutenant de police*:

> Monseigneur, MM les lieutenants & major de la bastille m'ont autorisé à avoir l'honneur de vous rendre compte du motif qui les a portés à se donner la peine de monter à ma chambre. Ils m'ont annoncé que votre intention étoit que l'on *me mît au pain & à l'eau*, si je jettois encore mes repas à ma porte. Il n'a jamais été question d'y jetter la totalité, mais bien une partie; encore lorsque ma patience étoit poussée à bout, & lorsqu'on m'apportoit des restes de table ou de la viande gâtée. C'est une observation que l'on aura sûrement oublié de vous faire.[25]

Bad behaviour was clearly liable to be punished by the guards, whether or not they had explicit directives from their superior.[26]

Dutailli's complaints were not limited to the quality of his meals, for in his first two letters he protests about the candles provided – he was given 'celle destinée aux Ecuries [...] au lieu de la chandelle moulée'[27] – and about the lack of heating:

> Et la reduction du bois egalement cette hiver ci, dont la fourniture na commencé qu'au *Ier de Novembre*. Vous voyez si l'on pouvoit negliger encore *un mois sur les six a gagner*. Quand a la demie buche reciée suprimée également, on sait que cet année ci les prisonniers de la Bastille sont condamnez a n'avoir que de 5 à 7 Rondins par jour, *de deux a trois pouces au plus de Diamètre*. vous voyez encore que je ne dois plus sortir de mon lit qu'a l'heure ou on m'apporte le diné, et y rentrer aussi tot le misérable soupé fait pour tacher de

---

25. Cited in Simon-Nicolas-Henri Linguet, *La Bastille dévoilée ou recueil de pièces authentiques pour servir à son histoire* (Paris, Desenne, 1789), p.73. This letter seems to have disappeared.
26. Linguet, *La Bastille dévoilée*, p.74.
27. BSP_407.

conserver quelques rondins de reserve a retrouver dans les grands froids.[28]

The *douceurs* of Bernardin, or the call to reason

Bernardin did not abandon his brother. From the end of March 1779 he asked for permission to visit Dutailli,[29] and a prison register indicates that he visited on a dozen occasions between the beginning of May and the end of November 1779.[30] Bernardin is announced, rather strangely, as M. Du Tailly, for instance: 'je vous prie Monsieur de donner l'entrée du château a M. du tailly a l'effet d'y voir et parler au S. Du Tailly son frere en prenant les précautions d'usage en pareil cas'. The absence of letters from Bernardin to his brother may be due precisely to these visits, in that they rendered written correspondence unnecessary.

The care and concern Bernardin expressed for his brother are evident in a letter from May 1781, by which point Dutailli had been in prison for almost two years:

> je ne vous offrirai point mon frere, mes tristes consolations, mais si quelques douceurs peuvent chasser l'ennuy de votre prison où on ne peut rien ajouter à l'honneteté de votre traittement phisique, je vous offre les petits frais d'amusement auxquels on n'a point d'egard tels que des estampes, des pinceaux, des couleurs, un surcroit de tabac enfin tout ce que vous imagineres propre a vous distraire. j'en remettrai les fonds à M[r]. le Secretaire de M[r]. le lieutenant de police.[31]

Bernardin's sincerity cannot be doubted. Bernardin's frequent use in the correspondence of the term 'honnêteté' (and its cognates) when discussing his brother's treatment at the Bastille suggests he believed that the carceral system abided by a certain rule of decency – or at least he wanted to imply this to his correspondents, whose pride he needed to spare. In any case, he was aware of his brother's needs, for in April 1780 (one year after

---

28. BSP_406.
29. Col E363, f.26 [IREL 638] 29 March 1779.
30. Arsenal, MS 12516 (Microfilm R 65892).
31. BSP_640 (24 May 1781).

the start of his imprisonment), he requested that Dutailli be given permission to walk in the gardens of the Bastille. Castries's ambiguous response does not indicate whether or not this request was met: 'J'ai reçu la lettre que vous m'avez écrite le 5 de ce mois en faveur de votre frère détenu à la Bastille. Je viens de l'envoyer à M. le Noir que j'ai autorisé à faire ce qu'il croira de plus convenable.'[32] It is difficult to imagine that Dutailli should have been been locked in his room and denied access to the garden for a year. Bernardin's requests do give some idea of the conditions in which his brother was held, yet his letters, although certainly demonstrating his efforts to help Dutailli, nonetheless betray the sense that he imagined this forced incarceration to be beneficial to rest and to artistic pursuits. On one occasion, for instance, he wrote of his brother's drawing skills: 'si vous voulés les etendre à votre patrie, representés sur le papier ces grands mornes de S^t domingue hérissés de pitons, entrecoupés d'affreuses ravines, ces marais où croissent des roseaux grands comme des arbres, ces paysages américains inconnus à nos artistes; amusés vous à les fortifier, à les deffendre avec peu de monde.' Bernardin also encouraged his brother to write: 'si le crayon se refuse à votre imagination, prenès la plume. le tableau présenté à l'ame est encore superieur à celui qui ne parle qu'aux yeux. on admirera toujours les vivantes et immortelles peintures d'homere et de Virgile. dans le lieu ou vous etes Voltaire fit une partie de la henriade.'[33] Alas! Dutailli was no Voltaire (nor for that matter the marquis de Sade), and he replied to his brother's encouragement: 'comment pourois je avoir egard aux Estampes, pinceaux, couleurs, surcroit de tabac que vous m'avez offerts, quand votre situation ne sauroit se partager? vous m'avez fait regreter souvent d'avoir recu les premiers petits secours.'[34] Dutailli's letters are full of bitterness and recriminations against both his brother (whom he accused of insufficient efforts in having him freed) and daily life at the Bastille, especially the marquis de Launay, governor of the fortress.

---

32. Col E 363, f.53.
33. BSP_410 (n.d.).
34. BSP_641 (25 May 1781).

But above all these concerns, which are entirely to be expected, these letters reveal Dutailli's mental deterioration. Although he did not endure physical violence, his imprisonment was certainly experienced as a kind of mental violence. His was a long period of detention, with few if any visits to the garden, and he was held in solitary confinement. Indeed he was practically held in silent confinement too; the turnkeys (the staff who came most frequently into contact with the prisoners) were forbidden from talking with the inmates, and the prisoners were prevented from communicating with each other.

Dutailli's reactions to his brother's advice

Bernardin was aware of the gulf separating him from Dutailli and of his limited influence over him: 'mes conseils vous irritent mais soyés bien sur que vous avés une grande part à mes sollicitudes et a mes prieres'.[35] And so the correspondence between the two brothers came to an end. Receiving nothing but recriminations, Bernardin grew weary. On 21 October 1780 he wrote 'Si je vais à la Bastille pour consoler un frère infortuné, je le trouve aigri et irrité par le malheur';[36] and a letter dated 29 February 1781 shows that the situation had deteriorated: 'Ce ne sont plus mes vaines consolations qui le soutiennent. Il les rejette avec fureur ce qui ne me permet plus ni de le voir ni de lui écrire.'

Following the publication of the *Etudes de la nature*, *Paul et Virginie* and his revolutionary writings, Bernardin was to appear to his readers as the 'consolateur' of his fellow men. It is ironic, then, that fate denied him this same role to his own brother. In fact, relations between the two brothers were always complicated, and documents show that every time he was in difficulty, Dutailli always turned to Bernardin for help. For example, according to a business register from Port Louis (dated 1777) Bernardin shared his gratuity of 1,000 *livres* 'avec sa sœur retirée dans un couvent à Dieppe et son frère arrivé depuis l'année dernière de St Domingue'.[37] On 19 August that same year Bernardin wrote to

35. BSP_0640.
36. Col. 363, f.31 [IREL 645].
37. Archives nationales, H/480.

Benjamin Franklin, explaining that Dutailli had entered 'au service de votre république'.[38] Bernardin was often torn between exasperation and compassion, as evidenced in a letter he wrote to Hennin in May 1783:

> Il me serait difficile d'exprimer le sentiment que m'inspire la situation de mon frère. D'un côté, son ton leste et maniéré, ses réponses extravagantes, et surtout l'apathie de son cœur, me font craindre sa présence; d'un autre côté, sa figure qui porte l'empreinte profonde du malheur, et sa position inexplicable m'inspirent une tendre pitié, et me ramènent à lui.[39]

A letter from Dutailli shows how he reproached his brother from his cell in the Bastille:

> J'ai recu, mon frere, la Lettre que vous m'avez fait l'honneur de m'ecrire dattée du 12 avril, en réponse a la mienne du 7 du même Mois. Vous me citez quelle est d'un ton de reproche quelle soutient comme toutes les autres. Vous avez trop épuisé la douceur de mon caractère pour n'avoir pas été réduit a la triste nécessité d'en venir enfin là.
>
> N'ayez plus la dureté de chercher des torts au foible, ni laisser ecouler des deux, trois mois a voir un frere si accablé, le distraire de l'horreur de se retrouver du Matin au soir entre quatres murailles & de l'amertume qui l'y dévore.[40]

Dutailli was aware that he treated his brother unfairly and harshly, as evidenced by some lines scribbled upside down and between the lines of his plan about Georgia:

> *Au Gouverneur (20 mois)*
> Il vous aura été peut etre rendu compte que jai traité bien durement mon pauvre frere la derniere fois qu'il vient me voir. il etoit tres difficile de ne pas etre outré de le rencontrer toujours a rendre coupable le foible pour sauver les apparences de la justice envers le fort. il n'est que l'instrument que l'on employe pour me dire ce que lon croiroit ne devoir pas se charger de madresser directement.[41]

38. *The Papers of Benjamin Franklin*, ed. Leonard W. Labaree (New Haven, CT, and London, 1950) vol.24. p.448-49.
39. BSP_0545.
40. BSP_0501.
41. Arsenal, MS 12452, f.169.

Dutailli's complaints: myth or reality?

The recent exhibition at the Arsenal strove to show that the regime at the Bastille, particularly in its final years, was not as terrible as some would claim, and that it does not merit its reputation as 'the embodiment of terrifying absolutist domination and despotism' that it had acquired in underground literature from the beginning of the eighteenth century.[42] My research has allowed me to uncover the conditions in which Dutailli was imprisoned. But who should be believed? Was Dutailli really offered 'toutes les douceurs qu'on peut procurer à un prisonnier'? His brother seemed to think so, writing to the maréchal de Castries in July 1780: 'on ne peut rien ajouter au bon traittement qu'il y éprouve ainsi qu'aux honnetetés de Mr les officiers et notamment de Mr le gouverneur'.[43] But that version is, of course, totally at odds with that expressed in Dutailli's letters.

Quétel provides some interesting statistics on the lengths of imprisonment at the Bastille: '50% sont libérés après moins de 6 mois; 60% y restent moins d'un an; ceux qui restent emprisonnés plus d'un an ne sont que 12%.' Dutailli therefore was part of the small percentage of prisoners who resided for a long time at the fortress, in his case twenty-two months. Dutailli wanted to leave prison purely and simply so that he might join the American battalions, but the accusation of treason meant that the king could not allow him to be liberated as long as the war between England and France continued. Indeed, several documents relating to Dutailli's liberation bear the laconic phrase: 'il n'y a pas moyen pendant la guerre de lui rendre la liberté'.[44] Quétel remarks upon the profound hardship of an extended imprisonment: 'bonne table, bon vêtement, distractions et douceurs de toutes les façons n'empêchent pas les prisonniers de s'ennuyer [...]. N'est pas stoïcien qui veut [...] De l'ennui au désespoir, il n'y a qu'un pas que franchissent de nombreux prisonniers.'[45] Above all

---

42. Hans-Jürgen Lüsebrink and Rolf Reichardt, *The Bastille: a history of a symbol of despotism and freedom*, trans. Norbert Schürer (London, 1997), p.6.
43. CO1. e 363 f.28 [IREL 640].
44. Col. 363, f.54. July 1780.
45. Quétel, *Histoire véritable de la Bastille*, p.322.

there was the dreadful solitary silence, for, as noted, the inmates could not speak to each other or to the turnkeys: 'Ce qu'il y a de plus terrible en prison, c'est la solitude. Dans la solitude absolue, bien des prisonniers devinrent fous.'[46] And this, undoubtedly, was the path taken by Dutailli.

The madness of Dutailli: did prison lead Dutailli to madness or did madness lead him to prison?

Those scholars who have examined the case of Dutailli have often concluded that he was mad. While Arvène Barine claims that madness ran in the family,[47] and Maurice Souriau sees in his 'treachery' the 'commencement de folie',[48] Mathurin de Lescure argues instead that it was despair that led him to insanity.[49] There is no question that Dutailli was hot-headed, but was he so different from all the other young men who set off to make their fortunes in the New World? Dutailli's letters and drafts, Lenoir's reports, Bernardin's letters – all reveal that the gradual deterioration of his mental health was linked to his despair at remaining in prison. In a letter to Sartine, Bernardin expresses concern about his brother's mental health: 'je me suis hâté de venir à son secours, dans une circonstance ou le poids de ses malheurs, une prison de sept mois et la gravité de son accusation, sont capables de troubler son esprit'.[50] That Dutailli himself was aware of slipping into madness, is evident in the following two scraps:

> helas! mon pauvre frere, jai la tète toujours sans dessus dessous, toujours si bouleversé que je ne sai comment pouvoir ecrire deux lignes de suite. je suis toujours aussi poussé dans le fond de cette Bastille par un tel excès d inhumanité, que je n'en puis plus.[51]
>
> Voici encore mon pauvre frere une nouvelle annee que je passe dans les Larmes. pour prix davoir mis mes esperances du coté de versailles. toujours prier de l'humanite l'innocence cinquante

---

46. Funck-Brentano, *Légendes et archives de la Bastille*, p.67.
47. Arvène Barine, *Bernardin de Saint-Pierre* (Paris, 1891), p.70.
48. Maurice Souriau, *Bernardin de Saint-Pierre d'après ses manuscrits* (Paris, 1905), p.188.
49. Mathurin de Lescure, *Bernardin de Saint-Pierre* (Paris, 1892), p.54.
50. 29 March 1979 Col E363, f.26 [IREL 638].
51. BSP_639.

Lettres & les cris; depuis plus de 22 mois faire pourir un ingenieur dans lhorreur de quatre murailles pour prix davoir cru des vertus & ministre Oh! mon frere obtenir que lon ne me fasse plus prier a [illegible] mais que l'on se hate de me donner la mort.[52]

Despite its ironic title, Joseph-Michel-Antoine Servan's *Apologie de la Bastille* was one of numerous works that sought to portray the Bastille as a feared and fearful place, and his description of the fortress perfectly illustrates Dutailli's case: 'Une Bastille est toute maison solidement bâtie, hermétiquement fermée et diligemment gardée, où toute personne, quels que soient son rang, son âge, son sexe, peut entrer, sans savoir pourquoi, rester sans savoir combien, en attendant d'en sortir sans savoir comment.'[53] If he knew the reasons for his imprisonment (for which he denied all guilt), he was entirely ignorant as to both the term of his incarceration and his future once outside the prison walls. The uncertainty about his jail term consumed him: 'je me trouve à la Bastille depuis dix-huit mois, dans les privations & les larmes, cherchant d'un objet à l'autre a rencontrer ce qui pouroit faire decider mon malheureux sort. Si j'etoit instruit de ce qu'il me seroit destiné, je saurois aller au devant, & je jouirois de quelques consolations.'[54] The handwriting itself of these scraps becomes more and more illegible and indecipherable. His remarks are sometimes so incoherent that the researcher begins to wonder exactly who is losing his head. Consider, for instance, how Dutailli bemoans the wretched state of his clothes, complaining that he is barefoot and that he has only one old dressing gown to wear:

> qu'il m'en coute pour avoir preférer rester dans la Bastille. Quelle deluge de nouvelles indignites sont venu my relancer mieux que jamais, a reprendre seulement depuis la comission pretendu qui ma fait marcher si longtems nuds pieds jusquau bas que je traine sans souliers sans mes souliers jusqu'aux lambaux de la robe de chambre que je traine egalement dans [illegible] de la muraille pour me tenir mieux chaudement contre les froits vigoureux ou nous sommes aussi [two illegible words] accablés.[55]

52. BSP_2649.
53. Quoted in Funck-Brentano, *Légendes et archives de la Bastille*. p.83.
54. 16 June 1780 Col E363, f.42 [IREL 458].
55. BSP_638.

The description given of Dutailli upon his arrival at the château de Ham confirms his own account:

> la situation dans laquelle il est arrivé, me fais reclamer vos bontes, pour pouvoir lui fournir les choses les plus urgentes dont il a besoin. Il est arrivé icy sans effets, avec un habit tres mince sur le corps, il seroit a desirer par l'humanité que l'on le vettis, luy fournir du bois et autres choses pour le mettre a labris des rigueurs de la saison, dautant que toutes les chambres dicy que l'on pouroit traiter de galetas sont tres mal fermée. etc.[56]

Lenoir recognised that Dutailli was losing his mind, as he wrote to Castries in October 1781: 'Permettez-moi de vous présenter une feuille concernant le Sr Du Tailly dont la tête se dérange journellement.'[57] In another letter composed that same month, Lenoir explains that Dutailli was offered his freedom on the condition of exile. Dutailli refused this offer, as he would have had no means of supporting himself, and it seems that this unrealisable opportunity of freedom accelerated his depression, for as Lenoir writes in the same letter: 'la tête du Sieur Du Tailly s'échauffe'.[58] Dutailli was never to recover from his time in prison. Following his incarceration at Ham, he was transferred to the monastery of St Venant at the request of his brother who judged him to be insane, as he no doubt was.[59]

Amongst the extensive correspondence between Bernardin and the authorities about a pension for his brother and requests for help in bringing him back to St Venant (from where he would regularly escape), there is a letter dated 19 August 1785 from Crosne, *lieutenant général de police*, in which he acknowledges that Dutailli's current mental state is due to his previous imprisonment in the Bastille: 'M. de Sartine ayant pris les ordres du roy pour le faire mettre a la Bastille d'ou il ne devoit sortir qu'à la paix. la tete de ce prisonnier s'étant dérangée pendant son séjour dans ce chateau.'[60]

56. Col. E363, f.70 [IREL 500], 4 January 1782.
57. Col. E363, f.58 [IREL 485].
58. Col. E363, f.59 [IREL 486].
59. The community of the Bons-Fils, a third order of the Franciscans, managed three establishments, including one at St Venant. It was a *maison de force* specialising in the care of mentally ill patients.
60. Col. E363, f.131 [IREL 594].

In conclusion, one might argue that, much as the Bastille was meant to be a reasonable site of correction where prisoners might enjoy 'des douceurs' and where great writers such as Voltaire and Sade developed their literary talents, it was nonetheless a place where immense violence was wrought upon the individual. As Foucault posits, 'la peine est une souffrance morale infligée à l'âme dans la privation de liberté'.[61] And it was this very loss of liberty behind the walls of the Bastille that so utterly ruined Dutailli.

---

61. Foucault, *Surveiller et punir*, p.22.

Violence, terrorism and the legacy of the Enlightenment: debates around Jean-Jacques Rousseau and the Revolution[1]

OURIDA MOSTEFAI

The transfer of Rousseau's ashes from Ermenonville to the Panthéon on the 20 Vendémiaire An IV (11 October 1794) gave rise to what, according to contemporary opinion, was one of the most spectacular celebrations of the revolutionary period (and one of the most costly, too):[2] 'C'était vraiment la plus belle des fêtes et la mieux ordonnée.'[3] Bringing together 'une foule immense' and 'une jeunesse nombreuse', the celebration gave the French people, recently emerged from the Terror, the opportunity to celebrate the revolutionary Army's recent military victories at Aix-la-Chapelle and Cologne. Leaving from Ermenonville, where Rousseau's remains had been kept on the marquis de Girardin's estate since his death on 2 July 1778, the procession was thronged with joyous and patriotic followers. There were fraternal feasts all along the way as well as an abundance of floral garlands, and willow and poplar branches. The people of Paris came in a procession of carriages decorated with tricolour ribbons and representations of the writer's works, to pay homage to Rousseau and to accompany him in his final

1. Translated by Matthew Smith.
2. This was the most costly event after the *Fête de l'Etre suprême*. According to Albert Mathiez, the suppliers' bills for the festival on 20 Vendémiaire totalled 18,273 francs, compared to 41,890 francs 19s.3d, for the larger event; see 'Le coût des fêtes publiques à Paris en 1794', *Annales historiques de la Révolution française* 6 (1929), p.503. Raymonde Monnier suggests that the accounts of the Commission de l'instruction publique mention the sums of 93,000 and 322,947 *louis* respectively; 'L'apothéose du 20 Vendémiaire An III (11 octobre 1794). Rousseau revisité par la République', *Annales J.-J. Rousseau* 42 (1999), p.403-28 (417-18).
3. The *conventionnel* Marragon, quoted by Monnier, 'L'apothéose du 20 Vendémiaire An III', p.417.

journey to the Panthéon, gathering in great number around the island prepared for this occasion at the centre of the Grand Bassin of the Tuileries (recently baptised the Palais National), and singing the anthem composed by Marie-Joseph Chénier in honour of 'le bienfaiteur de l'humanité'.

This festive scene remains troubled, however, by the unclear ties between the Revolution and *J.-J. Rousseau considéré comme l'un des premiers auteurs de la Révolution*, to cite the title of Louis-Sébastien Mercier's 1791 book.[4] Indeed, this seemingly triumphal reception of Rousseau did not pass undisputed, as is most clearly demonstrated by the Jacobins' contested participation in the procession and their exclusion from the official ceremony in spite of (or because of) their proclaimed support of Rousseau. What is more, people were not strictly speaking paying homage to Rousseau the writer or the great thinker, for as Pierre-Louis Ginguené states in *La Feuille villageoise*: 'Ce n'était point l'homme de génie, l'homme éloquent, le grand homme qu'on paraissait honorer, mais l'homme bon et sensible, l'apôtre des bonnes mœurs, le bienfaiteur de l'humanité.'[5]

The near-religious devotion of this 'Rousseaumania' speaks of an apotheosis, but this consecration masks a number of mixed feelings, as Jean Roussel carefully demonstrates in *Jean-Jacques Rousseau en France après la Révolution* (1972). The matter in question here concerns the mixed feelings and conflicting opinions surrounding the ties between Rousseau and the Revolution, especially in the period during and after the Terror. The Revolution is a curious child of the Enlightenment, and the turn-of-the-century is no less strange a decade, one that witnessed an explosion of new ideas as well as an evolution of various political stages, all of which laid claim to the Enlightenment without, however, being able to agree on the meaning of its legacy. There is no question that the Revolution recognised itself in the legacy of the *philosophes* – in the notions of reason, nature,

4. The previous year Charles François Lenormant's book *Jean-Jacques Rousseau aristocrate* had appeared; see Lionello Sozzi, 'Interprétations de Rousseau pendant la Révolution', *SVEC* 64 (1968), p.187-223 (187).
5. *La Feuille villageoise* 9 (1794), p.66. I have corrected the quote by Jean Roussel (with slight puctuation change), *Jean-Jacques Rousseau en France après la Révolution 1795-1830: lectures et légende* (Paris, 1972), p.14, which omits the words 'et sensible'.

happiness and virtue – but beyond these principles, it struggled to envisage a direct line of descent, so profound are their differences of thought. This explains not only the violent debates surrounding pantheonisation of the great men of the Enlightenment and of the Revolution (Rousseau, Voltaire, Marat, Mirabeau and even Descartes), but also the endless conflicts and disputes accompanying these events.[6]

Of all the Enlightenment thinkers, it was Rousseau who remained the primary focus of the Revolution. Throughout the revolutionary decade, Rousseau's influence was as constant as it was contradictory, resulting in what can aptly be described as a 'vague imprégnation rousseauiste'.[7] Constantly reinterpreted – indeed reclaimed – by opposing factions, many figures of Rousseau unfold and overlap in successive stages: the Rousseau of the Girondins, the Montagnards, the Jacobins and the Sans-culottes. Deriving from his works, his way of life and the ideology believed to be the driving force behind these, Rousseau's legacy at this time was at once widespread and rife with contradictions, so much so that it has proven impossible to measure the extent of his influence on the Revolution in any straightforward terms. Indeed, although the Revolution continued to lay claim to his name, this legacy remains a constant problem to its participants.

It comes as no surprise then that Rousseau's pantheonisation provoked such significant debates and conflicts. Indeed, confusion reigned throughout the official ceremonies as Rousseau's supporters and adversaries fought over his legacy. Thus the plan to erect a statue of Rousseau, announced immediately by the Revolution and ordered by the Constitutional Assembly as early as 21 December 1790, was never carried out. As for the idea of transferring his ashes to the Panthéon, it was met by countless protests staged by different factions. In his *L'Ami du peuple*, Marat launched an attack against 'l'outrage fait aux cendres de JJR', virulently denouncing the 'pantalonnades funèbres' that would

6. On the difficulties of cultural and political commemoration during the Revolution, see Yann Robert's article, 'The everlasting trials of Jean Calas: justice, theatre and trauma in the early years of the Revolution', p.103-19.
7. Gundula Gobel and Albert Soboul, 'Audience et pragmatisme du rousseauisme: les almanachs de la Révolution (1788-1795)', *Annales historiques de la révolution française* 234 (1978), p.608-40 (610).

dare place Rousseau alongside 'cadavres contagieux, des apôtres de l'imposture, des apologistes du despotisme, des corrupteurs de la vertu, des spoliateurs des pauvres, des oppresseurs de peuple'.[8]

Many joined Marat in opposing the transfer of Rousseau's ashes, from the marquis de Girardin who disapproved of the decision to 'arracher ses mânes au sein de la nature et à la clarté des cieux', to Louis-Sébastien Mercier who, in *Le Nouveau Paris*, had Rousseau utter the following: 'Moi dans un Temple? Pourquoi m'y a-t-on placé? Je reposais si bien dans l'Ile des Peupliers; c'était la dernière habitation que j'avais obtenue de l'amitié. J'étouffe à l'étroit dans ce sépulcre. L'immortalité n'est point en sûreté au Panthéon.'[9] A plethora of pamphlets both comic and serious was produced to protest the very idea of his transfer to the Pantheon. Many of these pamphlets were written as prosopopoeiae in which Rousseau rises from the Champs-Elysées to attack those seeking to 'abuser de [son] nom, [et] le faire servir à égarer l'opinion publique, à voiler le crime'.[10]

Delayed many times by various setbacks, Rousseau was eventually transferred to the Panthéon, but the peculiar order in which it all unfolded attests to the confusion occasioned by the sequence of political events during the Revolution. Jean Roussel sums it up appositely: 'Voulu par les Montagnards, qui ont voté le décret, le triomphe de Rousseau est célébré par ceux qui ont provoqué leur chute, et qui avaient été persécuté par eux.'[11] Such discrepancies between politics and chronology were a constant

---

8. Quoted by Hervé Guénot, 'De l'Ile des Peupliers au Panthéon: la translation des cendres de Rousseau', *Etudes Jean-Jacques Rousseau* 3 (1989), p.101-25 (109). The allusions are to Voltaire and Mirabeau, already transferred to the Panthéon.
9. Mercier, *Le Nouveau Paris*, quoted by Guénot, 'De l'Ile des Peupliers au Panthéon', p.104.
10. See in particular the *Lettre de Jean-Jacques Rousseau à l'Assemblée nationale* (1793); Théodore Desorgues, *Ode à J.-J. Rousseau* (1794); Dubrail, *Grande dispute au Panthéon entre Marat et Jean-Jacques Rousseau* (1794); Joseph Michaud, *Ermenonville, ou Le Tombeau de Jean-Jacques* (1794); Ptivar, *La Vérité, ou J-J Rousseau montrant à Robespierre le livre des Destins* (1794); Joseph-François-Nicolas du Saulchoy de Bergemont, *La Pelle au cul des Jacobins léguée par Jean-Jacques Rousseau au peuple français* (1797). Reprints of some of these texts can be found in *J.-J. Rousseau et la Révolution française*, *Etudes J.-J. Rousseau* 3 (1989), p.1-174.
11. Roussel, *Jean-Jacques Rousseau en France après la Révolution*, p.17.

feature of the Revolution: almanacs, calendars and *décadaires* (the new Republican calendars) circulating in November of a given year had necessarily been created months before, and were often of no use for the year they were dated. For instance, the Girondin almanacs written in 1792 were not put into circulation until 1793 – after the fall of the Gironde faction.

Thus, between the time Rousseau was granted acceptance into the Panthéon and that of the actual transfer of his ashes, many things had changed: in October 1791, the Constituent Assembly had proposed to accept Rousseau into the Panthéon as the 'père de la constitution'; in April 1792 the Convention had made the same request but this time calling the writer the 'père de l'égalité et des vertus sociales'; in the end Rousseau was panthéonised by the Thermidorian Convention on 11 October 1794. Following the fall of Robespierre, the Thermidorians celebrated Rousseau's entry into the Panthéon as an anti-Jacobin triumph, lauding his peaceful and virtuous character. In this way Rousseau's panthéonisation became an anti-Terror celebration. Speaking about the ceremony, *Le Courrier républicain* describes Rousseau's *Contrat social* as an anti-Jacobin manual: 'En voyant approcher de ce livre sublime quelques audacieux dont les vêtements sont encore dégoutants du sang qu'ils ont versé, il nous semblait entendre la voix de l'austère philosophe, prononçant ces mots: N'approche pas, sacrilège, il n'y a pas dans ce livre saint une page, une ligne où ta condamnation ne soit tracée.'

But Rousseau's arrival at the Panthéon can hardly be seen in isolation; rather, it must be considered together with Marat's arrival, which had just taken place, and had itself coincided with Mirabeau's eviction from this same site.[12] And it is not by chance that Rousseau's pantheonisation was so soon followed by Marat's 'depantheonisation' on 26 February 1795. Behind the figure of Rousseau lurk those of the *Terroristes* claiming his name: Robespierre, then Marat; Rousseau's pantheonisation became an occasion to denounce the violence of the Terror. Far from marking a definitive step toward reconciliation, as those

12. For an analysis of the complex phenomenon of pantheonisation, see Jean-Claude Bonnet, *Naissance du Panthéon: essai sur le culte des grands hommes* (Paris, 1998).

celebrating on 20 Vendémiaire had hoped, the figure of Rousseau actually reopened the debate on the violence of the Terror.

For the Revolution had reached an important turning point where a new distaste for violence led to its condemnation as at once useless, damaging and unbearable. In the wake of the *Confessions*' popularity, a new Rousseau begins to emerge. Now a non-violent apostle of a new sensibility, the image of Rousseau as opponent of the Terror is repeatedly evoked in order to condemn violence, specifically the political violence of the Jacobins. The character and works of the 'citoyen de Genève' are cited as proof that violence is not an integral part of human nature, but rather an effect of its corruption: Rousseau's anti-Hobbesian position finds full support, and his theory of man's natural goodness is reinterpreted in the political context of the Terror.

Among the many examples of this characterisation of the anti-terrorist, one pamphlet is worth considering. The *Grande dispute au Panthéon entre Marat et Jean-Jacques Rousseau* was published first anonymously and subsequently in the name of Dubrail, in October 1794, three months after 9 Thermidor and the fall of Robespierre, the day after Rousseau's ashes had been transferred to the Pantheon.[13] Three weeks before, the Thermidorian Convention had undertaken Marat's pantheonisation, a particularly ambiguous festival, and, in stark contrast to Rousseau's, this celebration proved considerably less successful. The organisers sought to play down Marat's calls to 'couper trois cent mille têtes' while playing up the image of the 'martyr de la liberté' and of the fearless journalist who was fiercely attached to the freedom of the press. The effect of Rousseau's pantheonisation was to stir up the unease left by Marat's own entry into the Panthéon: the difference between these two figures was overwhelmingly clear. The Thermidorian press was quick to pit Rousseau against Marat, who stood for the very *Terroristes* the Thermidorians were attacking.

---

13. For a stylistic analysis of this pamphlet, see Marie-Hélène Cotoni, 'Image et discours de "Jean-Jacques" dans la *Grande dispute au Panthéon entre Marat et J.-J. R. de Dubrail* (1794)', in *Rousseau and the eighteenth century: essays in memory of R. A. Leigh*, ed. Marian Hobson, J. T. Leigh and Robert Wokler (Oxford, 1992), p.369-84.

The *Grande dispute au Panthéon entre Marat et Jean-Jacques Rousseau* contributed to this campaign against Marat. The pamphlet depicts a scene of Parisian life: since 20 Vendémiaire – the day of Rousseau's arrival at the Pantheon – the residents of the Faubourg Marceau and the Rue Jacques (previously Saint-Marceau and Saint-Jacques respectively, both near the Panthéon) have been woken up each night by 'un bruit, un tintamarre horrible'. An argument ensues as to the source of this 'charivari': is it a parricidal plot instigated by 'quelques bandes d'aristocrates ou de royalistes', or Jacobin conspirators determined to carry out their 'délibérations liberticides'?

To put an end to a conflict on the verge of becoming a 'schisme dangereux', '12 ou 15 braves sans-culottes' volunteer to carry out an investigation and to end the dispute, 'armés de forts gourdins et bien résolus de corriger les ennemis et ceux du club électoral de leur sommeil, quels qu'ils fussent, royalistes d'outre-Rhin, ou clubistes aristocrates'. They hear a voice shrieking, 'Je te dénoncerai' and, nearing the temple, they see between the columns a singular assembly gathered inside the Panthéon: Marat, whom they immediately recognise, as well as Voltaire and Jean-Jacques Rousseau. There they are, witnesses of a strange dispute between Marat on one side (the high-pitched voice) and Voltaire and Rousseau on the other. Jean-Jacques wants to leave the Panthéon because he cannot abide the idea of sharing this dwelling with the monster who had called for 'trois cents mille têtes'. For his own part, Marat justifies his call for massacre by deeming it necessary to 'assurer la liberté publique et le succès de la révolution que toi-même avais préparée'. Outraged ('On n'y saurait tenir'), Jean-Jacques disavows any ties between his philosophy 'qui a pour base l'amour de l'humanité, et pour but le bonheur du peuple' and the horrific orders of Marat, whom Rousseau calls a 'prédicateur du meurtre'. At the centre of this dialogue lies the question of the political use of violence:

JEAN-JACQUES

Oui, j'ai prêché la philosophie, elle était dans mon cœur comme dans mes écrits; mais cette philosophie qui a pour base l'amour de l'humanité, et pour but le bonheur du peuple.

MARAT

C'est pour assurer ce bonheur que je demandais d'aussi grands sacrifices.

JEAN-JACQUES

La félicité d'une nation peut-elle être cimenté par le sang? Quand j'ai parlé d'une révolution n'ai-je pas dit que si elle devait coûter la vie d'un innocent, il ne fallait point la faire?

Rousseau's position is comparable to a refusal of political violence. To bolster this idea the pamphlet cites an idea of Rousseau's that was extremely popular during the Revolution. In his *Discours sur l'économie politique* published in the *Encyclopédie* in 1755, then in its own edition in 1758, Rousseau had stated the following: 'mais si l'on entend qu'il soit permis au gouvernement de sacrifier un innocent au salut de la multitude, je tiens cette maxime pour une des plus exécrables que jamais la tyrannie ait inventée, la plus fausse qu'on puisse avancer, la plus dangereuse, et la plus directement opposée aux lois fondamentales de la société'.[14] In 1764, he returned to this pacifist argument in his *Lettres écrites de la montagne* in response to the accusation of having approved of, even stirred up, political unrest in Geneva: 'comment approuverais-je qu'on voulût troubler la paix civile pour quelque intérêt que ce fût, moi qui lui sacrifiai le plus cher de tous les miens? [...] J'ai préféré l'exil perpétuel de ma patrie; j'ai renoncé à tout, même à l'espérance, plutôt que d'exposer la tranquillité publique: j'ai mérité d'être cru sincère, lorsque je parle en sa faveur.'[15] Rousseau reiterated this position in a letter written – later reprinted and widely distributed – at the time of his debate with Hume:

> Pour moi, je vous déclare que je ne voudrais pour rien au monde avoir trempé dans la conspiration la plus légitime; parce qu'enfin ces sortes d'entreprises ne peuvent s'exécuter sans troubles, sans désordres, sans violences, quelquefois sans effusion de sang, et qu'à mon avis le sang d'un seul homme est d'un plus grand prix que la liberté de tout le genre humain.[16]

---

14. Jean-Jacques Rousseau, *Discours sur l'économie politique*, in *Œuvres complètes*, ed. Bernard Gagnebin and Marcel Raymond (Paris, 1966), vol.3, p.256.
15. Rousseau, *Lettres écrites de la montagne*, in *Œuvres complètes*, vol.3, p.852.
16. Rousseau to Caroline-Frédérique de Salm-Grumbach, comtesse de

As Bronislaw Baczko has shown, this statement was to gain immense prominence with the Revolution.[17] Although not attested before 1789, this statement by Rousseau – recognised precursor to the Revolution and a figure of great authority – would subsequently be drawn on to condemn the violence committed in the name of the Revolution. The earliest attestation according to Baczko goes back to 1 February 1790. In his *Motion sur le discours adressé par le roi à l'Assemblée nationale* delivered to the Assemblée, Pierre Victor de Malouet, one of the Monarchien party leaders, stood up against the chaos and violence that had beset the country since the start of the Revolution. Left-leaning members of the Assemblée sought to justify the violence by asserting that such is the price of freedom. Malouet retorted, 'Je sais que la liberté vaut la peine d'être achetée; mais vous savez, Messieurs, que son illustre défenseur, Rousseau, la croyait trop chère payée par le sang d'un seul citoyen. Sans doute la liberté commande des sacrifices; mais ce n'est pas celui de l'ordre, des mœurs, des droits les plus sacrés de la société.'[18]

One year later, Malouet repeated his attack and once again condemned the Revolution's 'mouvements convulsifs'. He presented himself spokesperson for 'tous les hommes paisibles qui ne veulent point sacrifier leur repos et la génération actuelle aux générations futures; tous ceux qui, n'ayant éprouvé ni tort ni grâce de l'ancien gouvernement en regrettant la protection et la tranquillité'. He also spoke for the 'hommes mêmes qui, désirant passionnément la destruction des abus et le règne de la liberté, pensent comme Jean-Jacques qu'elle serait trop cher payée par la vie d'un seul homme'.[19] Thus we see how, from 1790 to 1794, Rousseau's maxim circulated from one text to another as it followed the vicissitudes of the Revolution.

Wartensleben, 27 September 1766, in *Correspondance complète de Jean-Jacques Rousseau*, ed. R. A. Leigh (Oxford, 1965-1998), vol.30, p.385.

17. Bronislaw Baczko, 'Thérèse, La Comtesse, Mme de Staël, Chateaubriand, et les autres', *Lire la correspondance de Rousseau*, ed. Jacques Berchtold and Yannick Séité, *Annales de la Société Jean-Jacques Rousseau* 47 (2008), p.5-74.
18. Pierre Victor de Malouet, *Motion sur le discours adressé par le roi à l'Assemblée nationale, dans la séance du jeudi 4 février* [Paris, 1790], p.4-5.
19. Quoted by Baczko, 'Thérèse, La Comtesse, Mme de Staël, Chateaubriand, et les autres', p.68.

In conclusion, and returning to our pamphlet, it is worth noting the role played by Voltaire who, by refusing to enter into the debate, opts instead to be no more than a spectator. There is no dispute now between Voltaire and Rousseau, in spite of the fact that neither of them has changed (and this is precisely how the pamphlet's narrator recognises them). Voltaire's scathing irony nevertheless remains unmistakable – 'Allons, Rousseau, de la philosophie. Vous la prêchiez si bien il y a vingt ans. Se peut-il en la donnant aux autres que vous en ayez gardé si peu pour vous' – as does Rousseau's tendency to take offence: 'Ne me retenez plus. Je veux aller à mon désert. Là j'herboriserai tout à mon aise, et je n'entendrai point.'[20] But beyond these easy caricatures, it is worth noting that the two *philosophes* are no longer at odds; a calmed Voltaire has become the mediator of the conflict, seeking nothing else but to hold back his former adversary with non-violent means. In spite of its title *Grande dispute*, the pamphlet presents no such thing: the text ends with the two *philosophes* coming to an actual agreement against the violence of the Terror. As the debate ends in silence and consent, it is the victory of the tomb – the place of peace and rest – that succeeds in silencing Marat. Angered by Marat, but held back by Voltaire, J.-J. ends up returning to his grave, and the pamphlet ends with a peaceful resolution, albeit not without irony: 'Les Sans-culottes se retirèrent très satisfaits de l'espérance que leur donnait l'issue de cette querelle, de n'être plus troublés dans leur sommeil, et en effet, depuis ce jour, on n'entend plus de bruit vers le Panthéon.'[21] In this popular pamphlet, where major political conflicts have been transposed to the level of everyday life, the problem of striking a peaceful political accord unfurls at night, thereby offering a positive solution to the Revolution's biggest political quandary: how to get out of the Terror. But things turned out otherwise: only a few months later, Marat was removed from the Panthéon and, as the legend has it, his ashes were tossed in the gutter. Effigies of Marat were collectively destroyed and in the streets, theatres and cafés, busts of Marat were broken and

---

20. Dubrail, *Grande dispute au Panthéon entre Marat et Jean-Jacques Rousseau* [Paris, 1794], p.7.
21. Dubrail, *Grande dispute au Panthéon*, p.15.

replaced by those of Rousseau.[22] In the end, the Panthéon itself could not guarantee immortality for Marat, or put an end to the violence.

---

22. Jean-Claude Bonnet, 'Les images négatives de Marat', in *La Mort de Marat*, ed. Jean-Claude Bonnet, (Paris, 1986), p.167-84.

IV

Violence and morality

Violence in the work of Bernardin de Saint-Pierre

MALCOLM COOK

In the following chapter I propose to offer a precise reading of the theme of violence that can be found in Bernardin de Saint-Pierre's *Etudes de la nature*, the first edition of which dates from 1784, and in his novel, *Paul et Virginie* which first appeared in the fourth volume of the third edition of the *Etudes* and which dates from 1788.

When Bernardin came to write the *Etudes*, living the life of a poor author in Paris in the 1770s and early 1780s, using a whole variety of sources, studies of science, astronomy, travellers' tales, classical literature as well as personal experience, he had already led the life of a true adventurer, having visited Russia, Poland and most especially the Ile de France, modern-day Mauritius. He had experienced violence at first hand, through warfare and human rivalry, and he was also familiar with the violence that could be found in nature – storms at sea, volcanoes, earthquakes, hurricanes and tempests.[1] Later, living in Paris in the 1790s, he was to experience the violence of the Revolution, managing to escape any personal injury but conscious of the daily threats. He would describe the fears of those living through the Terror in his unfinished novel, *L'Amazone*.[2] The novel for which he is now best known, *Paul et Virginie*, is open to a number of quite different interpretations, but it is clear from the correspondence that the author received from a variety of individuals that it was seen

---

1. On the violence suffered by Bernardin de Saint-Pierre's brother, see Odile Jaffré-Cook's article, 'The Bastille or the "Enfer de Dutailli de Saint-Pierre"', p.161-75.
2. The novel was clearly being worked on when Bernardin died in 1814, but no complete and finished version seems to exist. However, Louis Aimé-Martin did include a large extract in his edition of the complete works, entitled 'Fragmens de l'Amazone' in *Œuvres complètes de Bernardin de Saint-Pierre*, 2 vols (Paris, 1840), vol.2, p.482-510. We have recently discovered an extensive manuscript of the *Amazone* in the Musée des lettres et manuscrits, Paris.

primarily as a 'roman sensible', a dramatic and emotional love story with a tragic ending. It is now thought likely that the novel was written, at least in draft, as early as 1773.[3] At this time Bernardin, although still a relatively young man, had lived through conditions as difficult and as violent as can be imagined. When he returns from Mauritius a new phase of his life begins, one that is hard to envisage given his previous experience, the sedentary life of an author struggling to write for a living. He depends on charity as he composes the *Etudes* and only the success of this production gives him a life of some ease, the possibility of purchasing his own residence and, significantly, the reputation of a major cultural figure.[4] His vast experience, most unusual for a person living during the period, gives him authority and status and it allows him to analyse the world around him with a sense of stature and awareness. The *Etudes* represent a vast amalgam of themes and ideas; it is a work of synthesis whose complexity astounds us for its rich and diverse examples. Why, in 1788, did he decide to incorporate the novel *Paul et Virginie*? Could the novel do things the much longer treatise could not? These questions perplex us but it is almost certainly true that the success of the novel astonished him – he was not even the first to envisage a separate edition of the novel, seemingly unaware, at first, of the commercial potential of this short fictional masterpiece.[5]

Bernardin saw himself primarily as a man of science, a mathematician, who contested Newton's views on the cause of tidal movement, claiming in the *Etudes* that such movement was primarily the result of the thawing and freezing of the polar ice caps. Despite numerous letters from readers contesting his views,[6] he remained adamant until his death that he was correct, and sought every possible occasion to reinforce his ideas.[7] That said, as we

---

3. See Malcolm Cook, *Bernardin de Saint-Pierre: a life of culture* (London, 2006), p.57.
4. Cook, *Bernardin de Saint-Pierre*, p.88-104.
5. See Malcolm Cook, 'The first separate edition of Bernardin de Saint-Pierre's *Paul et Virginie*', *French studies bulletin* 109 (2008), p.89-91.
6. See the fourth *Etude*, in Bernardin de Saint-Pierre, *Œuvres complètes*, vol.1, p.163-93.
7. See, for example, the introduction to his short novel *La Chaumière indienne* (Paris, Didot le jeune,1791); 'Notes de l'avant-propos', in *Œuvres complètes*, vol.1, p.586-87.

can see from his care in the production of the so-called 'luxury edition' of *Paul et Virginie* of 1806, he was not blind to the beauty of artistic presentation.[8] He may well have seen himself as a man of science but there is ample evidence in his literary productions that he cared passionately about the print and the quality of illustrations that were to adorn these works.[9]

Bernardin tried to present himself as a lone figure, somebody who did not seek companionship, and this may have been true for a certain phase of his life as he struggled in his garret in the 1770s. However, by the Revolution, he was a figure of note and he was managing a busy social diary; the correspondence which is now appearing in *Electronic Enlightenment* will show to what extent his personality may need to be reassessed. The apparently solitary figure, friend of Rousseau – who walked with him in the countryside round Paris – had to learn to manage success and the obligations that readers imposed. Bernardin's philosophy is not easy to define; there is no doubt that Rousseau was an influence, but so too were the many experiences he had lived through, his voracious reading and a small group of influential friends, Hennin and Mesnard in particular.[10] Is it possible to assert that his philosophy was the result of particular scientific views? Is there a particular vision of the world that we can define by reading Bernardin's works, especially his *Etudes*? Does a coherent philosophy emerge from this vast work of synthesis?

According to Bernardin, there are two opposing tendencies in the world, violence and harmony. He claims, in the second *Etude*, that nature is kind and clement: 'Elle n'a répandu ses biens d'un pôle à l'autre qu'afin de nous engager à nous réunir pour nous les communiquer. Elle nous rappelle sans cesse, malgré les préjugés qui nous divisent, aux lois universelles de la justice et de l'humanité [...].'[11] This is a powerful statement of a particular

---

8. See Malcolm Cook, 'Bernardin de Saint-Pierre and Girodet: illustrating the "luxury" edition of *Paul et Virginie*', *Modern language review* 102 (2007), p.975-89.
9. See in particular his 'Préambule' to the edition of 1806, in the edition prepared by Jean-Michel Racault for the novel *Paul et Virginie* (Paris, 1999), p.287-99.
10. The letters to and from Hennin and Mesnard can be read in *Electronic Enlightenment*, http://www.e-enlightenment.com/services/index.html.
11. Bernardin de Saint-Pierre, *Œuvres complètes*, vol.1, p.159.

philosophy and one that may surprise us. For we also see in the *Etudes* that the world is violent, tempestuous, dangerous.[12] There are the physical dangers of storms and winds and there are social dangers that confront man:

> Il y a beaucoup de terres qui n'ont jamais été cultivées; mais il n'y en a point de connue des Européens, qui n'ait été souillée du sang des hommes. Les solitudes même de la mer engloutissent dans leurs abîmes des vaisseaux chargés d'hommes, coulés à fond par d'autres hommes. Dans les villes en apparence si florissantes par leurs arts et leurs monuments, l'orgueil et la ruse, la superstition et l'impiété, la violence et la perfidie sont sans cesse aux prises, et remplissent de chagrins leurs malheureux habitants. Plus la société y est policée, plus les maux y sont multipliés et cruels.[13]

Does the novel present us with a more satisfactory interpretation? For here too there are dangers: the dangers of a colony which is dependent on the violence of slavery; the dangers of an island which, while having undoubted natural charms, also offers constant challenges – the noises of the sea in the novel remind us of the precarious nature of this distant land: 'A l'entrée de ce bassin, d'où l'on découvre tant d'objets, les échos de la montagne répètent sans cesse le bruit des vents qui agitent les forêts voisines, et le fracas des vagues qui brisent au loin sur les récifs.'[14] The harmony and charm of this distant land is constantly threatened and undermined by the power and violence of the surrounding ocean. The word 'violence' is relatively rare in Bernardin's writing. Indeed, in the *Etudes* we find just sixteen occasions when the word is used, and it is found only once in the novel *Paul et Virginie*. It is used to describe three phenomena: the first, and by far the most important, is its use to describe nature and the natural world; Bernardin seeks to understand the relations between the creation of the world by a providential being and, at the same time, the evidence of misery and poverty in a world that he cannot explain and cannot easily comprehend.

---

12. On nature and violence, see also Olivier Ritz's contribution, 'Metaphors of popular violence in the Revolutionary debate in the wake of Edmund Burke', p.35-47.
13. Bernardin de Saint-Pierre, *Œuvres complètes*, vol.1, p.382.
14. Bernardin de Saint-Pierre, *Paul et Virginie*, ed. J.-M. Racault (Paris, 1999), p.115.

Man, naturally curious and avid for knowledge, sails the seas to find unknown lands and to confront a reality that is foreign and unfamiliar, and potentially dangerous. The sea is violent, fierce and men die in shipwrecks and through illnesses caught on board and in foreign climes. Bernardin describes such misery in his *Voyage à l'Ile de France* (1773). We read:

> Je ne saurais vous dépeindre le triste état dans lequel nous sommes arrivés. Figurez-vous ce grand mât foudroyé, ce vaisseau avec son pavillon en berne, tirant du canon toutes les minutes; quelques matelots semblables à des spectres, assis sur le pont; nos écoutilles ouvertes, d'où s'exhalait une vapeur infecte; les entreponts pleins de mourants, les gaillards couverts de malades qu'on exposait au soleil, et qui mouraient en nous parlant. Je n'oublierai jamais un jeune homme de dix-huit ans à qui j'avais promis la veille un peu de limonade. Je le cherchais sur le pont parmi les autres; on me le montra sur la planche; il était mort pendant la nuit.[15]

In the third *Etude* Bernardin gives objections to the perception of a providential creation of the universe. There is a randomness, a sense of a world that is unplanned, diverse, challenging; yet it is a world that combines perfect harmony with violent contrasts:

> Les rivières coulent au hasard. Les unes inondent nos campagnes, les autres s'engloutissent ou se précipitent en cataractes, sans qu'aucune d'elles ait un cours réglé. [...] Nos cabinets d'histoire naturelle sont pleins de monstres, de corps à deux têtes, de têtes à trois yeux, de brebis à six pattes. [...] [L]a rage et la fureur désolent tout ce qui respire, et l'épervier dévore, à la face du ciel, l'innocente colombe.[16]

But, he notes, 'la discorde qui divise les animaux n'approche pas de celle qui agite les hommes'. Man, he continues:

> est le seul être qui soit forcé, pour vivre, de cultiver la terre; [...] les insectes ravagent ses semences, les ouragans ses moissons, les bêtes féroces ses troupeaux, les volcans et les tremblements de terre ses villes; et la peste, qui, de temps en temps, fait le tour du globe, le menace de l'enlever quelque jour tout entier. Il a dû son intelli-

---

15. Bernardin de Saint-Pierre, *Œuvres complètes*, vol.1, p.34.
16. Bernardin de Saint-Pierre, *Œuvres complètes*, vol.1, p.162.

gence à ses mains, sa morale au climat, ses gouvernements à la force, et ses religions à la peur.[17]

Man lives in a hostile universe, where nature constantly poses a threat; and man himself, corrupted by civil society, distanced from a natural state of purity, has further aggravated the situation by his customs and criminal morality. Bernardin explains that his *Etudes* are the result of many years of reading and preparation; they are rich in examples of natural and human phenomena – but is it possible to see a clear and distinct plan in this long and arduous journey? When one arrives at a conclusion, is there a real sense of clarity? Is that indeed what Bernardin intended or is he simply giving us an image of a world that is complex and ill-defined, one that is impossible to encapsulate in any simple philosophy? The confusion of readings of major authors combined with personal anecdotes further complicates the text. Allusions to Rousseau abound, giving the work a sense of authority and power, and we can see Rousseau's ideas lurking in this thick undergrowth. Bernardin was, without doubt, influenced by his reading of Rousseau and no doubt also by his discussions with him. But there are differences: Bernardin is proposing a system, he is proposing scientific ideas that he is keen to promote, against the Academy and against many major thinkers of the past, Newton in particular. He wishes to assert his own authority but he can do this only if he can prove that others are mistaken. How did Bernardin have access to so many authors, to so many books, at a time when he was poor and apparently isolated? Was it through access to the Royal Library? Was it through friendships with richer figures, people like d'Alembert, Hennin, Mesnard?

These are questions that we are not yet able to answer; but we can say with certainty that Bernardin recognised that the world was a paradox, one that contained immense natural beauty and yet one that contained inherent violence. He is moved by natural beauty and he can find the prose to describe such wonders. Yet he is also aware of the constant menace, of the threat to well-being that nature, in its extreme forms, can offer. Is it possible, in such a

---

17. Bernardin de Saint-Pierre, *Œuvres complètes*, vol.1, p.163.

view of the world, to believe in a providential being, a God that created and maintained harmony and beauty?

Bernardin attempts to explain the plan of the *Etudes* from the very first part. But is the architecture clear, is there a real sense of a planned work moving towards a particular ambition?

> L'homme seul est exposé à la famine, et jusqu'aux insectes regorgent de biens. Presque partout il est esclave de son semblable, et les animaux les plus faibles se sont maintenus libres contre les plus forts. La nature, qui l'avait fait pour aimer, lui avait refusé des armes, et il s'en est forgé pour combattre ses semblables. Elle présente à tous ses enfants des asiles et des festins; et les avenues de nos villes ne s'annoncent au loin que par des roues et par des gibets. L'histoire de la nature n'offre que des bienfaits, et celle de l'homme que brigandage et fureur. Ses héros sont ceux qui se sont rendus les plus redoutables. Partout il méprise la main qui file ses habits et qui laboure pour lui le sein de la terre; partout il estime qui le trompe, et révère qui l'opprime. Toujours mécontent du présent, il est le seul être qui regrette le passé et qui redoute l'avenir. La nature n'avait donné qu'à lui d'entrevoir qu'il existât un Dieu, et des milliers de religions inhumaines sont nées d'un sentiment si simple et si consolant. Quelle est donc la puissance qui a mis obstacle à celle de la nature? Quelle illusion a égaré cette raison merveilleuse d'où sont sortis tant d'arts, excepté celui d'être heureux? O législateurs! Ne vantez plus vos lois. Ou l'homme est né pour être misérable, ou la terre, arrosée partout de son sang et de ses larmes, vous accuse tous d'avoir méconnu celles de la nature.
>
> Qui ne s'ordonne pas à sa patrie, sa patrie au genre humain, et le genre humain à Dieu, n'a pas plus connu les lois de la politique, que celui qui, se faisant une physique pour lui seul, et séparant ses relations personnelles d'avec les éléments, la terre et le soleil, n'aurait connu les lois de la nature. C'est à la recherche de ces harmonies divines que j'ai consacré ma vie et cet ouvrage.[18]

This powerful critique sets the tone of the *Etudes* and shows the extent to which Bernardin is trying to come to terms with a paradox he finds it hard to understand. How was such potential lost? How did man lose the chance of finding happiness, how did he come to corrupt a universe that promised so much? The *Etudes* do not resolve in a satisfactory manner this paradox and

---

18. Bernardin de Saint-Pierre, *Œuvres complètes*, vol.1, p.157-58.

Bernardin promises, eventually, to find the solution. But the promised *Harmonies de la nature* are not published in his lifetime and the extant versions that we have need to be further assessed.[19] Will the perspective of an author who has lived through the traumas of a violent revolution allow a new vision to be formed, one based on an optimistic analysis of a new regime? In short, are the *Etudes* the work and thoughts of a man who has known the injustice and the harshness of the *ancien régime*? Is there a political vision of a new world, one that is transformed, just and based on republican morality? Are the *Etudes*, in short, the work of a disillusioned author? Will the *Harmonies* provide the answers?

In 1784 Bernardin was hardly known. His *Voyage à l'Ile de France* had not met with remarkable success. But the correspondence shows us the extent to which he was brought to the attention of the public following the success of the *Etudes* and this same correspondence shows us the different kinds of reader who were attracted by his work: scientists, priests, intellectuals, other authors, readers from a wide variety of social classes. The world described by Bernardin is a world of contrasts, where what is natural has been corrupted by man; man has introduced his own forms of violence into a natural world that is itself composed of harmony and contrasts. Like Rousseau, Bernardin had a passionate interest in the education of children. It is one of the major themes of the *Etudes* and there is a constant implicit question that is being asked: is it surprising that men are violent given the fact they undergo an education that destroys their innocence and their simplicity. We read:

> La sage nature, en donnant tant de force aux habitudes du premier âge, a voulu faire dépendre le nôtre à qui il importe le plus de le faire, c'est-à-dire de nos parents, puisque c'est des affections qu'ils nous inspirent alors que dépend celle que nous leur porterons un jour. Mais, parmi nous, dès qu'un enfant est né, on le livre à une nourrice mercenaire. Le premier lien qui devait l'attacher à ses parents est rompu avant d'être formé. Un jour viendra peut-être où il verra sortir de leur pompe funèbre de la

---

19. At the time of writing, a new edition of the complete works is being planned, one that will seek to provide an authoritative text of the *Harmonies* to replace the edition prepared by Aimé-Martin in his edition of the complete works.

maison paternelle avec la même indifférence qu'ils en ont vu sortir de son berceau. On l'y appelle, à la vérité, dans l'âge où les grâces, l'innocence et le besoin d'aimer devraient l'y fixer pour toujours; mais on le lui en fait goûter les douceurs que pour lui en faire sentir aussitôt la privation. On l'envoie aux écoles; on l'éloigne dans des pensions. C'est là qu'il répandra des larmes que n'essuiera plus une main maternelle. C'est là qu'il formera des amitiés étrangères, pleines de regrets ou de repentir, et qu'il éteindra les affections naturelles de frère, de sœur, de père, de mère, qui sont les plus fortes et les plus douces chaînes dont la nature nous attache à la patrie.

Après avoir fait cette première violence à son jeune cœur, on en fait éprouver d'autres à sa raison. On charge sa tendre mémoire d'ablatifs, de conjonctifs, de conjugaisons. On sacrifie la fleur de la vie humaine à la métaphysique d'une langue morte. Quel est le Français qui pourrait supporter le tourment d'apprendre ainsi la sienne?[20]

This is clearly some way removed from the kind of natural education that Bernardin would favour and he uses the term 'violence' to describe this attack on a young mind. We can begin to get a clearer picture of the philosophy that is the driving force of the *Etudes*. He recognises that nature is full of catastrophic events, of natural disasters and violent phenomena but in this harsh environment, rather than seek to reduce human misery, man introduces a political and moral dimension that further aggravates him and makes a painful situation worse.

There appears to be no ideal solution but in this violent universe there are moments of consolation and hope: there is the beauty of nature, the sublime, moments of ecstasy. Nature, Bernardin says, is a mixture of harmony and contrasts: 'La Nature oppose les êtres les uns aux autres, afin de produire entre eux des convenances.' He quotes the Bible: 'Chaque chose a son contraire, l'une opposée à l'autre, et rien ne manque aux œuvres de Dieu' (Siracides 42:25).[21] He concludes: 'Je regarde cette grande vérité comme la clef de toute la philosophie.'[22]

20. Bernardin de Saint-Pierre, *Œuvres complètes*, vol.1, p.238.
21. Sirach or the Book of Ecclesiasticus (not to be confused with Ecclesiastes) is considered apocryphal by some Christian groups.
22. Bernardin de Saint-Pierre, *Œuvres complètes*, vol.1, p.271.

The very force and violence of nature can give us an image of the sublime that surrounds us:

> Si l'on ajoute à chaque plante ses harmonies élémentaires, telles que celles de la saison où elle paraît, du site où elle végète, les effets des rosées et les reflets de la lumière sur son feuillage, les mouvements qu'elle éprouve par l'action des vents, ses contrastes et ses consonances avec d'autres plantes et avec les quadrupèdes, les oiseaux et les insectes qui lui sont propres, on verra se former autour d'elle un concert ravissant dont les accords nous sont encore inconnus. Ce n'est cependant qu'en suivant cette marche qu'on peut parvenir à jeter un coup d'œil dans l'immense et merveilleux édifice de la nature. J'exhorte les naturalistes, les amateurs des jardins, les poètes même, à l'étudier ainsi, et à puiser à cette source intarissable de goût et d'agrément. Ils verront de nouveaux mondes se présenter à eux; et sans sortir de leur horizon, ils feront des découvertes plus curieuses que n'en renferment nos livres et nos cabinets, où les productions de l'univers sont morcelées et séquestrées dans les petits tiroirs de nos systèmes mécaniques.[23]

There is an irony here in that violence itself can be beautiful when represented as part of the majesty of nature. We find examples of this nature, in, for example, *Paul et Virginie* where the hurricane that will cause the death by drowning of the heroine is itself astonishing in its force and drama. Bernardin admires the paintings of Vernet and Proudhon, saying of the seascapes of the former: 'La nature proportionne toujours les signes de destruction à la grandeur du danger. Ainsi, par exemple, les signes de tempête du cap de Bonne-Espérance surpassent en beaucoup de points ceux de nos côtes. Il s'en faut bien que le célèbre Vernet, qui nous a offert tant de tableaux effrayants de la mer, nous en ait peint toutes les horreurs.'[24] Are we able, given these views, to understand better the phenomenal success of the novel *Paul et Virginie*? A novel that can appear to some to be a simple straightforward account of young love on an island paradise is in fact offering a much wider interpretive field. There is confusion on the island, a harsh contrast between the idyllic landscape, nature

---

23. Bernardin de Saint-Pierre, *Œuvres complètes*, vol.1, p.308.
24. Bernardin de Saint-Pierre, *Œuvres complètes*, vol.1, p.309.

unspoilt by man, and the violent reality of a colony dependent on the slave trade, carrying with it the prejudice and the evil of the European homeland.

The old man has found a personal solution on the island. He avoids people, lives the life of a hermit and so avoids the threat of contact with the dominating fatherland. He can admire the beauty of the violence and can seek his own happiness by attempting to do good works. He explains: 'Pour moi, je me laisse entraîner en paix au fleuve du temps, vers l'océan de l'avenir qui n'a plus de rivages; et par le spectacle des harmonies actuelles de la nature, je m'élève vers son auteur, et j'espère dans un autre monde de plus heureux destins.'[25] Towards the end of the *Etudes* Bernardin explains his aims in the work. They may be the same as those of the novel that was eventually to follow but which in fact probably precedes the composition of the larger work. He writes:

> J'ai exposé, dans cet ouvrage, les erreurs de nos opinions, les maux qui en sont résultés pour les mœurs et le bonheur social; j'ai réfuté ces opinions, et jusqu'aux méthodes de nos sciences; j'ai recherché quelques lois de la nature; j'en ai fait une application, j'ose dire heureuse, à l'ordre végétal; mais tout ce grand travail serait vain, à mon avis, si je ne l'employais à trouver remèdes aux maux de la société.[26]

In this chapter I have attempted to offer a reading of the *Etudes de la nature* and sought to understand how Bernardin manages to combine a picture of a violent, savage and natural world with the image of a man who is corrupt and vicious. The solution must lie in the realisation that violence and grandeur in nature can be pleasing and majestic, sublime and magnificent. Man is unable fully to explain or understand the complexity of the world in which he lives. For man himself is corrupt and corrupted by the world in which he is brought up. It is here, perhaps, that we detect most clearly the influence of Rousseau, a figure much quoted in the *Etudes*. Children are born in purity and innocence but are tainted by the education they receive; man wanders in a world that is violent, ferocious, powerful, but immensely beautiful and

---

25. Bernardin de Saint-Pierre, *Paul et Virginie*, p.212.
26. Bernardin de Saint-Pierre, *Œuvres complètes*, vol.1, p.418.

pleasing. According to Bernardin, man cannot find true happiness in a world that he alone has corrupted and yet which he cannot fully comprehend. That perhaps is the moral lesson of the *Etudes*; it is certainly the lesson of the novel, *Paul et Virginie*, which in so many ways is an exemplification of the philosophy expounded in the parent text.

Violence and the monster: the *Private lives* of the duc d'Orléans

REBECCA SOPCHIK

When the duc d'Orléans, previously the duc de Chartres and later known as Philippe Egalité, died under the guillotine on 6 November 1793, he fell victim to not only the Revolutionary Tribunal, but also to a significant slander campaign that had lasted for almost ten years. This underground pamphletary literature against him, including the important genre of the *Vies privées* (*Private lives*), underwent a remarkable transformation in tone, changing from tongue-in-cheek, titillating banter to crude, moral outrage, as has been noted by Robert Darnton in his study of libels of the era.[1] This transformation is logical, given the changes in the political climate and the emerging conceptualisation of the Revolution by its participants as a battle of good against evil. What is more surprising, however, are the various ways in which the different pamphleteers deploy violence – be it physical or rhetorical – to further political agendas and dehumanise individuals, and the consequences of this violence on questions of narratorial authority, literary genre and the reading public, questions that have been by and large overlooked by recent scholarship on this genre.[2] These differences in violence become salient when we note that in the four *Vies privées* written against the duc d'Orléans, a significant portion of the pamphlets' plots are actually remarkably consistent, with many pre-revolutionary events changing little from the earliest *Vie* in 1784 to the last one in An II.[3] In

---

1. Robert Darnton, *The Devil in the holy water, or the art of slander from Louis XIV to Napoleon* (Philadelphia, PA, 2010); and *Dictionnaire des Vies privées*, ed. Olivier Ferret, Anne-Marie Mercier-Faivre and Chantal Thomas, SVEC 2011:02.
2. On the use of rhetorical violence to dehumanise and exclude political groups, see Olivier Ritz's article 'Metaphors of popular violence in the revolutionary debate in the wake of Edmund Burke', p.35-47.
3. There is a fifth *Vie privée* concerning Orléans through the lens of his wife

this series, strategies of revision, narratorial intervention and intertextuality are intricately linked with violence and the gradual process of dehumanisation, which transform Orléans from a ridiculously ignorant and debauched aristocrat into a monstrous enemy, increasingly distant from civil society in thought, behaviour and emotions, who must be eliminated at all cost.

The genealogy of the duc d'Orléans

The evolving representation of the genealogy of Orléans gives us a first glimpse of the complex relationship between violence, dehumanisation and the presence of the narrator in the four *Vies privées*. This section of the *Vies*, drawing on the period's recognition of the importance of blood lines and inheritance, serves to characterise Orléans, at times even before his actual appearance, through the manipulation of violent episodes in his ancestry. Here genetics (or in one case, divine wrath) trumps even education which, thanks especially to Rousseau's *Emile*, had come to be seen over the course of the eighteenth century as an important part of an individual's development.

The first pamphlet, the 1784 *Vie privée ou Apologie de très-sérénissime prince Monseigneur le Duc de Chartres*, probably written by Charles Théveneau de Morande, only goes back one generation to his mother, her many lovers and her husband.[4] The duc's supposed father, the elder duc d'Orléans, is ridiculed as being 'naturally inept' and completely blind to his wife's debaucheries with, among others, a certain coachman Lefranc, who is assumed to be the actual father of Orléans.[5] In keeping with the light tongue-in-cheek tone of the title, violence is absent from this first presentation of the duc's genealogy, in favour of a portrait of aristocratic libertinage recounted through the impersonal expressions of rumour such as 'Des gens malhonnêtes [...] ont donné

---

which will not be considered here, due to its purpose to defend the duc: *Vie secrète de Louise-Marie-Adélaïde Bourbon Penthièvre, duchesse d'Orléans, avec ses correspondances politiques* (London, Imprimérie Werland, 1790).

4. Charles Théveneau de Morande, *Vie privée ou Apologie de très-sérénissime prince Monseigneur le Duc de Chartres* (Paris [A cent lieues de la Bastille] (London, J. Hodges), 1784).

5. Morande, *Apologie*, p.3-4.

à croire que' and 'On ajoute enfin que' that bestow upon the text an air of delicious scandal without becoming overtly moralising.[6]

The second pamphlet, *Vie de Louis-Philippe-Joseph, duc d'Orléans, traduit de l'anglais*, by M. R. D. W. and published in 1789, goes back further in time to retrace his lineage, starting with the failed regicide attempted by his great-grandfather, the Regent, who as a result of his ambition for the throne tries unsuccessfully to poison Louis XV and instead poisons himself when the cups are switched.[7] Despite the failure of this attempt, the episode serves to foreshadow the threat of the Orléans family as political usurpers.[8] The author pauses the narrative in order to underline the importance of this act: 'A ce trait on reconnaît déjà la scélérate ambition du Régent et sa haute audace.'[9] The 'déjà' implies the consequences for the future duc d'Orléans's own political ambition, while the use of the impersonal 'on' affirms the neutrality and the universally recognised veracity of this assertion. The narrator's subjective 'je' intervenes a few paragraphs later, but here it is to acknowledge the Regent's positive qualities: 'Je suis ici nécessairement entraîné au plaisir de réfléchir et d'écrire, que [...] [le Régent] préféra la mort au soupçon d'un pareil crime.'[10] The violence is restricted to this one episode, with the rest of Orléans's lineage in this account engaging in behaviour consistent with the earlier 1784 pamphlet.

The third pamphlet, the anonymous 1793 *La Vie et les crimes de Philippe, duc d'Orléans*, resembles the 1784 genealogy in that the duc's ancestry is reduced to his parents and the attempted regicide of the Regent is removed.[11] His illegitimate birth as the son

---

6. Morande, *Apologie*, p.4. Olivier Ferret, 'La *Vie privée... du duc de Chartres* et les *Mémoires secrets*', in *Le Règne de la critique: l'imaginaire culturel des Mémoires secrets*, ed. Christophe Cave (Paris, 2010), p.397-413.
7. M. R. D. W., *Vie de Louis-Philippe-Joseph, duc d'Orléans, traduit de l'anglais* (London, Imprimérie du Palais Saint-James, 1789). The claim that the work is a translation is a fiction on the part of the author, which inscribes his work in the tradition of French libellers in England who learned that country's style of virulent scandal-mongering and appreciated its freedom of the press. See Darnton, *Devil in the holy water*, p.314-39.
8. Ferret, *Dictionnaire des Vies privées*, p.374.
9. M. R. D. W., *Vie de Louis-Philippe-Joseph*, p.7.
10. M. R. D. W., *Vie de Louis-Philippe-Joseph*, p.8.
11. *La Vie et les crimes de Philippe, duc d'Orléans* (Cologne, 1793).

of a coachman is relegated to a footnote, where some of the most scandalous and injurious details can be found throughout the text. The author's royalist leanings appear early on with the duc's excessive villainy being attributed to his lowly heritage: 'L'on sait que le Duc d'Orléans s'est vanté lui-même d'être le fils d'un cocher. La bassesse, qui forme le fond de son caractère, rend très vraisemblable cette assertion.'[12] Besides the new element of the duc's pride in his lowly birth, what is most remarkable in 1793 is that the suppression of violence in his genealogy coincides with the early dehumanisation of Orléans as a monster: 'Ce fut le 13 avril de l'année 1747, que le ciel dans sa colère ordonna à la nature de produire celui qui devait être un jour l'opprobre du genre humain et l'auteur des maux de son pays.'[13] Thus from the moment of his birth, Orléans is linked with early modern ideas of monstrosity as being the product of God's wrath.[14] This idea of monstrosity is reinforced by the author's denial of a connection between Orléans and his parents, which recalls another theory of monstrosity that defines the monster as that which does not resemble its parents:[15] 'Louis Philippe d'Orléans naquit, et avec lui le germe des passions les plus outrées, des inclinations les plus vicieuses. Ce n'était point le sang qui les lui avait transmises.'[16] To underline this lack of resemblance between Orléans and his parents, the author reiterates, on the unlikely chance that the reader missed it before: 'Philippe d'Orléans ne dut donc *qu'à lui-même* son organisation vicieuse; ce fut *en lui-même* qu'il trouva la source féconde de ses désordres et de ces sentiments dépravés *qu'il se plut à développer* dans le cours d'une vie profondément criminelle.'[17] This emphasis on Orléans's radical difference from other human beings and his fundamental lack of all humanising blood ties relegates him from the beginning to the edge of humanity, even pushing him into the territory of the inhuman. Defined by his criminality, and more importantly by his enjoyment of his malevolence, violence becomes a marker of his

12. *Vie et les crimes*, p.4.
13. *Vie et les crimes*, p.3.
14. Ambroise Paré, *Des monstres et prodiges*, ed. Jean Céard (Geneva, 1971).
15. Marie-Hélène Huet, *Monstrous imagination* (Cambridge, MA, 1993).
16. *Vie et les crimes*, p.3.
17. *Vie et les crimes*, p.4. Emphasis added.

inhumanity in that the infliction of violence and cruelty testifies to a borderline animalistic indifference, if not complete lack of pity, towards the victims of his crimes and debaucheries. This portrait is all the more frightening because the responsibility for his character is not the result of genealogy, but rather lies in him alone, as the author repeatedly states. Even education fails to redeem him: 'L'éducation, dont le but est de rectifier les défauts naturels, ou au moins de les rendre moins saillants [...]: l'éducation ne produisit point sur lui cet effet ordinaire; elle ne changea rien à une empreinte morale trop fortement exprimée pour que rien pût en altérer le caractère primitif.'[18] The monster Orléans defies Rousseau's model in *Emile* of the power of education to prevent the corrupting effect of society on the child since he has already been born corrupt. The absence of violence in his ancestry is all the more frightening, therefore, because it means that Orléans is an anomaly, a freak of nature coming from heavenly wrath, whose destructive appearance is unpredictable and thus even more terrifying.

In the last pamphlet, *Vie de L.-P.-J. Capet, ci-devant duc d'Orléans, ou Mémoires pour servir à l'histoire de la Révolution française* by Pierre Turbat and published in An II after Orléans's execution, we return to a genealogy similar to the 1789 model, although the presence of the author is much stronger in this version.[19] After a proliferation of the personal pronoun 'je' in the foreword, this author reappears in the portion of the genealogy devoted to the duc's mother to remind the reader that the purpose of the family tree is its connection with Orléans: 'celui dont j'écris l'histoire était le fruit de ses crapuleux adultères'.[20] The author's presentation of himself as a simple historian also serves to remove the rumour quality from reported events such as 'on dit qu'elle se prostituait à ses valets,' giving them rather the air of historical fact.[21] In this version the history of Orléans's lineage begins once again with a violent ancestor with a fondness for poison. In An II,

18. *Vie et les crimes*, p.4.
19. Pierre Turbat, *Vie de L.-P.-J. Capet, ci-devant duc d'Orléans, ou Mémoires pour servir à l'histoire de la Révolution française* (Paris, Imprimérie de Franklin, 1793).
20. Turbat, *Vie de L.-P.-J. Capet*, p.13.
21. Turbat, *Vie de L.-P.-J. Capet*, p.13.

however, the violence is successful (though non-political) and goes back one more generation to his great-great-grandfather, thus illustrating how deeply corruption is embedded in the nobility. While the author claims that this ancestor might be innocent of this accusation of having poisoned his wife, Henriette d'Angleterre, his characterisation does not change. Rather, the author places murder on a par with sexual deviancy and robbery, since all three acts merit the same label of 'monstre':

> il est à peu près démontré qu'il n'a point commis ce crime, mais il n'en est pas moins un monstre; comment le qualifier autrement, il aimait avec fureur le jeune *Devardes*, il passait la moitié de sa vie à s'habiller en femme, et pour varier ses plaisirs, lui et ses courtisans allaient la nuit sur le Pont-Neuf détrousser les passants.[22]

Smutty public behaviour is thus vilified, becoming intrinsic proof of a capacity for or predisposition to violence. It is this potential to commit violent acts that is important; actual guilt concerning one particular act is brushed aside as unessential. The rest of the Year II lineage, in line with the earlier pamphlets, is clearly negative, though not violent, consisting of the immoral behaviour that was typical of Old Regime pamphletary literature, such as debauchery, incest, gluttony and promiscuity. And while Orléans's birth is still illegitimate, his father is hinted as likely to be aristocratic, in keeping with the republican bias of the author.

The episode of the prince de Lamballe

In the episode of the decline and death of Orléans's brother-in-law, the prince de Lamballe, violence and the process of dehumanisation become more closely entwined, while different rhetorical strategies are deployed to convince the reading public of the duc's guilt.

In the 1784 pamphlet, the tone is playful, beginning with the joke that the author is writing on behalf of a *Société d'amis du prince* committed to defending Orléans's honour and reputation. Regarding the death of Lamballe, the author cites in quotations

---

22. Turbat, *Vie de L.-P.-J. Capet*, p.12.

another pamphlet that was suppressed by this *Société* in order to indirectly levy the charge that Orléans brought about Lamballe's death out of greed for the Penthièvre family's immense fortune and position as Grand Admiral:[23]

> Ce n'était pas assez pour l'héritier de la maison d'Or[léans] de suivre en tout les goûts de Philippe-Auguste, il fallait encore pour satisfaire une autre de ses passions déshonorantes, qu'il entraînât dans l'abîme de la débauche et du désordre le prince de Lamb[alle], fils infortuné du duc de Pinthièvre. On a attribué la mort de ce Prince à l'effervescence de ses sens, et à sa complaisance extrême pour le duc de Ch[artre]s. Mais elle a encore une autre cause que je vais dévoiler. Depuis longtemps le duc de Ch[artre]s avait projeté de se marier avec la sœur du prince Lamb[alle]; une de ses vues principales était d'accumuler sur sa tête les biens immenses de la maison de Pinth[ièvre] et la charge de Grand-Amiral.[24]

The author then mounts a weak defence of the duc's innocence:

> Nous croirions faire injure aux sentiments de M. le duc de Ch[artre]s si nous nous permettions de répondre à cette diffamation que l'enfer seul peut avoir produite: aucune âme bien née ne formera même le moindre soupçon sur la fausseté de cette imputation. [...] Il est bien plus juste de dire et de croire que ces deux Princes contemporains et compagnons de débauche, encouraient les mêmes dangers, mais qu'un seul des deux a été la victime de ses désordres et du poison qu'il avait recueilli dans les lieux les plus infâmes, et avec les femmes les plus impures de Paris.[25]

The weak arguments, appealing to the supposed delicate feelings of Orléans and to the instincts of the high-born, clearly show that the truth about Lamballe's death lies in the charges against him and not in his defence. Nevertheless, in this pamphlet it never

---

23. As Olivier Ferret notes, the practice of quotation is one of the principal characteristics of this text. The libel referenced throughout the 1784 pamphlet is probably the 1781 *Lettre de Danguy, danseur de l'Opéra, péri dans le feu du 8 juin dernier, à sa mère, touchant les véritables causes de l'incendie de cette salle*. This text is regrettably not in the catalogue of the BNF and cannot be located. See Ferret 'La *Vie privée...*', p.398-400.
24. Morande, *Apologie*, p.12.
25. Morande, *Apologie*, p.13.

becomes clear exactly how Orléans is responsible for Lamballe's untimely end. There is never any proof causally linking the duc's motives and Lamballe's death – at most, as the author states in his justification, the two participate in the same debauchery, with only Lamballe succumbing.

In the 1789 pamphlet, however, Orléans's role is made much more obvious: he allegedly actively plots to prevent Lamballe from producing descendants and to kill him at an early age so that Orléans will inherit all the Penthièvre riches through his wife. As in 1784, the direct cause of Lamballe's death is venereal disease, however here alcohol also contributes to the degradation of his health. Even more importantly, the causal connection between Orléans's motives and behaviour and Lamballe's dissolute lifestyle and ultimate death is drawn much more explicitly:

> Le Duc de Chartres, en épousant Mademoiselle de Penthièvre, conçut l'idée de devenir l'unique héritier de son beau-père. Pour y parvenir, il lia une amitié très étroite avec le prince Lamballe, devenu son beau-frère. Il se mit de toutes ses parties, le mena dans tous ses lieux de débauche, lui fit connaître les femmes les plus prostituées, l'excita à boire de ces liqueurs brûlantes qui dessèchent la poitrine.
>
> Par l'impulsion du Duc de Chartres, il se livra à la passion inextinguible d'une créole infectée, au point qu'elle gangrena ses parties extérieures comme les fibres internes. Il fallut lui faire l'amputation des testicules, opération à la fois cruelle et douloureuse, dont il mourut.[26]

The explicitly grisly detail of Lamballe's death only exacerbates the impression of the duc's responsibility. This is compounded by the addition of a footnote to this episode which begins with Orléans's hypocritical discourse on his brother-in-law's painful end, in which he pretends to be saddened by the other man's self-destructive behaviour: 'Que je suis fâché du libertinage de mon frère de Lamballe [...], c'est un homme sans raison, il se tue, il s'empoisonne, je l'aime autant que je l'estime, il me fera mourir de douleur de le voir lui-même abréger ses jours.'[27] Just in case the reader misses the irony in Orléans's supposed lament, it is

26. M. R. D. W., *Vie de Louis-Philippe-Joseph*, p.29.
27. M. R. D. W., *Vie de Louis-Philippe-Joseph*, p.29-30.

immediately followed by the reaction of the author, who models the appropriate outrage towards such immorality: 'Peut-on pousser plus loin la scélératesse, la perfidie?'[28] His fury nonetheless quickly returns to a more neutral tone which he uses to provide additional details concerning Orléans's culpability: 'Pour restaurant, après les ébats des prostituées qu'il lui présentait, il lui faisait avaler ces liqueurs emmiellées et mortelles, pour rendre toutes les ressources de la guérison inutiles. A ce trait seul, connaissez, lecteur, le duc de Chartres.'[29] This last sentence is particularly important in that it marks a single violent act as revealing Orléans's entire character, in a similar way that his ancestor's attempted regicide defined him and his political ambition in the same pamphlet. Through the technique of a direct address to the reader which interrupts the third-person narration, the author intervenes to model the correct interpretation of the duc's character. This overall message communicated to the reading public is that Orléans's obvious hypocrisy and dissimulation conceal a lack of pity and of respect for familial bonds, all of which make him a dehumanised monster.[30]

The connections between Orléans's motives and his destructive actions become even more explicit in the 1793 version. The word 'avarice' opens the episode and is then used repeatedly to tie together the series of events dealing with Orléans's marriage, his greed and his plot against Lamballe. Furthermore, while the violence in 1789 centres on the ravages of the disease on Lamballe and his torturous death, in 1793 the reader receives less grisly details:

> Dévoré du désir d'absorber cette riche succession, le duc pour y parvenir imagina le plus affreux expédient. Il se lia étroitement avec le prince de Lamballe, et profitant de l'ascendant que sa scélératesse déjà profonde lui donnait sur la jeunesse confiante et inexpérimentée de ce dernier, il l'entraîna dans toutes sortes d'excès. Ce projet lui réussit; l'infortuné prince de Lamballe,

28. M. R. D. W., *Vie de Louis-Philippe-Joseph*, p.30.
29. M. R. D. W., *Vie de Louis-Philippe-Joseph*, p.30.
30. Moral sense theories of the time considered pity the natural response to the sight of suffering; Lester Crocker, *Nature and culture: ethical thought in the French Enlightenment* (Baltimore, MD, 1963), ch.2.

victime des séductions de son perfide parent, mourut à la fleur de son âge sans laisser d'héritier.[31]

The focus here is on Orléans's culpability, as the author hypothesises in a footnote as to how exactly he accomplished his crime: 'Bien des gens assurent que le duc de Chartres fit avaler dans une orgie au prince de Lamballe, une poudre qui le rendit impuissant; d'autres disent même que ce fut un poison lent.'[32] In the end, however, the conclusion is that it does not even matter how or even whether he committed this specific crime (a technique that we have previously seen in the genealogy in the later An II pamphlet), that he is nonetheless responsible because of all his other criminal acts: 'Mais est-il besoin, nous le répétons, de prêter à ce monstre un crime sur l'existence duquel on n'a pas la plus complète certitude; il y en a assez de réels à lui reprocher. Il suffit d'ailleurs de savoir que ce fut lui qui causa la mort de son beau-frère.'[33] Moreover, the dehumanisation of Orléans through his lack of natural feeling and hypocrisy receives a much more lengthy treatment here than in the previous pamphlet. While including the same hypocritical remark by Orléans from 1789 in a footnote to the episode, the author expands on and exaggerates the earlier version, and re-emphasises the duc's culpability in Lamballe's death. Whereas in 1789 Orléans: 'feignit d'en être affecté; et dans le fond de l'âme, il se louait et s'applaudissait d'avoir réalisé ses intentions sanguinaires',[34] in 1793 'Cette mort prématurée mit le comble aux vœux de Philippe; mais il déguisa sa joie; il affecta même d'être vivement affligé. Ceux qui le connaissaient déjà assez pour apercevoir la noirceur de son âme, ne furent point la dupe de ces sentiments fins; ils regardèrent toujours le duc de Chartres comme l'assassin du prince de Lamballe.'[35] In 1793 Orléans no longer merely pretends to be affected by Lamballe's death, but also explicitly hides his joy in his criminal success. The ideas of unmasking and just punishment appear in the mention of a public who is wise to his double-

---

31. *Vie et les crimes*, p.10-11.
32. *Vie et les crimes*, p.11.
33. *Vie et les crimes*, p.11-12.
34. M. R. D. W., *Vie de Louis-Philippe-Joseph*, p.31.
35. *Vie et les crimes*, p.11.

faced behaviour and in the label of *assassin*. The violence thus shifts towards emphasising Orléans's responsibility, while also highlighting and developing his monstrous character, especially through public opinion which corroborates the author's conclusions.

The An II pamphlet includes even fewer violent details and surprisingly presents a nuanced attribution of responsibility for Lamballe's tragic end, although ultimately guilt for his death lies with Orléans. While greed remains the driving force, and libertinage the weapon of choice, here Lamballe has a much greater role in his own degeneration. Unlike the 1789 and 1793 versions, in which it is Orléans who incites him into all dangerous excesses, here Lamballe is not entirely absolved of responsibility in that he destroys his own health by trying to keep up with Orléans's greater sexual stamina and by excessively consuming wine and liquor: 'Philippe, doué d'une constitution vigoureuse, passait les nuits sans éprouver trop de fatigues; Lamballe, d'un tempérament plus faible, avait besoin de réparer ses forces épuisées. Il se livra au goût du vin; les liqueurs spiritueuses succédèrent; ses sens se dépravèrent.'[36] With Lamballe's health deteriorating significantly, Orléans re-enters the picture to finish what he started.

> [Il] lui fit prendre des palliatifs qui détruisirent pour jamais les sources de la vie; bientôt sa santé fut entièrement délabrée, et dans les instants où la nature combattait encore, le duc de Chartres proposait une nouvelle orgie: enfin, Lamballe succomba; des maux affreux l'accablèrent, une opération douloureuse et terrible fut ordonnée par les gens de l'art; peu de temps après le malheureux termina ses jours.[37]

This acknowledgement of Lamballe's responsibility could come from the author's desire to depict the entire nobility as corrupt and degenerate (with Orléans being merely the instigator of others' natural inclinations). In An II, with the duc safely guillotined, the urgency to denounce him personally is possibly somewhat diminished, though it is still necessary to depict the

---

36. *Vie et les crimes*, p.21.
37. Turbat, *Vie de L.-P.-J. Capet*, p.21-22.

corruption of the aristocracy in order to sustain the momentum of the Revolution.

Pleasure in blood, and the addition of violence

Although some gory detail is suppressed from the Lamballe episode in the Year II pamphlet, this last work contains a violent episode that is absent from the earlier pamphlets, despite the fact that it describes an event from the duc's adolescence, thus falling in the period of time covered by all the tracts. The event happens as follows: at the age of fourteen, Orléans attends a ball during which two young men fight, one of them ends up being stabbed by the other. What is notable about this episode, and what receives the greatest attention, however, is Orléans's reaction:

> le prince voulut voir le blessé, il vit couler son sang, et ne fut point ému; je vis même dans ses yeux, qu'il éprouvait un certain plaisir, et je fus indigné de son sang-froid lorsqu'il demanda s'il y avait du danger, et qu'il dit: *Je croyais qu'un mourant portait une figure plus hideuse*, sur-le-champ il forma avec gaieté une contre-danse, où il se livra au plaisir avec un abandon qui me donna une telle idée de son âme, que je n'ai jamais rencontré ce prince sans éprouver une sensation désagréable.[38]

In this episode, the narrator noticeably intervenes, presenting himself as a direct witness in order to increase the credibility of and to model the appropriate reaction to this important incident and Orléans's monstrosity. What merits this condemnation of Orléans's character as 'barbare et inhumain'[39] is especially his perversion of the natural sentiment of pity into the malicious feeling of pleasure towards another's pain.[40] His enjoyment of the light-hearted *contre-danse* exposes his joyous indifference to the sight of the dying man's torment. Appearing at the tender age of fourteen, this barbaric reaction to suffering marks his character, separating him permanently from the rest of humanity, and establishes a clear precedent for the Lamballe episode.

38. Turbat, *Vie de L.-P.-J. Capet*, p.16.
39. Turbat, *Vie de L.-P.-J. Capet*, p.16.
40. James A. Steintrager, *Cruel delight: Enlightenment culture and the inhuman* (Bloomington, IN, 2004), p.5.

We may ask ourselves at this point why this episode appears only in the last pamphlet. Why does the author choose thus to revise Orléans's adolescence when most of the other episodes concerning this time period are taken from previous versions? One possible explanation draws on the diverging goals of the two last pamphlets. In 1793, the royalist pamphleteer's aim is to denounce Orléans's actual deeds by exposing his responsibility for the violence and the intense discord of the Revolution. Since he is still alive at the time, he remains a serious threat to society; hence the urgency to accumulate proof of these allegations. In the case of the Year II pamphlet, however, Orléans has recently been guillotined. Therefore denouncing him here may serve to justify the reasons why his death was necessary. The constant emphasis throughout the pamphlet on his perverse influence and corruption (for example, in the episode concerning the death of Lamballe) supports this idea.[41] It may also serve to condemn the aristocracy as a whole, with Orléans being seen as stereotypical of his class and of the threat of an aristocratic plot infiltrating the Revolution. The dehumanisation of *les grands*, accomplished through assertions that they are of a different species, and the fact that their manner of thinking is unnatural, all participate in this effort:

> on conviendra que tous les grands, de quelque pays qu'ils soient, sont dès leur berceau environné de flatteurs, qu'au moment où l'aurore de la raison commence à poindre, cette noble canaille se croyait d'une espèce différente de la nôtre, qu'à l'instant où le germe des passions est développé, ces tigres sacrifiaient sans pitié à leurs désirs, l'innocence d'une vierge, l'union de deux époux et la propriété du pauvre.[42]

The episode at the ball thus demonstrates the continuity of the aristocrats' monstrosity. Their perverted, inhuman nature is not the result of the extraordinary circumstances of the Revolution, but rather inherent in their degenerated class, and was visible

---

41. The scene at the ball also foreshadows another instance of pleasure in the observation of violence in which the narrator once again directly intervenes: the murder of Orléans's sister-in-law, the Princesse de Lamballe, during the September Massacres. Turbat, *Vie de L.-P.-J. Capet*, p.44-45.
42. Turbat, *Vie de L.-P.-J Capet*, p.vii.

prior to the fall of the monarchy. Furthermore, pleasure in the suffering of another individual would not only separate Orléans (and the nobility) from natural feeling but also from enlightened thinking. The influence of the works of Montesquieu, Rousseau and Beccaria in the late eighteenth century resulted in the rejection of even state-sanctioned spectacular punishment in favour of the increasingly popular belief that suffering should be inflicted for utilitarian and social reasons (aristocratic pleasure would hardly be considered either of those).[43] Inner characteristics thus gain importance in highlighting the hidden monstrosity of the aristocracy in order perhaps to support the acts of Terror that have already been committed and to illustrate the need for them to continue.

Rhetorical violence

Beyond narratorial strategies involving the author and his imagined public, the different manifestations of violent rhetoric in these pamphlets also contribute to the effort to dehumanise Orléans, illustrating how literary techniques can be put to the service of political goals. This appears even at the most basic level, in the occurrence of certain denunciatory terminology such as *monstre* and *scélérat*, whose frequency increases, peaks in 1793, and then decreases in An II. This repetition serves as a pedagogical tool to convey continually the message of the duc's monstrosity which, in combination with the violent episodes and other striking incidents of virulent rhetoric, leads to the logical conclusion that Orléans must be removed from society.

Furthermore, the third and fourth pamphlets mark the appearance of comparisons between Orléans and extremely violent historical figures. In 1793, the anonymous author pronounces in a footnote: 'Oh, il faut l'avouer, les Tibère, les Caligula, les Néron ne sont que des enfants auprès de Philippe d'Orléans.'[44] These figures, infamous for their tyranny and incredible cruelty, contribute to the dehumanisation of Orléans through their incar-

---

43. Jean-Clément Martin, *Violence et révolution: essai sur la naissance d'un mythe national* (Paris, 2006). p.39-40.
44. *Vie et les crimes*, p.71.

nation of monstrosity, as illustrated in the *Encyclopédie* article 'Tyrannie', in which the chevalier de Jaucourt notes that the name Nero has become a proverb to designate a monster in the government.[45] The figure of Nero reappears in An II in order to highlight the two men's responsibility for the assassination of a family member (Nero ordered the murder of his mother Agrippina; Orléans voted for the death of his cousin Louis XVI). The author then expands this already monstrous allusion to include the duc's entire family: 'car Philippe ressemblait à Néron, il aurait voulu que toute sa famille n'ait qu'une tête, afin d'avoir le double plaisir de la couper et d'en hériter'.[46] These allusions to brutal historical figures contribute to the work done by the genealogies, linking Orléans to a lineage of famous violent tyrants, and illustrate the threat of revolutionary violence being co-opted and perverted for personal gain (either financial or political).

Lastly, the paratexts of the different pamphlets – the subtitles, frontispiece captions and opening quotes – saliently expose the underlying message of the different works through their deployment of different literary techniques such as irony and intertextuality. The bantering tone of the 1784 pamphlet is clearly conveyed through the subtitle of the work: 'Contre un libelle diffamatoire écrit en mil sept cent quatre-vingt-un, mais qui n'a point paru à cause des menaces que nous avons faites à l'Auteur de le déceler.' Thus the first game in a pamphlet full of teasers is for the reader to discover that the pamphlet is an amusingly bad defence of Orléans, full rather of titillating details of his sexual adventures, unbelievable ignorance and poor excuses for his bad behaviour.

The 1789 pamphlet opens with an acrostic poem constructed with the letters of 'Le duc d'Orléans'. Drawing on the earlier pamphletary tradition that incorporated poems and bawdy songs

---

45. Louis, chevalier de Jaucourt, 'Tyrannie', in *Encyclopédie, ou Dictionnaire raisonné des sciences, des arts et des métiers, par une société de gens de lettres*, ed. Denis Diderot and Jean Le Rond d'Alembert, University of Chicago: ARTFL Encyclopédie Project (Spring 2013 Edition), Robert Morrissey (ed.), http://encyclopedie.uchicago.edu/.
46. Turbat, *Vie de L.-P.-J. Capet*, p.25.

into the text, it nonetheless communicates outrage at Orléans rather than teasing satire:

> *L'exécrable adultère infecta* son berceau,
> Et sa mère impudique, illustrant sa naissance,
> Dans *l'école du crime* allaita son enfance;
> Une *infâme* leçon, un *horrible* tableau
> *Corrompirent* bientôt sa première innocence,
> Des maîtres *criminels* lui versant leur *poison*,
> Ont surpassé les vœux, les desseins de sa mère.
> Reconnaissance, amour et désir de bien faire
> Le choquaient, l'indignaient, *révoltaient* sa raison,
> Et son cœur respirant *le fiel et l'imposture*,
> Annonça que ce prince aux forfaits préparé,
> N'aimant que *les pervers* dont il est entouré,
> Serait avant trente ans *l'horreur de la nature*.[47]

Humour has disappeared between 1784 and 1789, replaced in the poem by a lexicon of horror and righteous fury and by references to crime and a corrupted innocence, which are quite typical of the genre at this time. The author's suppression of the poem in later editions of the pamphlet implies that the lightness of the poetic genre was no longer seen as fit to capture the repulsion one should feel towards Orléans. Denunciation can thus be seen as becoming more serious, meriting a more serious form and no longer the appropriate domain for more 'playful' poems and songs.

The epigraph to the 1793 pamphlet is a quote attributed to Voltaire: 'Ainsi que la vertu, le crime a ses héros.'[48] This brief and direct reference to crime and its supposed chief perpetrator coincides well with the rest of the text: direct, hardly verbose in description, though lengthy in the accumulation of historical events and personal episodes that prove the opening assertion. The transformation of Racine's formulation in *Phèdre* 'Ainsi que la vertu, le crime a ses *degrés*' [emphasis added] removes any

---

47. M. R. D. W., *Vie de Louis-Philippe-Joseph*, p.1. Emphasis added.
48. The exact quote from chant 5 of Voltaire's *Henriade* is 'Le crime a ses héros; l'erreur a ses martyrs' (see Ferret, *Dictionnaire des Vies privées*, p.379). The probable appeal of this *chant* to the republican author attacking Orléans appears two lines later: 'Souvent des scélérats ressemblent aux grands hommes.'

element of ambiguity or nuance from the original quote, creating an attack devoid of semantic or formal play, and serving to place Orléans in a company of illustrious criminal heroes of the Revolution. We may note, moreover, that despite this indirect reference to Racine, Orléans is actually more reminiscent of a Cornelian hero, such as Cléopâtre in *Rodogune*, in his complete and magnificent malevolence.

The An II pamphlet is accompanied by a detailed frontispiece, an engraved portrait of Orléans that exaggerates his resemblance to the Bourbons (and to Louis XVI in particular), emphasising his round face and prominent nose. Along with his dates of birth and death, the caption bears the inscription 'Infidèle aux tyrans, et traître à sa Patrie'. Accompanying the portrait of Orléans as a sort of posthumous monument summing up his entire existence, this attack is even more direct than the 1793 epigraph in that it is not just an adapted quote but was rather created for the express purpose of resuming his life. Remarkable for his criminality in 1793, in An II he is classified as a true enemy of the human race, faithful neither to despots nor to his country in general. The end of the pamphlet resurrects the caption and adds an explanation that further dehumanises him, completing the justification for his execution: '[la postérité] confirmera ce vers qui le distingue particulièrement des monstres de son espèce. – Infidèle aux tyrans, et traître à sa Patrie.'[49] A monster among monsters and thus even more distant from humanity, the pamphleteer leaves no question that Orléans merited execution.

Over the course of the pamphletary campaign against Orléans from 1784 until after his death in An II, violence comes to permeate the entire text: in gory details added to previously existing episodes, in the addition of new events, or in rhetorical form, conveyed through narratorial interventions, malicious terminology, historical allusions or in less nuanced and more direct attacks in the paratext. This increase in violence generally accompanies the overall effort on the part of the pamphleteers to dehumanise Orléans, thus discrediting him politically and personally and eventually serving to advocate his execution or to justify his death after the fact. In the end, however, the violence is

---

49. Turbat, *Vie de L.-P.-J Capet*, p.56.

not restricted to the subject matter. As the lesson to be retained from the pamphlets becomes clearer throughout the course of the slander campaign, as the attacks become more virulent and the episodes become more violent, the author's interventions to model the appropriate reaction to the subject matter result in a deliberate, forceful removal of the reader's autonomy, for he is no longer seen as able to judge the 'facts' for himself. He is now either the passive receptor of the political and moral lessons distributed by an all-knowing author and a member of a public wise to Orléans's deceit; or by daring to reach different conclusions and disagree, he himself is an enemy to the Revolution who must be eliminated at all cost.

'Avec une telle violence que...':
Sade's use of the term *violence*[1]

JEAN-CHRISTOPHE ABRAMOVICI

Violence seems so utterly pervasive in Sade's work as to appear as nothing more than tautological and self-evident, consigned to the background of critical assessments of his writings.[2] When critics do broach the subject of violence, more often than not they do so incidentally or in a roundabout way, when analysing, for instance, the place of the reader, or recurrent motifs in Sade's imaginative world such as the volcano, the machine or the sadistic instrument. These apparently evasive tactics are not, however, signs of the critic's faltering courage or guilty modesty: what can one say about the violence of Sade's texts, other than that one feels it?[3] At best one can attempt to describe certain of its workings, and to show that it is not just a matter of representation, but primarily of language and writing.[4]

Do the instances of the word 'violence', in *Les Cent vingt journées de Sodome* and the *Justine* trilogy, indicate the writer's critical reflexion on the violence that he depicts? Do they serve to qualify the Sadean act? In each and every case they reveal the (too frequently underestimated) literary labour of a writer who, for

1. Translated by Thomas Wynn.
2. For other accounts of violence in Sade, see Michèle Vallenthini, 'Violence in history and the rise of the historical novel: the case of the marquis de Sade', p.93-102; and Thomas Wynn, 'Violence, vulnerability and subjectivity in Sade', p.139-60.
3. We must indeed recognise this response, which is quite the contrary of the hagiographic tradition that defends the notion that the works of the 'divin marquis' are innocuous. For a clarification of the violence of the 'effet-Sade', by an author who is nonetheless associated with the Surrealist movement, see Anne LeBrun, *Soudain un bloc d'abîme, Sade* (Paris, 1986). See also Will Mc-Morran's article, 'The sound of violence: listening to rape in Sade', p.229-49.
4. Hence the high stakes involved when it comes to translating Sade into foreign languages. Until now, Sade has been very badly served by his English translators, although it is gratifying to learn that there is now a renewed interest in providing better translations of his works.

each of his novels, made use of notebooks, plans, sketches, drafts and so on, before re-reading and ruthlessly correcting himself, hunting down the least repetition.

Although there are only nine instances of the word 'violence' in the whole of *Les Cent vingt journées de Sodome*, taken as a whole they reflect the novel's structure in a rather troubling way. Just as there is the deliberate, thematic gradation of the passions (simple, complex, criminal and murderous) described by the four 'historiennes', so there is the aesthetic gradation actualised in the move from the relatively comfortable reading of the first part to the brutal confrontation with the following parts. Whereas La Duclos, first of the 'historiennes', offers supplementary narrative features (descriptive details, anecdotes, witticisms, addresses to her listeners) that attenuate her stories' contents, the dry enumeration of the passions in the rest of the novel forces the reader to confront directly the increasingly violent content.

Moreover, it is in this completed section of the novel (comprising the introduction and the first part) that one finds seven of the nine instances of the word 'violence'. We read in the portrait, still somewhat vague, of the président de Curval that this character's profound hatred for his pious daughter Adélaïde leads him, on the day she deprives him of the pleasure of sex with a poor young girl, to 'se port[er] contre elle à de telles violences qu'elle en fut quinze jours au lit'.[5] The plural noun, rarely used by Sade, has here a euphemistic effect, which is required at the novel's 'threshold' given the necessity to 'disposer [le] cœur et [l'] esprit [du lecteur] au récit le plus impur qui ait jamais été fait depuis que le monde existe' (p.69).

Once this story properly begins, the veil that had been cast over the acts of cruelty can now be lifted, even if the narrator continues to respect scrupulously the gradation that is in keeping with the plan of *Les Cent vingt journées*. In the first part of the novel La Duclos narrates a series of passions that she, as a former prostitute, has experienced as object, agent or witness. She depicts a harsh but accepted violence that is considered inseparable from an occupation which she, blessed with a truly libertine

---

5. D.-A.-F. de Sade, *Les Cent vingt journées de Sodome*, in *Œuvres*, ed. Michel Delon, 3 vols (Paris, 1990-1998), vol.1, p.36.

character, exercised with a faultless professionalism. She was hardly alarmed by the sodomy enthusiast she describes on the third day: 'en écartant mes fesses d'une main, [il] se branlait très voluptueusement de l'autre et déchargea en attirant à lui mon anus avec tant de violence, en le chatouillant si lubriquement, que je partageai son extase' (p.116). She experienced less pleasure, however, with the 'inconnu' described on the twenty-seventh day: he hurt her breasts ('il les serre et les comprime avec une telle violence que je lui dis brusquement: "Vous me faites mal!" Alors on cesse, on me relève [...]') and her buttocks ('on les palpe et les comprime avec une violence sans égale') (p.279). A high-class prostitute, La Duclos has the privilege of being able to impose limits to her clients' 'caprices', and of refusing to suffer an act of brutality that would be devoid of pleasure. Similarly, she knows when to calibrate the number of blows she is asked to inflict, and how to introduce the right amount of force into the sex act that is necessary to the client's pleasure. In addition, at the end of the twenty-ninth day she demonstrates to the libertine masters at Silling her expertise in masturbation: 'Il était impossible d'y mettre plus de volupté; elle agitait sa main avec une légèreté [...] ses mouvements étaient d'une délicatesse et d'une violence [...]' (p.302).

The word 'violence' is not restricted to such descriptions of sexual passions, and indeed there are three examples to consider. The first has philosophical import in a novel devoid of extended abstract argument: in a muffled echo of Rousseau's *Second discours*, La Duclos justifies her taste for and practice of theft as a means of using 'la force et la violence' in order to 'rétablir l'équilibre' and 'cette égalité, première loi de la nature' (p.176). The two other instances occur in the description of Curval's orgasm: 'Je n'ai jamais vu des décharges de cette violence-là' (p.249), exclaims the duc de Blangis. Speaking as a sort of amateur materialist doctor, Curval justifies his excesses by means of a short physiological description (p.249):

> les objets de nos passions donnent une commotion si vive au fluide électrique qui coule dans nos nerfs, le choc reçu par les esprits animaux qui composent ce fluide est d'un tel degré de violence, que toute la machine en est ébranlée, et qu'on n'est pas plus le maître de retenir ses cris à ces secousses terribles du plaisir qu'on ne le pourrait aux émotions puissantes de la douleur.

One might note, for the record, that Sade himself had personal experience of these 'secousses terribles', probably as a result of a badly treated case of syphilis.[6]

Even though violence, both carried out and narrated, continues to intensify and increase beyond the first part of *Les Cent vingt journées*, it is only in the novel's fourth and final part that the last two instances of the word 'violence' occur. They appear in the synopsis of two murderous passions:

> 89. Celui du trente janvier, de Martaine, et qu'elle a conté le cinq février, coupe les tétons et les fesses d'une jeune fille, les mange, et met sur les plaies des emplâtres qui brûlent les chairs avec une telle violence qu'elle en meurt. (p.363)

> 107. Celui du vingt-neuf décembre, de Champville, qui aimait à fouetter des femmes grosses, veut la mère et la fille toutes deux grosses; il les lie chacune sur une plaque de fer, l'une au-dessus de l'autre; un ressort part, les deux plaques se rejoignent étroitement, et avec une telle violence, que les deux femmes sont réduites en poudre, elles et leurs fruits. (p.366)

The subordinating conjunction 'avec une telle violence que' emphasises the goal and the end point of the violent act. In both cases it is, crudely and simply, death. Just as death puts an end to the victims' ordeal, so the conjunction completes both the narrative sequence and the detailed description of torture. Equivalent to the 'Que vous dirois-je' used by medieval narrators to cut short a combat scene, whose outcome it indicates (by designating the victor), the conjunction catalyses and restarts the narrative in equal measure, since one passion is only concluded so as to make way for another.

The effacement of narrative linkages, and the stylistic denuding that so characterise the incomplete parts of *Les Cent vingt journées* serve to reinforce formally the violent content of

---

6. See the famous 'La vanille et la manille' letter that Sade sent to his wife at the end of 1784: 'c'est véritablement une attaque d'épilepsie et, sans d'ennuyeuses précautions, je suis bien sûr qu'on s'en douterait au faubourg St-Antoine [that is, beyond the walls of the Bastille] et des convulsions et des spasmes et des douleurs'. See *Correspondance du marquis de Sade et de ses proches enrichies de documents, notes et commentaires*, ed. Alice Laborde, 20 vols (Geneva, 1999-), vol.19, p.91-92. See also *50 Lettres du marquis de Sade à sa femme*, ed. Jean-Christophe Abramovici and Patrick Graille (Paris, 2009), p.233-34.

these sections.[7] It is as if the 'historiennes' (who stimulate the narration and the libertines) can neither physically bear the violence nor verbally articulate it any longer. Sade resolves this conflict by denying them a voice.

The instances of the word 'violence' in the *Justine* novels are both more numerous and more semantically diverse. Comparing the three versions allows one a keen insight into Sade's ventures as a writer, for he mixes techniques of amplification (extending the length and number of the episodes, the cruel details, the dissertations and so on) with experiments in narrative voice (first-person narrator in *Les Infortunes de la vertu* and *Justine ou Les Malheurs de la vertu*; omniscient narrator in *La Nouvelle Justine*). The increasing number of examples of the term 'violence' partly follows the general movement dynamic of augmentation and addition. If the leap from the *Infortunes* to *Justine* (three to sixteen cases) is particularly sizeable, the increase from *Justine* to *La Nouvelle Justine* (from sixteen to thirty-nine instances) is in proportion to the increase in pages between the two versions. On a number of occasions the term is used in ways that may be considered secondary or negligible. Firstly, there are idioms, such as 'faire violence' and 'violence du tourment'; there is one instance in *Les Infortunes de la vertu*, three in *Justine* and five in *La Nouvelle Justine*. Sade is reluctant to make use of such set expressions which mask reality under euphemistic or imagistic terms; 'cette bête dont tu parles sans cesse sans la connaître et que tu appelles nature', as the preface to *Les Cent vingt journées* puts it, inveighing against such language.[8] Similarly, the philosophical uses of the term 'violence' are rather rare; there are no examples in *Les Infortunes de la vertu*, two in *Justine* and six in *La Nouvelle Justine*, and these are only found in Père Clément's eulogy of the passions and in the Bishop of Grenoble's justification of authoritarian political power. Unlike crime or murder, violence is less a category of thought than a mode of action, and as such is more likely to be depicted than debated.

7. See Jean-Christophe Abramovici, 'Les Cent vingt journées de Sodome: lecture et isolisme', in *Lectures, livres et lecteurs du XVIIIe siècle*, ed. Jean Marie Goulemot, *Cahiers d'histoire culturelle* (2003), p.95-103.
8. Sade, *Les Cent vingt journées de Sodome*, in *Œuvres*, vol.1, p.69.

Some examples of the term disappear with the change of narrative voice that occurs between *Justine* to *La Nouvelle Justine*. In order to convey the intensity of her distress, the heroine makes use of hyperbole, speaking of a 'crise de douleur morale de la violence de celle que j'éprouvais',[9] or, at the only times when she considers suicide, lamenting that she is ready 'à céder avec violence aux effets de [s]on désespoir'.[10] Confronted with Justine's astonishing physical and mental resistance, the reader might not go as far as suspecting her of hypocrisy, but may at least have occasion to find her ambiguous. Explicitly ironic, the narrator of the third version portrays Justine with a mix of commiseration and mockery, but now stands between the reader and the heroine, screening her attempts to solicit a little compassion.

The word 'violence' is used first and foremost to qualify the libertine act, with one example in *Les Infortunes*, six in *Justine* and seventeen in *La Nouvelle Justine*. The tone of decency and the allusiveness that are characteristic of the *conte* as a genre explain why the *Infortunes* are so lacking in such depictions. In contrast, the representation of sexual brutality continues and intensifies as one moves from *Justine* to *La Nouvelle Justine*. In both novels, it is this brutality that determines the portrayal of the rapes repeatedly suffered by the heroine,[11] just as it does the depiction of tastes that one might call, for want of a better term, sadomasochistic: 'Plus on lui donne de plaisir, plus les coups qu'il porte ont de violence.'[12]

It is, nonetheless, indicative of a change in the representation of this primary brutal force, that the subordinating conjunction 'avec une telle violence que', which is absent from the 1791 edition, appears no less than five times eight years later. Whereas in *Les Cent vingt journées* the conjunction served to make death the

---

9. Sade, *Justine ou Les Malheurs de la vertu*, in *Œuvres*, vol.2, p.237.
10. Sade, *Justine ou Les Malheurs de la vertu*, in *Œuvres*, vol.2, p.308
11. In *Justine* Sévérino 'retire l'instrument avec violence et s'engloutit lui-même au gouffre qu'il vient d'entrouvrir...' (*Œuvres*, vol.2, p.279); in *La Nouvelle Justine*, Rodin 'pousse avec violence' in order to rape Justine; and later in the same novel the heroine 'est déchirée. Le dard monstrueux de Cardoville, en s'introduisant avec violence, va renouveler les blessures faites par Volcidor' (*Œuvres*, p.564, 1096).
12. Sade, *La Nouvelle Justine*, in *Œuvres*, vol.2, p.612.

ultimate end-point of all 'passions', in *La Nouvelle Justine* it contributes to a sort of aestheticisation of the Sadean scene. There is, of course, no lack of corpses in this third version, but given that they are, as it were, nonchalantly pushed into the margins, these bodies are no longer meticulously tallied up, as in *Les Cent vingt journées*' final 'récapitulation'.[13] Instead, this little grammatical phrase tethers the libertine act to its effect on the victimised body, an effect that might be rendered aurally: 'avec une telle violence, que la pauvre fille, transpercée à la fois dans mille endroits de son corps, jette des cris qui s'entendraient d'une lieue'; 'avec une telle violence, que Justine jetait les hauts cris'. Or visually:

[Rodin] flagelle avec une telle violence, que le sang paraît aussitôt.
[Sylvestre] arrache en cinq ou six endroits la peau des cuisses et des fesses, avec une telle violence, que le sang coule à chaque plaie.
[Siméon] la fustige de la main droite avec une telle violence, qu'en moins de soixante coups, ses cuisses sont inondées du sang que son derrière distille.[14]

Prolonging and crowning the violent act, this bloodletting is a kind of orgasm, with which it is often conflated: 'Antonin redouble de violence, et son foutre échappe *malgré lui*.'[15] Those final words remind us that the Sadean libertine is rarely in control of his ejaculation; the crisis that in most cases accompanies the orgasm denies the libertine his mastery of the scene and his actions. His predilection for those spurts of blood might thereby be better understood, as welcome proxies for that dreaded orgasm, and can be controlled and displaced upon the other, as in the case of Gernande and his wife: 'il resserre [les ligatures] de toute sa force, afin, dit-il, que le sang jaillisse avec plus de violence.'[16]

It is not so much that the Sadean imagination becomes less violent from *Les Cent vingt journées* to *La Nouvelle Justine*; it is rather

---

13. Sade, *Les Cent vingt journées de Sodome*, in *Œuvres*, vol.1, p.382.
14. Sade, *La Nouvelle Justine*, in *Œuvres*, vol.2, p.689, 853, 530, 621, 1000.
15. Sade, *La Nouvelle Justine*, in *Œuvres*, vol.2, p.699. Emphasis added.
16. Sade, *La Nouvelle Justine*, in *Œuvres*, vol.2, p.874.

that the place allotted to the reader is modified. Whereas the reader was merged with the unknowing victims of Silling, and fated to a textual death, in the trilogy he is invited to share the libertine's perspective, to feel – even despite himself – this 'violence des désirs' that a conversation between the innocent Joséphine and Sulpice stirs in Jérôme.[17] This constrained violence (indeed, this violence of constraint) is exemplified in those erect penises that seem ready to erupt with spurts of blood, in unison with the victimised bodies that suffer blow upon blow. 'On ne banda jamais de cette violence-là',[18] says Jérôme, who later relates his encounter with the famous Almani whose sexually excited body encapsulates violence's new function in the *Justine* trilogy: 'Almani, interrompis-je avec chaleur, vous bandez, sans doute, en vous y livrant [au crime]. – Jugez-en, me dit le chimiste, en me mettant à la main un vit gros comme le bras, et dont les veines violettes et gonflées semblaient prêtes à s'ouvrir sous la violence du sang qui circulait dans elles.'[19] The images and stylistic variations around the word 'violence' have not, we have seen, come about by chance. The contrasting ways in which the term is used in *Les Cent vingt journées* and the *Justine* novels reflect two different aesthetics, two relationships with the reader. In the 'ultimate' novel of 1785, the correlation between violence and death partakes of a deadly process, a spiral that draws in the reader, trapping him as a victim by means of the 'tutoiement' in the final passions. The association of violence with desire makes the reader of the *Justine* trilogy, on the other hand, a privileged spectator of the improbable heroine's ordeal, and invites him to overcome his humanist efforts to resist, and thus to participate in joyfully trampling underfoot a series of moral hypocrisies. And by doing this, Sade brings off, without ambush or irony, the snare that he had set in *Les Cent vingt journées*: 'Sans doute, beaucoup de tous les écarts que tu vas voir peints te déplairont, on le sait, mais il s'en trouvera quelques-uns qui t'échaufferont au point de te coûter du foutre, et voilà tout ce qu'il nous faut.'[20]

17. Sade, *La Nouvelle Justine*, in *Œuvres*, vol.2, p.718.
18. Sade, *La Nouvelle Justine*, in *Œuvres*, vol.2, p.752.
19. Sade, *La Nouvelle Justine*, in *Œuvres*, vol.2, p.780.
20. Sade, *Les Cent vingt journées de Sodome*, in *Œuvres*, vol.1, p.69.

The sound of violence: listening to rape in Sade

WILL MCMORRAN

> que votre imagination se représente tout ce
> que la débauche peut en tel cas dicter à des
> scélérats
>
> Sade, *Justine*[1]

In his contribution to this volume, Jean-Christophe Abramovici accurately observes that criticism on the marquis de Sade generally relegates to the background the violence in which his works are immersed. Where violence is discussed it is only tangentially, in the study of particular motifs, rather than as the focus of attention itself. Insisting that this is not because Sade's critics lack courage, Abramovici asks, 'what can one say about the violence of Sade's texts, other than that one feels it?'[2] There is apparently nothing more to say on the matter, other than to show that Sadean violence 'is not just a matter of representation, but primarily of language and writing'.[3] This kind of approach to Sade's works, with the emphasis on the language rather than the representation of violence, has its origins in Roland Barthes's highly influential work on Sade in the 1960s and early 1970s – firstly, in 'L'arbre du crime', his contribution to the 1967 *Tel Quel* issue on *La Pensée de Sade*, and secondly, in his short monograph, *Sade, Fourier, Loyola*. While previous generations of Sade scholars had defended their author's works on scientific, moral or philosophical grounds, Barthes defended them on literary grounds by

---

1. D. A. F. de Sade, *Justine ou Les Malheurs de la vertu*, in *Œuvres*, ed. Michel Delon, 3 vols (Paris, 1990-1998), vol.2, p.233.
2. Jean-Christophe Abramovici, '"Avec une telle violence que..." Sade's use of the term *violence*', p.221-38. The original French reads 'que peut-on dire de la violence des textes de Sade, sinon qu'on l'éprouve?' For other accounts of violence in Sade, see the contributions by Michèle Vallenthini, p.93-102, and Thomas Wynn, p.139-60.
3. The original French read '[la violence] n'est pas seulement affaire de représentations, mais d'abord de langue et d'écriture'.

examining them in exclusively linguistic terms: in 'L'arbre du crime', he insisted, 'le seul univers sadien [...] est l'univers du discours'[4] – a position he subsequently summarised in *Sade, Fourier, Loyola* when he proclaimed, 'écrite, la merde ne sent pas'.[5] Barthes's linguistic line of argument immediately became the standard defence and legitimisation of the literary rehabilitation of Sade – and has remained so to this day. Laurence Lynch thus affirms that 'Sade's violence is indeed that of language',[6] Geoffrey Bennington that 'the only "real" cruelty in Sade is that worked in the body of a language'[7] and Philippe Roger, one of Barthes's former students, that Sade 'ne met à mal que le langage'.[8] Even Nancy Miller, a pioneering feminist critic of the eighteenth-century novel, echoes Barthes's line when she states, 'Justine is neither a comic nor a tragic heroine; she is the object of a verb'.[9]

The linguistic approach to Sade has not been without its opponents. Annie Le Brun labels Sade a perpetual prisoner – 'autrefois de la Bastille, hier de sa malédiction, aujourd'hui de la critique'. Looking back on what academics in particular have done to Sade, she laments 'on rendait Sade fréquentable en le neutralisant [...] c'était grâce à la notion d'écriture qu'on était parvenu à ce beau résultat: vingt années d'analyse textuelle aboutissaient à exclure Sade de lui-même'.[10] From an entirely different perspective, Roger Shattuck takes Sade's critics to task for failing to engage with the sexual violence of the Sadean text: 'Almost all the literary and philosophical discussions of Sade I have mentioned sponge away the depravity and the bloodiness of his narratives by considering only his ideas.'[11] Having condemned Barthes's 'cavalier defanging' of Sade's works, Shattuck condemns

---

4. Roland Barthes, 'L'arbre du crime' in *Tel Quel* 28 (1967), p.23-37 (37).
5. Roland Barthes, *Sade, Fourier, Loyola* (Paris, 1971), p.141.
6. Lawrence Lynch, *The Marquis de Sade* (Boston, MA, 1984), p.129.
7. Geoffrey Bennington, 'Sade: laying down the law', *Oxford literary review* 6:2 (1984), p.38-56 (54).
8. Philippe Roger, *Sade: la philosophie dans le pressoir* (Paris, 1976), p.190.
9. Nancy K. Miller, *French dressing: women, men and ancien régime fiction* (London and New York, 1995), p.131.
10. Annie Le Brun, *Soudain, un bloc d'abîme* (Paris, 1993), p.16.
11. Roger Shattuck, *Forbidden knowledge: from Prometheus to pornography* (San Diego, CA, 1997), p.255.

more recent critics such as Peter Cryle: 'Cryle deals confidently with form and simply ignores the challenge of Sade's content.'[12] Although Shattuck's criticism is misdirected, as Cryle is one of the very few to reflect ethically upon the nature of the critic's relationship to the Sadean text,[13] it is arguably valid for the majority of Sadean criticism from Barthes to the present day. Discussions of the violence in Sade's works, and its ethical implications, have largely been left to Sade's opponents, from Andrea Dworkin to Laurence Bongie among others. While much has made been made of the 'turn to ethics' over the last thirty years within both the Continental tradition of post-structuralist criticism and theory, and the Anglo-American humanist tradition of literary criticism and moral philosophy, Sade studies seem to have turned away from ethics over the same period. Chantal Thomas, another former student of Roland Barthes, ridicules Simone de Beauvoir's 1951 essay, 'Faut-il brûler Sade?', for confusing 'l'encre et le sang'[14] – the word of violence for violence itself. As uneven as Beauvoir's essay may now seem, her conclusion that the most valuable aspect of Sade's writing is its capacity to worry the modern reader is as relevant today as it was sixty years ago: 'Sade a vécu jusqu'à la lie le moment de l'égoïsme, de l'injustice, du malheur et il en revendique la vérité. Ce qui fait la suprême valeur de son témoignage, c'est qu'il nous inquiète. Il nous oblige à remettre en question le problème essentiel qui sous d'autres figures hante ce temps: le vrai rapport de l'homme à l'homme.'[15] There is an echo of Beauvoir's *inquiétude* in Michel Delon's declaration thirty years ago, 'Il est donc temps de rendre Sade à son temps dans une étude érudite et précise sur les discours du XVIIIe siècle, mais aussi au nôtre dans une interrogation permanente de ce qui, en lui, nous concerne.'[16] Sadean criticism, however, has almost entirely concentrated on the former at the expense of the latter, restoring Sade to his

12. Shattuck, *Forbidden knowledge*, p.249, 255.
13. See, in particular, Peter Cryle, *Geometry in the boudoir: configurations of French erotic narrative* (New York, 1994).
14. Chantal Thomas, *Sade* (Paris, 1994), p.175.
15. Simone de Beauvoir, *Faut-il brûler Sade?* (Paris, 1955), p.82.
16. Michel Delon, 'Sade comme révélateur idéologique', *Romanistische Zeitschrift für Literaturgeschichte* 5 (1981), p.103-12 (111-12).

eighteenth-century literary and philosophical contexts but leaving to one side any anxieties the modern reader may have about the characteristic violence of his fiction.

The way out of this linguistic impasse is, perhaps ironically, suggested by Barthes himself. At the end of 'The Death of the author' (published the same year as 'L'arbre du crime') Barthes concluded, 'The birth of the reader must be at the cost of the death of the author.'[17] It is about time that Sadean criticism made room for the reader as well as the text, and for the ethical and affective questions that the process of reading Sade inevitably raises. This chapter therefore takes up the challenge of Abramovici's question – 'what can one say about the violence of Sade's texts, other than that one feels it?' – by examining this violence not just as a matter of words on a page but as part of a reading process that includes images seen in the mind's eye and words heard in the mind's ear.

If readers experience the Sadean text aurally as well as visually, their situation echoes the circumstances in which many of Sade's characters find themselves in their own storytelling encounters. The aural and the visual are always connected in Sade, from the interplay of *dissertation* and *orgie* in *La Philosophie dans le boudoir*, to the first person narratives of *Justine ou Les Malheurs de la vertu*, the *Histoire de Juliette* and *Les Cent vingt journées de Sodome*. The internal narrations incorporated in Sade's fiction are typically introduced by a dramatic visual spectacle: like Manon, Justine creates a scene at an inn; in 'Emilie de Tourville,' a young woman is found covered in blood in a forest; the fugitive Sophie, in *Aline et Valcour*, is also found in a forest just as she has given birth to a child. Their stories immediately follow. As Justine discovers to her cost, moreover, her various interlocutors cannot listen to her without also looking at her:

> Justine en larmes va trouver son curé; elle lui peint son état avec l'énergique candeur de son âge [...] Elle était en petit fourreau blanc; ses beaux cheveux négligemment repliés sous un grand bonnet; sa gorge à peine indiquée, cachée sous deux ou trois aunes de gaze; sa jolie mine un peu pâle à cause des chagrins qui la

---

17. Roland Barthes, 'The death of the author', *Aspen magazine* 5/6 (1967). Reprinted in *Image – music – text*, trans. Stephen Heath (London, 1977), p.142-48 (148).

dévoraient, quelques larmes roulaient dans ses yeux et leur prêtaient encore plus d'expression. 'Vous me voyez, monsieur', dit-elle au saint ecclésiastique [...] 'Oui, vous me voyez dans une position bien affligeante pour une jeune fille [...].'[18]

As Justine's repetition of 'vous me voyez' reflects, the *curé* sees Justine only too well.

While Sade's libertines typically look and listen, as well as indulging their other senses, at the same time, the absence of the visual is occasionally represented as a source of eroticism. In the *Nouvelle Justine*, in a passage that Barthes describes as the invention of radio, Mme de Verneuil is obliged to wear 'un casque à tuyau, organisé de manière que les cris que lui faisaient jeter les douleurs dont on l'accablait ressemblaient aux mugissements d'un bœuf'[19] as she is raped and tortured by her son and his accomplices. The sound is transmitted to a neighbouring room where her husband, unaware of his son's involvement, listens in ecstasy to his wife's screams: 'Oh! Foutre, qu'est ceci?' dit Verneuil en entendant cette musique, et se ruant sur la d'Esterval [...] 'il est impossible de rien entendre de plus délicieux [...] que diable lui font-ils donc, pour la faire beugler ainsi?'[20] As Barthes observes, 'le casque transmet sa douleur aux autres libertins, comme par radio, sans qu'ils voient la scène: ils peuvent, plaisir suprême, l'imaginer, c'est-à-dire la fantasmer'.[21] If the absence of the visual here serves an erotic function, it is not one that Sade's generally voyeuristic libertines typically pursue. Nevertheless, Barthes's suggestion that the aural may hold pleasures beyond the visual for Sade's libertines is apparently corroborated by the striking declaration in *Les Cent vingt journées de Sodome*: 'Il est reçu, parmi les véritables libertins, que les sensations communiquées par l'organe de l'ouïe sont celles qui flattent davantage et dont les

---

18. Sade, *Justine ou Les Malheurs de la vertu*, in *Œuvres*, vol.2, p.135.
19. Sade, *La Nouvelle Justine ou Les Malheurs de la vertu*, in *Œuvres*, vol.2, p.950.
20. Sade, *La Nouvelle Justine*, in *Œuvres*, vol.2, p.950.
21. Barthes, *Sade, Fourier, Loyola*, p.147. Barthes simplifies slightly the delights this scene offers the libertines: for Verneuil, the pleasure really comes with the subsequent revelation of his son's involvement in the rape and murder of his wife. For those in the know, like his son, it is Verneuil's ignorance of the facts that intensifies their own pleasure.

impressions sont les plus vives.'[22] If Sade here seems to challenge the sensorial hierarchy that places the visual above the aural, when the storytelling eventually begins in Silling it becomes clear that the aural is subordinate to the visual even in its absence. Duclos, the first of the *historiennes* to tell her story, is interrupted as soon as she begins by a dissatisfied Curval who demands a meticulous attention to visual detail: 'il faut à vos récits les détails les plus grands et les plus étendus [...] je n'ai nulle idée du vit de votre second récollet, et nulle idée de sa décharge. D'ailleurs, vous branla-t-il le con et y fit-il toucher son vit? Vous voyez, que de détails négligés!'[23] Each of the *historiennes* has been chosen for all the perversions she has witnessed at first hand: when she speaks, it is to say what she has seen. When the libertine listens, it is to form a mental picture of what she has seen.

While Verneuil is free to create his own fantasy from the aural cue of his wife's screams ('en laissant tout deviner à mon imagination'),[24] Curval and his peers are less interested in creating a fantasy of their own than in re-creating as precisely as possible the previously enacted fantasies of other libertines. Visualisation is not the end but the means to an end. In this respect they anticipate ironically the model of reception assumed by American campaigners against pornography in the 1980s, and epitomised by Robyn Morgan's slogan, 'Pornography is the theory, rape the practice'. According to this rigidly mimetic view, theory inevitably entails practice, even if, for the libertines in Silling, it is a case of 'monkey hear, monkey do' rather than 'monkey see, monkey do'. The way in which reception is linked to enactment, or performance, in Silling further reinforces the subordination of the aural to the visual: the role of the mind's ear is to inspire a feast for the eyes. The four libertines listen to the *historiennes* in the theatrical (or amphitheatrical) setting, of the *salon d'histoire*: the *historienne*, seated upon a raised throne 'se trouvait alors placée comme est l'acteur sur un théâtre, et les auditeurs, placés dans les niches, se trouvaient l'être comme on

---

22. Sade, *Les Cent vingt journées de Sodome* in *Œuvres*, vol.1, p.39.
23. Sade, *Les Cent vingt journées de Sodome* in *Œuvres*, vol.1, p.84.
24. Sade, *La Nouvelle Justine*, in *Œuvres*, vol.2, p.950.

l'est à l'amphithéâtre.'[25] If this suggests a distinction between the performer and her audience, such a distinction does not tell the whole story: between the storytelling throne and the libertines' *niches* is the space in which the *historienne*'s script will be performed by a cast already dressed for the part:

> les gradins du bas de son trône seront garnis de seize enfants, arrangés de manière à ce que quatre, c'est-à-dire deux filles et deux garçons, se trouvent faire face à une des niches; ainsi de suite, chaque niche aura un pareil quatrain vis-à-vis d'elle: [...] les petits garçons et les petites filles des quatrains seront toujours différemment et élégamment costumés, un quatrain à l'asiatique, un à l'espagnole, un autre à la turque, un quatrième à la grecque, et le lendemain autre chose, mais tous ces vêtements seront de taffetas et de gaze: jamais le bas du corps ne sera serré par rien et une épingle détachée suffira pour les mettre nus. A l'égard des vieilles, elles seront alternativement en sœurs grises, en religieuses, en fées, en magiciennes et quelquefois en veuves.[26]

The emphasis in the *salon* is on the visible, from the 'quatre niches de glaces fort vastes et ornées'[27] to the colour and material of the equally ornate costumes. If the model of pornographic reception delineated in Silling anticipates the views of the anti-pornography campaigners of the 1980s, it is worth nothing that in both cases the power assigned to pornography is contingent on a view of men as inherently predisposed to violence. For Catherine MacKinnon, showing pornography to men 'is like saying "kill" to a trained guard dog. [...] Sooner or later, in one way or another, the consumer wants to live out the pornography further in three dimensions. Sooner or later, in one way or another, they do. *It* makes them want to [...]'.[28] For MacKinnon, and indeed for Sade, pornography works because of what men already are – dogs trained to kill. (As Alan Soble observes, 'MacKinnon does to men what she believes men and pornography do to women, that is,

---

25. Sade, *Les Cent vingt journées de Sodome* in *Œuvres*, vol.1, p.56. For more on the theatrical setting of Silling, see Mladen Kozul, 'L'inachèvement des *Cent vingt journées de Sodome* de Sade', *Cahiers d'histoires des littératures romanes/Romanistische Zeitschrift für Literaturgeschichte* 1-2 (1995), p.60-71 (61-63).
26. Sade, *Les Cent vingt journées de Sodome* in *Œuvres*, vol.1, p.61-62.
27. Sade, *Les Cent vingt journées de Sodome* in *Œuvres*, vol.1, p.56.
28. Catharine A. MacKinnon, *Only words* (Cambridge, MA, 1993), p.19.

reduce them to the status of their genitals, to the status of pure sex item and object.'[29]) If the libertines act out the scripts provided by the *historiennes*, it is because they are well-suited to the roles they have to play. The scripts themselves, however, are of limited power: within Sade's fiction more generally, the listener only hears what he or she wants to hear. Reception, whether visual or aural, has no transformative power – there are no convincing conversions in Sade's fiction. Juliette's embrace of virtue in response to her sister's narration at the end of *Les Infortunes de la vertu* and *Justine ou Les Malheurs de la vertu*, is transparent in its absurdity – a token of respectability dropped in the uncompromising retelling of the same story in *La Nouvelle Justine*. For all of their apparent openness to new experiences, the libertines in Sade are no more capable of change than Justine. As Clément, one of the monks in *Justine* observes, we are what we are: 'Pouvons-nous devenir autres que nous ne sommes?'[30]

If the aural inspires much of the violence in Sade's fiction, what role does it play for the reader? In the following passage, from *Justine ou Les Malheurs de la vertu*, Justine narrates her rape upon her induction to the monastery of Sainte-Marie-des-Bois:

> Vous me permettrez, madame, dit notre belle prisonnière en rougissant, de vous déguiser une partie des détails obscènes de cette odieuse cérémonie; que votre imagination se représente tout ce que la débauche peut en tel cas dicter à des scélérats [...]
>
> Allons, dit Sévérino dont les désirs prodigieusement exaltés ne peuvent plus se contenir, et qui dans cet affreux état donne l'idée d'un tigre prêt à dévorer sa victime, que chacun de nous lui fasse éprouver sa jouissance favorite.
>
> Et l'infâme, me plaçant sur un canapé dans l'attitude propice à ses exécrables projets, me faisant tenir par deux de ses moines, essaie de se satisfaire avec moi de cette façon criminelle et perverse qui ne nous fait ressembler au sexe que nous ne possédons pas, qu'en dégradant celui que nous avons. Mais, ou cet impudique est trop fortement proportionné, ou la nature se révolte en moi au seul soupçon de ces plaisirs: il ne peut vaincre les obstacles; à peine se présente-t-il, qu'il est aussitôt repoussé [...] Il écarte, il presse, il déchire, tous ses efforts sont superflus; la fureur de ce monstre se

---

29. Alan Soble, *Pornography, sex and feminism* (New York, 2002), p.17.
30. Sade, *Œuvres*, vol.2, p.261.

porte sur l'autel où ne peuvent atteindre ses vœux; il le frappe, il le pince, il le mord; de nouvelles épreuves naissent du sein de ces brutalités; les chairs ramollies se prêtent, le sentier s'entrouvre, le bélier pénètre; je pousse des cris épouvantables; bientôt la masse entière est engloutie, et la couleuvre, lançant aussitôt un venin qui lui ravit ses forces, cède enfin, en pleurant de rage, aux mouvements que je fais pour m'en dégager. Je n'avais de ma vie tant souffert.[31]

For the monks of Sainte-Marie-des-Bois, the rape of Justine is an aural, visual and tactile experience. But what does the reader experience when he or she reads a scene of violence such as this? What, in particular, did *you* hear as you were reading this passage? Did you hear the words of the text in your head and, if so, did you hear them in the same voice throughout? Would you identify that voice as your own, as that of the narrator, or as that of the author? Or did the voices change, and change gender, with the different characters in the text? Did you hear Séverino speak in a voice distinct from that of Justine? Did you hear Justine scream?

If such questions relate to the aural dimension of the reader's experience of the scene it is because this is arguably the most neglected aspect of textual reception. Martin Jay and other historians have persuasively delineated the ocularcentrism of Western culture from the Enlightenment (or 'EnLIGHTenment,' as he puts it) to the present day. While Jay notes the visual nature of metaphors for the mind ranging from Plato's cave to Locke's *camera obscura*, Hume's image of the mind as 'a kind of theatre, where several perceptions successively make their appearance; pass, re-pass, glide away, and mingle in an infinite variety of postures and situations,'[32] has proven to be particularly durable since its original formulation in his *Treatise of human nature*. It has, for example, recently been adopted by neuroscientists such as Bernard Baars in order to explain the nature of consciousness,[33] although Daniel Dennett has condemned the 'ghostly dualism' of what he describes as the 'persuasive imagery of the Cartesian

---

31. Sade, *Œuvres*, vol.2, p.233-34.
32. David Hume, *A Treatise of human nature*, ed. David Fate Norton and Mary Jane Norton (Oxford, 2000), I.iv. 6.165.
33. Baars claims that 'all unified theories of cognition today are theater models'; see *In the theatre of consciousness: the workspace of the mind* (New York, 1997), p.ix.

theatre'.[34] According to this Cartesian theatre, as Susan Blackmore elaborates, 'there is some place inside "my" mind or brain where "I" am. This place has something like a mental screen or stage on which images are presented for viewing by my mind's eye [...] The show in the Cartesian theater is the stream of consciousness, and the audience is me.'[35] While Blackmore and Dennett reject this ocularcentric view of consciousness, they are obliged to admit that the theatrical metaphor has a 'natural appeal' – that it 'may feel like this'.[36] The experiments of psychologists from Roger Shephard to Stephen Kosslyn have indeed suggested that the mind's eye is more than just a figure of speech, and that the creation of 'depictive' mental imagery is an intrinsic part of mental processing.[37]

The ocularcentrism Jay ascribes to Western culture is as deeply embedded in the language we use when describing the reading process as it is in the language we use when describing the way the mind works. Reading is generally 'seen' to entail both vision, as the eye deciphers the words on the page, and visualisation, as this deciphering prompts the production of mental imagery. Consequently, the lexis of textual analysis is dominated by the visual, as we observe, study, scrutinise, examine and explore the text in front of us. There is, however, more to the mental process of reading than vision and visualisation – the theatre, after all, is an aural experience as well as a visual one. In much of the recent discussion of mental imagery among philosophers, psychologists and neuroscientists, the aural tends to be marginalised by the visual – attention is largely focused on the mind's eye rather than the mind's ear (or ears?). This ocularcentrism is indeed so pronounced that the aural equivalent of mental images are typically labelled in visual terms as 'auditory images' – presumably because the tautology of an 'auditory sound' is less tolerable than that of a 'visual image'. The philosopher, Peter Kivy, however,

---

34. Daniel Dennett, *Consciousness explained* (Boston, MA and London, 1991), p.107.
35. Susan Blackmore, *Consciousness: an introduction*, 2nd edn (London, 2010), p.54-55.
36. Blackmore, *Consciousness*, p, 54, 55.
37. See Roger Shepard and J. Metzler, 'Mental rotation of three-dimensional objects', *Science* 171 (1971), 701-703; and Stephen M. Kosslyn, William L. Thompson and Giorgio Ganis, *The Case for mental imagery* (Oxford, 2006).

goes against this visual grain when he rejects the 'Lockean, Addisonian idea' that 'silent reading produces a kind of theatrical performance before the mind's eye' on the basis that 'simple introspection reveals that a running display of mental "images" is palpably not what the silent reader of novels and other fictional narratives experiences'.[38] For Kivy, the inner sense activated by the reading of fiction is not visual but aural: 'It is not a movie or a play in the mind's eye: it is a story telling in the mind's ear.'[39] The analogy Kivy settles on is thus with the silent reading of musical scores rather with the spectacle of the theatre. His confidence in the universality of his own introspective experience, however, is misguided: the experience of mental imagery during the reading process is an experience common to many, if not most, readers. Kivy indeed quotes Wittgenstein's observation, 'I simply read, have impressions, see pictures in my mind's eye, etc. I make the story pass before me like pictures, like a cartoon story.'[40] If Kivy is misguided in his exclusion of the visual, he nevertheless provides a useful reminder that, as J. O. Urmson had earlier claimed, 'in reading a literary work to oneself, one is simultaneously performer and audience, just as when one plays a piece of music to oneself'.[41] Kivy's insistence on the importance of the mind's ear when reading is moreover corroborated by the recent scientific research that shows that 'silent reading activates inner speech'.[42]

---

38. Peter Kivy, *The Performance of reading: an essay in the philosophy of literature* (Oxford, 2009), p.59. In this 'simple introspection' Kivy follows Edmund Burke's own refutation of Locke on similar grounds: 'I am of the opinion that the most general effect even of these words [simple abstracts and aggregates] does not arise from their forming pictures of the several things they would represent in the imagination, because on a very diligent examination of my own mind, and getting others to consider theirs, I do not find that one in twenty times any such picture is formed'; see *A Philosophical enquiry into the origin of our ideas of the sublime and beautiful*, ed. Adam Phillips (Oxford, 1990), p.149.
39. Kivy, *The Performance of reading*, p.63.
40. Ludwig Wittgenstein, *Zettel*, 2nd edn (Oxford, 1981), section 243, p.43.
41. J. O. Urmson, 'Literature' in *Aesthetics: a critical anthology*, ed. George Dickie and Richard Sclafani (New York, 1977), p.334-41 (337).
42. Marianne Abramson and Stephen D. Goldinger, 'What the reader's eye tells the mind's ear: silent reading activates inner speech', *Perception & psychophysics* 59:7 (1997), p.1059-68.

When we read we perform – or subarticulate – the text and listen to that performance in our mind's ear.

What role might the aural play in the reader's reception of Justine's rape? As the questions posed immediately after the passage above aim to suggest, the way in which the rape is narrated, as an event retrospectively narrated by its victim, is likely to have an impact on the reader's experience of the scene. Our subarticulation of the text duplicates Justine's narration, while our reception of that subarticulation duplicates the situation of Justine's listeners, Juliette and Corville. This duplication may not, however, extend to the nature of the voice we construct for Justine's account of her rape, or for her narration more generally. While some readers may be entirely unaware of any voice as they read, for example, others may construct the voice they hear as Justine's, as their own, as the author's, or, indeed, as a neutral voice without any clearly defined agency. The readers' aural experience of the novel as a whole may moreover find them switching between some or all of these possibilities. Certain cues in the text, for example, may prompt a shift in, or reinforcement of, the gendering of the voice – such as a phrase in which the sex of the speaker is emphasised (as in the case of 'dit notre belle prisonnière', for example). This gendering would often have to be fractionally retrospective, as the sex of the speaker may only be revealed after some of his or her speech has been reported (as in the case of 'Allons, dit Séverino', for example). Such a model of reading implies a potentially transvestite reader, for whom the gender of the characters in the text determines the gender of the voice heard in the process of reading. According to an alternative model, however, the gender of the reader may be a more decisive element in the construction and reception of voice than the gender of the characters in the text. Whether the reader's inner speech conforms exclusively to one of these models or alternates between the two is likely to vary between readers, and even between readings by a single reader. The difference between these two ways of reading may be one of effort as well as imagination: the former implies a more animated – indeed animating – reading performance, while the latter implies a comparatively passive, even functional, mode of reading, more like a 'read-through' of a script than a theatrical performance.

In 'Qu'est-ce qu'un auteur,' Foucault asked bluntly, 'Qu'importe qui parle?'[43] In terms of our inner speech, when reading a scene in which male and female are polarised by an act of sexual violence, I suspect it does matter whether that voice is gendered male, female, androgynous or is genderless, and whether that voice varies or remains consistent throughout. If, for example, male readers hear Justine's voice, or some kind of feminised voice narrating, it may have a different effect to hearing their own voice narrating the scene. While the former may make Justine more of a subject, and thereby make the violence against her more vivid, the latter may have a modulating, rehabilitating function – it may make the material less other, less distant and therefore less shocking. It may alternatively, however, create anxieties of its own for the male reader in particular: hearing oneself performing a Sadean script in one's own voice may reinforce the uncomfortable sense of gendered complicity in the violence being represented – our sense that, as Marcel Hénaff observed, 'De scripteur à lecteur, c'est à dire de Maître à Maître, le rapport n'est pas de contrat, mais de *complot*. Lire c'est déjà conspirer.'[44] The anxiety may go deeper than a concern about guilt by association, moreover: perhaps the deeper fear for the heterosexual male reader comes with the unwelcome recognition that he shares a gender and sexual orientation with these rapists. Equally, it is plausible to imagine that hearing a female voice will produce subtly distinct effects for a female reader than the masculinised voice of an authorial projection. While the shared gender of voice in the case of the former may encourage identification with the character, and consequently bring the violence a little closer to home, the latter may (in contrast to the case of the male reader) foreground the sense of an antagonistic, aggressive, masculine other. The difference between these two is largely one of focus, however: in neither case is there any escape from the relentless dynamic of male aggression and female victimisation. If there is a counterpart to the male reader's anxiety of sharing a gender with

---

43. Michel Foucault, 'Qu'est-ce qu'un auteur?' *Bulletin de la Société française de philosophie* 3 (1969). Republished in *Dits et écrits*, 2 vols (Paris, 1994), vol.2, p.817-849 (817).
44. Marcel Hénaff, *L'Invention du corps libertin* (Paris, 1978), p.77.

the rapists in *Justine*, it may be the female reader's anxiety about sharing a gender with their victims. Lucienne Frappier-Mazur evokes such an anxiety when she describes the Sadean text as 'un texte qui peut agresser le lecteur, et la lectrice encore plus, de façon parfois intolérable'.[45]

Exploring the reception of Richardson's *Clarissa* in the early 1980s, Terry Castle suggested that the novel 'tends, often in very subtle ways, to polarise male and female readers' and 'encourages us to examine the ways in which the gender of the reader (along with resulting differences of socialisation and *power*) may condition those meanings he or she finds in the text'. Although she has no empirical evidence, Castle speculates: 'Do male and female readers respond differently to the "black transaction" at the heart of the text? My suspicion is that they do, at least initially.'[46] While any attempt to reduce either 'male' or 'female' to a singular reading of any work of fiction would be a hopelessly reductive exercise, Castle's suggestion that the reader's gender may exert a particular influence in the reception of narratives of sexual violence is entirely plausible. The use of 'on' in Abramovici's question (again, 'que peut-on dire de la violence des textes de Sade, sinon qu'on l'éprouve' in the original French) may therefore be doubly misleading in implying or assuming a unanimity among critics as well as a universality of experience among readers. What can be said about representations of sexual violence is moreover as vulnerable to gender as the reading of such representations. As Linda Williams has observed of the academic study of pornography more generally, 'the group of scholars that has most effectively engaged with pornography over the last decade has been the one group that has found itself the least

---

45. Lucienne Frappier-Mazur, *Sade et l'écriture de l'orgie* (Paris, 1991), p.5. Following the panel at which a shorter version of this paper was delivered, more than one (female) Sade scholar suggested that reading Sade may be more distressing for female readers than their male counterparts. This was firmly rebuffed by other (male) Sade scholars, leading to something of an impasse, as neither side could logically claim to know what it is like to read Sade from the point of view of another gender. The very fact that this division was gendered, however, was itself suggestive that gender might be an important element in the reception of Sade.
46. Terry Castle, *Clarissa's ciphers: meaning and disruption in Richardson's Clarissa* (Ithaca, NY and London, 1982), p.28.

vilified for demonstrating an interest in pornography. "Pro-sex feminists" [...] have had a distinct advantage over heterosexual men in this regard'.[47] In contrast to some of their female counterparts, such as Jane Gallop or Chantal Thomas, Sade's male critics have perhaps understandably remained almost universally silent about the pornographic effects of his fiction on themselves as readers – as if they were, in Robert Browning's memorable words, 'dead from the waist down'.[48]

The role played by the aural in the reception of a literary text is not limited to the inner speech most readers experience upon reading, but is also a potentially revealing element in the scene that this inner speech describes. As the epigraph for this chapter reflects, Justine indeed invites her listeners, and by extension the reader, to imagine the scene for themselves. She nevertheless leaves far less to the reader's imagination than such an apparent disclaimer would imply, and provides an account of her rape that is intensely visual. Before looking at the visual aspect of this scene, however, it is worth listening to what its aural aspect has to tell us about our reception of fictional violence – and in particular about our relationship to the figure of the victim of such violence. The issue of readers' empathy for fictional characters has been a particular preoccupation of analytical philosophers in recent years;[49] one way of posing the question of empathy in relation to Justine is to ask whether we hear her scream when she tells us, 'je pousse des cris épouvantables'. A lot may rest on the practical

---

47. Linda Williams, *Hard core: power, pleasure, and the 'frenzy of the visible'*, 2nd edn (Berkeley and Los Angeles, CA, 1999), p.xi.
48. Jean Marie Goulemot is the exception that proves the rule in this regard: 'Dois-je par ailleurs le confesser, je ne suis pas de ceux que Sade a laissés indifférents, et j'entends par là sensuellement indifférents, et que n'ont pas troublés les scènes érotiques et les prémisses d'une violence dont les débordements rejettent et excluent par leurs excès mêmes'; see 'Beau marquis parlez-nous d'amour?', in *Sade, écrire la crise*, ed. Michel Camus and Philippe Roger (Paris, 1983), p.119-32 (119).
49. See, for example, Kendall Walton, *Mimesis as make-believe: on the foundations of the representational arts* (Cambridge, MA, 1990); Noël Carroll, *Beyond aesthetics: philosophical essays* (Cambridge, 2001); and Gregory Currie, *The Nature of fiction* (Cambridge, 2008). For an influential early example of this kind of approach to fiction, see Colin Radford and Michael Weston, 'How can we be moved by the fate of Anna Karenina?' *Proceedings of the Aristotelian Society, supplementary volumes* 49 (1975), p.67-93.

issue of the pace at which our reading of the scene is conducted: at their usual reading pace, most readers may not have time, or take time, to enact and hear these *cris épouvantables* in their mind's ear. Given the details of these screams are not supplied by the text, the reader would have to make a particular imaginative effort to do so, supplying his or her own soundtrack to supplement the Sadean script. Although it is certainly possible that a reader immersed in the action may do just that, there is a limit to our ability to 'auralise' that may correlate to a limit to our ability to empathise. Even if we hear Justine scream, it will not have the same impact as an actual scream: it is impossible to turn up the volume in the mind's ear, to make a scream much louder than a whisper. However immersed we are in the scene, there is a limit to the extent to which our inner sense can bring that scene to life, and this may correlate in some way to the limit of our capacity to empathise with Justine. If we cannot hear Justine scream, however, we can still hear her when she tells her audience, 'Je n'avais de ma vie tant souffert'. This sentence lingers at the end of the paragraph, offering a pause, and a space, for Justine's pain to dwell a little longer on the reader's consciousness – an invitation for a sadistic imagination to relish perhaps, but also for a more empathetic, if not masochistic, response to Justine as a subject, rather than an object, of suffering.

If the text leaves much to the reader's imagination in aural terms it is because Justine's focus as narrator is essentially visual. Although she cannot see what is being done to her, she nevertheless describes what is happening to her body in visual terms intensified by vivid animalistic imagery, the tigerish Sévérino assaulting Justine with a penis that turns from (battering) ram ('bélier') into serpent ('couleuvre'). Justine seems therefore to be visualising and describing her rape from the rapist's point of view, thereby placing us in the same viewing position as her rapist. This impression is reinforced by the focus upon Sévérino's agency ('Il écarte', 'il presse', 'il déchire') in overcoming a series of impersonal objects ('les obstacles,' 'l'autel', 'le sentier', 'les chairs') rather than a human subject. If, as Nancy Miller suggests, Justine is less a heroine than 'the object of a verb,' Sévérino is clearly its subject in this particular episode. The reader's visualisation of Justine's rape threatens to implicate him or her in a conspiracy of seeing from which Justine is excluded. This begs the uncomfortable question, to what extent is our attitudinal point of view affected by our visual point of view? Does seeing through the eyes of a rapist mean seeing as a rapist, or are the subject-positions readers adopt independent from their viewing-positions? The mobility of our subject-positions in fantasy is often stressed and it may be that, in a scene such as this, readers flit between various positions. It is worth noting, however, that one cannot occupy two visualising positions in relation to a mental image concurrently – although we can rotate an image of an object in our minds, we cannot simultaneously see it from two different perspectives. If our subject-positions are potentially unstable, so too are the mental images themselves. For all of the visual description offered by Justine, there are obvious limits to what the reader may see as well as hear when reading a scene like this. The text, for example, offers little description of the chamber in which Justine's rape takes place, and gives only limited physical portraits of the characters. The reader must therefore make images from fragmentary visual details – filling in the gaps in the text. Visualisation, like vision, is fragmentary by its very nature, however,[50] so what one sees in the mind's eye may be no more than fragments of fragments – a series of fleeting snapshots rather than a continuous movie.

Why focus on the mental imagery of the reader? Firstly, because, mental imagery – aural as well as a visual – is an aspect of reception that literary criticism largely ignores, although the growing interest in cognitive approaches to literature may reflect an imminent shift in critical approaches towards matters of affect. When encountering texts that represent sexual violence, however, mental imagery is an aspect of reception that becomes an urgent and troubling one for many readers – and one that is simply not addressed by the linguistic or semiological approach that has dominated Sadean criticism since Barthes. Given that texts do not exist in a vacuum but are scripts transformed by their readers into inner sight and sound, it would seem reasonable to

50. 'Images are fragmentary. We recall glimpses of parts, arrange them in a mental tableau, and then do a juggling act to refresh each part as it fades'; see Steven Pinker, *How the mind works* (London, 1998), p.294.

subject this readerly transformation to critical scrutiny. Secondly, there is increasing scientific evidence to suggest that the Barthesian insistence on the separation of the sign from its referent underestimates the way the two are linked in our mental processes. Neuroscientific research in particular is showing more and more clearly, as Annie Murphy Paul observes, that the brain 'does not make much of a distinction between reading about an experience and encountering it in real life; in each case, the same neurological regions are stimulated'.[51] Researchers from Emory University, for example, have shown that metaphors involving texture (such as 'The singer had a velvet voice' and 'He had leathery hands') activate the sensory cortex – the part of the brain responsible for perceiving texture through touch.[52] A study by Spanish researchers has moreover shown that words with strong olfactory associations – such as 'cinnamon' or 'perfume' or 'coffee' – activate the primary olfactory cortex, which, as the name suggests, is responsible for our sense of smell.[53] Barthes's famous declaration in defence of Sadean obscenity – 'écrite, la merde ne sent pas' – turns out not to be so self-evident after all. As Joseph Joubert, an earlier reader of Sade, suggested, Sadean language can indeed smell: 'au fond de ces scènes monstrueuses [...] Je crois même y respirer quelque chose de l'odeur de ce livre infect.'[54]

The libertine view that the aural offers advantages over the visual in stimulating mental imagery is also borne out by modern science. Vision and visualisation both use the same part of the brain, the visual cortex, and numerous experiments have shown the ways in which the two may interfere with each other. According to the so-called 'Perky effect,' for example, holding a mental image can be shown to interfere with seeing 'faint and fine visual

51. Annie Murphy Paul, 'Your brain on fiction', *The New York times*, 17 March 2012, http://www.nytimes.com/2012/03/18/opinion/sunday/the-neuroscience-of-your-brain-on-fiction.html?pagewanted=all.
52. Simon Lacey, Randall Stilla and K. Sathian, 'Metaphorically feeling: comprehending textural metaphors activates somatosensory cortex', *Brain and language* 120:3 (2012), p.416-21.
53. Julio González, Alfonso Barros-Loscertales, Friedemann Pulvermüller, Vanessa Meseguer, Ana Sanjuán, Vicente Belloch and César Ávila, 'Reading cinnamon activates olfactory brain regions', *NeuroImage* 32:2 (2006), p.906-12.
54. Joseph Joubert, *Pensées, essais et maximes*, 2 vols (Paris, 1842), vol.2, p.224. Quoted in Françoise Laugaa-Traut, *Lectures de Sade* (Paris, 1973), p.135.

details'.[55] Our own everyday experience also shows us that it is easier to visualise an object with one's eyes closed. Conversely, as Wittgenstein observed, 'While I am looking at an object I cannot imagine it.'[56] The potential interference between eye and mind's eye has obvious implications for the reading process: our visual awareness of the text on the page, and our visualisation of the imagery represented in the text, may be in competition with each other. The more aware we are of the white page and its black marks, the less vivid our imagining of the content of those marks is likely to be. At the same time, a reading that is vivid in its visualisation of textual content is likely to be less conscious of the visual aspect of the page itself. Something like these two ways of reading is described by Denis Donoghue, and subsequently Robert Eaglestone, as 'graphi-reading' and 'epi-reading' respectively: 'Graphi-reading reads the words and refuses to pass beyond, or create a world behind, them',[57] while 'Epi-reading transposes the written words on the page into a somehow corresponding situation of persons, voices, characters, conflicts, conciliations'.[58] While Sade critics, under the continued influence of Barthes, clearly fall into the category of graphi-readers, those hostile to the rehabilitation of Sade, such as Andrea Dworkin, might be categorised as epi-readers. To adopt Chantal Thomas's terms, the former might be accused of seeing only the ink and not the blood, while the latter might be accused of seeing only the blood and not the ink.

No two readings of the rape of Justine, or indeed of Sade's fiction more generally, will be the same. While some readers experience more vivid mental imagery than others, the context in which reading takes place also informs and shapes our responses to the text. Reading Sade for the first time is a very different experience to reading him for the hundredth time, while reading him in a classroom full of students is very different to reading him alone in a bedroom – the ideal setting, according to Chantal

55. Catherine Craver-Lemley and Adam Reeves, 'How visual imagery interferes with vision', *Psychological review* 99 (1992), p.633-49.
56. Wittgenstein, *Zettel*, section 621, p.108.
57. Denis Donoghue, *Ferocious alphabets* (London, 1981), p.101. Quoted in Robert Eaglestone, *Ethical criticism: reading after Levinas* (Edinburgh, 1997), p.4.
58. Eaglestone, *Ethical criticism*, p.3.

Thomas, for any reading of Sade.[59] If Sade's critics have too often forgotten the sensory and somatic power of the Sadean text, it may be because the process of close textual analysis is not conducive to an appreciation of this power. Donoghue's separation of critics into epi-readers and graphi-readers belies the fact that poring over a particular paragraph, sentence, or even word, in a text is more likely to produce a 'graphi-centric' response than an 'epi-centric' response. The closer one gets to a text the more difficult it becomes to see through it, and the critic's sensitivity to the violence in Sade's fiction will almost inevitably (and perhaps necessarily) be diminished by the repeated re-reading that textual analysis demands. Nor is it possible to respond sensorially to a text and analyse one's sensorial response at the same time: self-consciousness stifles the imagination. Such obstacles to remaining sensorially receptive have, however, been exacerbated by a certain critical snobbishness towards any approach that dwells on anything other than the form or the philosophy of Sadean fiction. Barthes described sadism as 'le *contenu* grossier (vulgaire) du texte sadien',[60] and there is, in much of the criticism on Sade since Barthes, the sense that any discussion of the violent content is itself inherently vulgar and unsophisticated. Timo Airaksinen, for example, insists, 'The structure and style of the written text are so important that what is said becomes secondary. Even the length of the text and its repetitive nature are more important than what Sade actually says.'[61] The problem with this form of reading is that it is so far removed from how non-academic readers read. If, as Peter Kivy suggests, 'The job of the critic, like the job of the performer, is to make the work available for appreciation',[62] then the graphi-reading which has characterised Sadean criticism over the last forty years constitutes a critical failure. In order to make Sade's works available for appreciation it is first of all important to present them in a form that is recognisable to the general reader (who is much more likely to epi-read than graphi-read).

---

59. 'Sade se lit de préférence au lit, et dans toutes les postures de l'abandon' (*La Dissertation et l'orgie*, 2nd edn [Paris, 2002], p.8).
60. Barthes, *Sade, Fourier, Loyola*, p.175.
61. Timo Airaksinen, *The Philosophy of the marquis de Sade* (London, 1995), p.148.
62. Kivy, *The Performance of reading*, p.98.

For this reason alone it is important that Sadean criticism moves beyond the linguistic and the philosophical to address the anxieties that the violence in Sade arouses in many if not most readers. In 'The death of the author', Barthes asserted, 'it is language that speaks, not the author'. As we have already seen (and heard), however, it is in a very real sense the reader who speaks, not language. One of the tasks of the critic is therefore to listen to what the reader is saying.

Violence in the novels of Charlotte [de] Bournon-Malarme[1]

MICHEL DELON

The experience of violence is much in evidence during the years of the French Revolution and Empire. One of the functions of literature, which had an expanding readership at this time, was to make sense of this experience and to exorcise the threat it represented.[2] The novels of Charlotte Bournon-Malarme, who in 1815 restored the aristocratic particle '*de*' to her name along with the title of countess, offer a particularly fertile corpus for research both in their quantity and in the lack of critical attention hitherto paid to them. This novelist (1753-1830?) is a close contemporary of Félicité de Genlis (1746-1830) and equals her in creative output. According to Quérard, she produced no fewer than forty-two novels between 1780 and 1827, eight under the *ancien régime*, twenty-two during the time of the Revolution and Empire and twelve during the Restoration, most of which comprise multiple volumes.

The novelist appears to have suffered both censorship and repression under the *ancien régime*, having been imprisoned in the Bastille in 1782 for a satirical tale, but it is the revolutionary period, which she spent away from France, that features in her novels as a time of extreme violence. Political upheaval, though, is simply a form of excess that originates in individuals. In 1801, Madame Bournon-Malarme published *Le Temps passé, ou Les Malheurs de Mad. de Mo*** émigrée*. The story opens with a fire which the unfortunate young heroine escapes. The narration of the blaze, which occurs in King Street in London, is only our first encounter with the misfortunes that repeatedly befall her

---

1. Translated by Teresa Bridgeman.
2. On the exorcism of violence in late eighteenth-century theatre, see Pierre Frantz's article 'Violence in the theatre of the Revolution', p.121-35.

throughout the two volumes. Like the motif in an overture, it sets the tone for the whole work, which sees the young woman emigrate, first to Germany and then to England. Her emigration has been for political reasons but it appears to represent the moral and almost metaphysical status of an individual who is never at home, who never reaches a stable and satisfactory situation. Despite such a catalogue of misfortunes we are in no doubt that the novel will provide a satisfactory conclusion. As Amelina, the unfortunate émigrée, remarks to a fellow Frenchwoman:

> Je le conçois, aujourd'hui on ne s'enorgueillit plus du titre de Français; et j'avoue que, depuis que ma patrie est devenue le théâtre des atrocités, je voudrais être née partout ailleurs. Cependant, ma chère compatriote, l'excès du mal conduit au bien; espérons qu'un jour à venir, bientôt peut-être, les monstres qui assouvissent leur sanguinaire fureur sur tant de milliers d'innocentes victimes paieront de leurs coupables têtes les crimes affreux dont ils se sont souillés.[3]

A note clarifies the reference to the events of 18 Brumaire and the establishment of the Consulat under Napoleon: 'Au moment où j'écris, le génie bienfaisant de la France plane de nouveau sur cette contrée qui fut si malheureuse; en créant un nouveau gouvernement, il lui a rendu la tranquillité intérieure, et c'est de la cime du Saint-Bernard qu'il prend son vol pour assurer la paix aux Français, que le fléau de la guerre désole depuis si longtemps' (vol.1, p.40). A further note, in the second volume, again praises the happy advent of Napoleon: 'Jours de deuil, vous êtes à jamais proscrits! Le héros des deux mondes veille sur la France' (vol.2, p.119). The promise of a conclusion is political in nature but the detailed account of the events which assail Amelina remains a psychological and personal one.

When she narrates her story to those who have rescued her from the fire, Amelina avoids any political explanations: 'Je n'entrerai dans aucun détail sur les causes des désordres qui ont désolé la France, c'est à l'histoire qu'il appartient de traiter ce

---

3. Charlotte (de) Bournon-Malarme, *Le Temps passé, ou Les Malheurs de Mad. de Mo*** émigrée*, 2 vols (Paris, Maradan, An IX [1801]), vol.1, p.40.

sujet aussi vaste qu'il sera difficile à traiter, parce que l'impartialité n'en saisira pas toutes les nuances' (vol.1, p.46). It is at a performance of La Martelière's play *Robert chef des brigands*, adapted from Schiller, that her persecution begins, as if the play were a symptom, alerting her to her situation. The daughter of a great aristocratic family whose members occupy senior positions in the army and the Church, Amelina is arrested first in Paris and then in Hamburg after fleeing there. She falls into the hands of a German Jacobin who wears 'un uniforme français de garde nationale, avec les épaulettes de commandant' (vol.1, p.76), and locks her up in a ruined castle until she agrees to marry him. Having settled once again in Paris, she is arrested after being betrayed to the authorities by her husband who has tired of her and is now living with a mistress. She manages to escape and leaves for Germany and then England. In London, the jealousy of another woman has caused the fire in which she has almost lost her life. Now that her story has been told there is a chance that Amelina will find rest: despite the destruction of her family, she still has an uncle living in England and one of her rescuers is an Englishman of good family who has fallen in love with her and is prepared to marry her. But the narrative starts up afresh, as does the cycle of misfortunes with a new series of persecutors who are in love with her. She cannot reach her uncle and her protector is obliged to leave her. Amelina once again flees across Europe, from prison to prison: 'Il était sans doute de la terrible destinée d'Amelina de rendre sensibles les cœurs les plus pervers' (vol.1, p.208). Irish, Italian and English persecutors succeed those in France and Germany and the passions of love follow the revolutionary Terror. The heroine deplores a 'malheureux sort qui la précipitait continuellement d'abîmes en abîmes' and which on each occasion turns her into the 'victime d'un homme qui s'était montré à elle sous les dehors de l'honnêteté' (vol.2, p.187). The violence she experiences is not so much that of history, in the form of the French Revolution, as a psychological violence which pursues her across the various European countries. The villains represent an ideal form of villainy and the heroine is no less ideally beautiful and good. A description of one of her persecutors could apply to them all: 'Il n'avait que des inclinations vicieuses; fripon par calcul, athée par principes, et libertin par gout.' Such was his character at the age of twelve and such it remains so at fifty-six (vol.2, p.54). As for the heroine, her appearance at the end of the tale has been affected by her fresh woes, but she has nevertheless remained herself: 'Tout le monde trouva Amelina maigrie; [...] mais l'ensemble de ses traits n'avaient rien perdu de ses charmes. Ses yeux, moins vifs, étaient devenus plus tendres' (vol.2, p.208). The excess of virtue appears to be less due to some sort of historical dialectic than to the providential principle of compensation, an influential concept at this time.[4]

In An VIII (1799-1800), Mme Bournon-Malarme published *Miralba, chef des brigands* which presents a more subtle analysis of violence. An English Lord falls in love with an Italian adventuress, follows her to her own country and soon becomes her victim there. She leads him into an ambush and locks him up in an underground prison that communicates with the lair of a group of brigands. Two types of violence are then contrasted with each other. As represented by the courtesan and her accomplices, violence is venal and self-serving; as represented by Miralba, the good-hearted brigand, it is intended to serve social justice. The meanings of the terms *brigand* and *honnête homme* are re-evaluated. The brigand denounces 'les gens soi-disant honnêtes': 'Ne vous avisez pas de confondre la chose parce que la stérilité des langues n'a pas diversifié le mot. Il y a voleur et voleur, comme il y a homme et homme [...] Notre état est sans aucun doute d'alléger les propriétés de ceux qui en sont abondamment pourvus; mais nous le faisons avec ménagement et discrétion.'[5] Now not so much a prisoner of the brigands as the guest of their captain, the English aristocrat is charmed by the latter's moral elegance and adopts some of his arguments. Miralba has more virtues 'que beaucoup d'hommes que l'on appelle *honnêtes gens*, mais il fait un métier qui les ternit toutes' (vol.1, p.198). Adopting a number of the principles put forward by his host, he attempts to transform his

---

4. See, for instance, Antoine de La Salle's *La Balance naturelle* (London,1788) and *La Mécanique morale* (Geneva [Auxerre],1789), and Hyacinthe Azaïs's *Des compensations dans les destinées humaines* (Paris, Garnery, 1809). See also Jean Svagelski, *L'Idée de compensation en France 1750-1850* (Lyon, 1981).
5. Bournon-Malarme, *Miralba, chef des brigands*, 3rd edn, 2 vols (Paris, Lecointe et Durey,1821), vol.1, p.174. On violence and moral re-evaluation, see Catriona Seth's article, 'The "dix août" (10 August 1792) in literary texts', p.75-92.

relationship with his own servant: 'je ne veux plus que la dure expression de *maître* soit en usage parmi nous' (vol.1, p.197).

Miralba acts as though he were running a business with a team of three thousand men operating throughout Europe. In addition to the cavern, drawn from the traditional imagery of robbers, he owns a dozen residences and castles. The cavern itself is most luxuriously appointed. Between his thieving operations he organises concerts and firework displays there. He dominates his world like a true prince. He narrates his personal history, revealing that he came from a well-heeled family, and has been rejected by his father. Chance misfortunes have turned him into a criminal and led him to join a band of thieves whose captain he rapidly became, causing the group to expand its ambitions and adopt a new set of principles. He aspires to use violence only where strictly necessary and condemns those scoundrels who take some sort of pleasure in seeing their victims 'expirer dans les souffrances les plus affreuses' (vol.2, p.69).[6] It is not possible for the prosperity of such a band of 'hommes libres et indépendants' – rather than brigands – to last. Miralba soon becomes the victim of a jealous mistress who lives with him and brings about his downfall out of revenge. He is finally besieged in a fortress beside the sea by the regular troops stationed in the region who outnumber his own band by two to one. He commits suicide by blowing up the tower. The English aristocrat returns to the path of familial and patriotic duty, marrying a young lady of his own class. The conclusion to be drawn is that 'Miralba était bon, généreux, sensible; mais il fut criminel et méritait d'être puni' (vol.2, p.274). There is no question of revolution, here, but the social claims made by the figure of the brigand (analysed by Eric Hobsbawm)[7] are those associated with popular uprisings. The band practises a redistribution of wealth and operates as an antisociety, as in Schiller's *Die Raüber* (the source of La Martelière's

6. Miralba is only cruel in cases of treachery, and on such occasions he makes the traitor's death 'doublement effrayante par les affreux tourments d'un long et douloureux supplice' (vol.1, p.169).
7. Eric J. Hobsbawm, *Primitive rebels: studies in archaic forms of social movement in Europe in the 19th and 20th centuries* (Manchester, 1959), and *Bandits* (London, 1969). On the transition from social reality to literary representation see *Cartouche, Mandrin et autres brigands du XVIIIe siècle*, ed. Lise Andriès (Paris, 2010).

adaptation) and the band of Independents who inhabit the heart of Bohemia's forests in Ducray-Duminil's *Victor ou L'Enfant de la forêt*. Revolt is destined to fail. The final chapter shows a return to traditional order: 'La suite est si simple et si naturelle qu'elle dispense d'aucun détail. Je me contenterai donc de dire que [...].' There then follows the announcement of marriages, before the novelist adds: 'que, que ... Supposez, lecteur, pour conclusion, tout ce que vous voudriez qui fût' (vol.2, p.282-84).

A third example, taken from her novel *Alicia, ou Le Cultivateur de Schaffhouse* (1805) exorcises revolutionary violence through both a personal psychological explanation and its contextualisation in a wider European space. The hero is a young English lord on his Grand Tour who falls in love with a relative who has been shut up by her stepmother in a Spanish convent. Throughout the embedded story of the 'Histoire de la sœur Maria' the convent features strongly as a locus of intrigues and brutalities modelled on the southern European monasteries to be found in English Gothic fiction, from Ann Radcliffe to Matthew Lewis. From the gloom of the confessional to its veiled nuns, Catholicism is portrayed as a religion that combines mystery with a troubling darker side.[8] This anticlericalism is matched by a condemnation of the Terror in France: 'L'insolence, l'injustice et la licence étaient à l'ordre du jour.'[9] The setting shifts between France, England and Spain before ending in Switzerland, a country which allows the building of bridges and brings consolation. 'Des prairies fertiles, des terres excellentes, une maison simple, mais grande et bien distribuée, une basse-cour considérable, de beaux et bons vergers' (vol.2, p.194) form the perfect antithesis to catastrophe and misfortune. The love affairs of a number of couples are perturbed by the villainy of an Irishman who appears under several different aliases but who seems to the young Englishman, who encounters him in Paris, to be 'extrêmement aimable', with plain manners and morals that are apparently gentle and honest. 'Il parle plusieurs langues' (vol.1, p.23); this proof of culture is quickly contradicted by his duplicity and loss

---

8. See Maurice Lévy, *Le Roman gothique anglais 1764-1824* (Paris, 1995), p.259-60.
9. Bournon-Malarme, *Alicia, ou Le Cultivateur de Schaffhouse*, 2 vols (Paris, Cretté, An XIII [1805]), vol.2, p.112.

of all credibility. A seducer with many victims, most of whom die, he kidnaps and incarcerates women. Behind his many different masks and identities his first name is Robert, the classic first name of brigands and a name so powerful that Robert's enemies dubbed him 'Roberspierre'.[10]

This personal and psychological expression of violence could end in pathos. Melodramas and novels would focus their brutality on striking objects and would then exorcise it in the form of a final explosion.[11] The principle of an eye for an eye required that the bodies of those who had tortured and caused suffering in others should be subjected to mutilation, a practice closer to those of the *ancien régime* than to the administrative neutrality of the guillotine. The final dwelling of the robber chief appears to offer an allegory of his character: 'Cette tour, qui n'offrait au dehors qu'un aspect effrayant par sa prodigieuse hauteur et ses alentours arides et sablonneux, renfermaient les appartements les plus délicieux.'[12] The brigand himself is troubled by the same contradictions: 'Miralba fut porté au vice par la rigueur de sa destinée: son cœur est bon, honnête et franc' (vol.2, p.264). This tension is pushed to its limits and resolves itself in suicide. The brigand blows up the tower and its ruins are then searched by soldiers looking for weapons. This spectacular explosion echoes that of the Castel Sant'Angelo at the end of Révéroni Saint-Cyr's *Pauliska ou La Perversité moderne*, which had appeared two years earlier.[13] The ancient fortress is gutted and the man behind the plots against the beautiful Pauliska is lost in the catastrophe he has wrought: 'Nous apprîmes le lendemain que Salviati, victime de sa propre vengeance, avait péri avec une grande partie de ses compagnons.'[14] The explosion serves at once to lay bare hidden secrets and to muddy the waters; it both reveals and conceals.

10. And so one slips from Robert to Roger, the father of Victor in Ducray-Duminil's novel; see Michael Tilby, 'Ducry-Duminil's *Victor ou L'Enfant de la forêt* in the context of the Revolution', *SVEC* 249 (1987), p.407-38.
11. See Simone Bernard-Griffiths and Jean Sgard, *Mélodrames et romans noirs* (Toulouse, 2000).
12. Bournon-Malarme, *Miralba*, vol.2, p.87.
13. See Pierre Saint-Amand's article, 'Gothic Explosions: Révéroni Saint-Cyr's *Pauliska ou La Perversité moderne*', p.61-72.
14. Jacques-Antoine de Révéroni Saint-Cyr, *Pauliska ou La Perversité moderne*, ed. Michel Delon (Paris, 1991), p.210.

The damned soul in *Alicia* also takes his own life. He swallows poison and dies seized with convulsions: 'Le misérable comble tous les crimes dont il s'est rendu coupable en devenant son propre assassin. Je ne fais pas de différence du suicide à l'homicide.'[15] *Peut-on s'en douter? ou Histoire véritable de deux familles de Norwick* provides a detailed account of the intricacies of a plot to avenge a past offence devised by the head of one family against another. His plans end in failure. The eldest son, whom he sought to help, is injured: 'Son œil droit ne tenait qu'à l'aide de quelques filaments, et tombait sur sa joue, qui dégoûtait de sang.' The father 'faisait des rugissements horribles, une écume noirâtre sortait de sa bouche, tous ses traits étaient dans d'effroyables convulsions'. As for the mother, she begins a confession but 'un vomissement de sang l'empêche de finir'.[16] The hell-born family is wiped out by its own excesses. Its punishment is overt, spectacular and exemplary. In *Hannibal*, published a few years later, two young female accomplices attack a couple whose marriage they wish to prevent. They finally neutralise each other, bringing about their own downfall. One of them, who has throughout the novel been filled with imaginative ideas for new traps for her victims, now wishes to get closer to them. She is prevented from doing so and is devoured by the guard dogs. She has left her former accomplice, now her rival, in possession of an explosive device which detonates, leaving the second culprit to be torn to pieces in her turn.

Lancelot Montaigu, ou Le Résultat des bonnes fortunes, published in 1816, aspires to bring an end to the novel of libertinage that had flourished in the eighteenth century and in the early years of the nineteenth. Unworthy of his medieval name, Lancelot is a 'libertin sans délicatesse, ni principe'[17] who escapes an oversimplified form of Manichaeism. He pursues his lust in England, Italy, Portugal, Spain and Switzerland, while his virtuous brother is arrested in Paris and becomes the confidant of the son of a

---

15. Bournon-Malarme, *Alicia*, vol.2, p.238.
16. Bournon-Malarme, *Peut-on s'en douter? ou Histoire véritable de deux familles de Norwick*, 2 vols (Paris, Mme Masson, An X [1802], vol.2, p.146, 161, 166.
17. Bournon-Malarme, *Lancelot Montaigu, ou Le Résultat des bonnes fortunes*, 3 vols (Paris, Pigoreau,1816), vol.1, p.92.

member of the *parlement* whose entire family has been massacred in 'la boucherie révolutionnaire' (vol.2, p.75): 'de tous côtés, le mot *liberté* se fait entendre; je le lis sur chaque porte, et c'est en me le répétant qu'on m'a ôté la mienne' (vol.2, p.84). The virtuous Englishman is beset by misfortunes, but the crimes of Lancelot the libertine eventually catch up with him. The seduction of a young Swiss woman leads to the intervention of her father and brother in which Lancelot's thigh is broken, leaving him with a weakened leg. He now limps. The symbols of a glorious eighteenth century are condemned to lose their lustre. A hot air balloon ascent ends in disaster as the balloon catches fire. The libertine city of Venice, capital of the Carnival, has become funereal: 'Ce n'était plus cette ville brillante de richesse, siège des plaisirs et de la galanterie; la Révolution en avait fait le séjour le plus triste et le plus ennuyeux' (vol.3, p.6). A jealous woman provokes a duel between the two brothers who have failed to recognise each other. Lancelot loses an eye in the fight. He has now sustained two blows to his body: 'Estropié et défiguré [...] il abjura, et de bonne foi, le désir insatiable de se rendre célèbre par ses innombrables bonnes fortunes' (vol.3, p.197). He recovers from his errant ways and returns to England where he marries an elderly woman in order to provide a young and meritorious girl with status and fortune. Revolutionary France has brought a halt to the practice of branding criminals but, by an innate justice, the libertine bears the marks of his immoral conduct.

It is the nature of such novels to portray physical fragility and emotional vulnerability in a brutal, disordered and complex world. They thrill their readers in the course of adventures which place the representatives of virtue in conflict with opponents who may assume many guises. Criminals conceal their true appearance behind a range of masks, and time does not bring experience and maturity but instead conceals an earlier evil: 'Un séjour de dix-huit à vingt ans dans les Indes orientales l'a tellement changé qu'il n'est pas reconnaissable.'[18] The old hurt nevertheless remains as painful as on the day it was inflicted and the change of appearance merely enables a return to France in search of vengeance. The loss of religious and social reference points is

18. Bournon-Malarme, *Peut-on s'en douter?*, vol.2, p.185.

criticised for the violence it has encouraged, but the unfurling of passions appears to be as much the consequence of individual temperament and family situation as of the historical moment and political context, where the Inquisition matches the French Terror and Catholic coercion is as powerful as Jacobin repression. A novelist such as Charlotte Bournon-Malarme offers her readers variations on the same theme: violence is committed against innocents until the criminal's confession makes the distant cause of his or her animosity known once again. This final narrative in the chain serves as an explanation of the plot of the novel and adds weight to the moral conclusion. It permits a shift from physical brutality to words and gives meaning to the fiction. An old injury has caused the criminal to leave the path of righteousness and has led him into a life of crime and he is now finally able to tell his story. Here, the position of Miralba, the robber chief, is unusual. He spontaneously tells his erstwhile prisoner, the English nobleman who is now his guest, the story of his life. The truth of his personal history is not revealed at the moment of death and the position of his narrative, set in the middle of the second volume, is in keeping with the contradictory judgements he attracts. He attributes his errors and his crimes to the circumstances in which he has found himself: 'Les circonstances m'ont fait la loi.' At the moment of farewell he reiterates this view: 'regrettez que les circonstances m'aient conduit sur un chemin épineux, et qui se termine toujours par un précipice'.[19]

The concluding pages of another of her novels which appeared in An XII resemble a Last Judgement. The characters are reviewed and their futures decided: 'Hood et son neveu Smith, qui n'avaient été fripons que par circonstances, redevinrent honnêtes gens, et restèrent au service, l'un de sir Adolphe Lymington, l'autre d'Ethelbert.'[20] Their return to virtue is rewarded by continued domestic service and the old order is perpetuated. The influence of circumstances is also referred to in the title of a novel which had appeared the previous year, *L'Infidèle*

---

19. Bournon-Malarme, *Miralba*, vol.2, p.50, 258.
20. Bournon-Malarme, *Les Trois Générations, ou Drusilla, Wilhelmina et Georgia*, 3 vols (Paris, Gérard, An XII [1804]), vol.3, p.254.

par circonstance. The first-person narrator of this tale blames the circumstances of his youth for his libertine behaviour which has brought about the failure of his marriage. On the final page of his confessions he still hopes for forgiveness: 'Peut-être pourrais-je tracer l'histoire de quatre autres années, où le sentiment et la raison feraient oublier celles qui n'ont été qu'un tissu d'égarements.'[21] He pleads for indulgence and the right to be forgotten. These references to circumstance fit with two contemporary currents of thought. The first took the view that criminal law should be based on investigation and expertise, establishing the precise circumstances of the crime in order to come to an understanding of it in human and social, as opposed to theological, terms.[22] The definition of 'circonstances atténuantes'[23] in law brought with it the need for moderation and a scale of punishments, allowing each case to be considered individually. The second involved an approach to politics that sought to define a social context in order to establish the margins of possibility for action.

In the realm of politics, Mme de Staël embarked in 1798 on *Des circonstances actuelles qui peuvent terminer la Révolution et des principes qui doivent fonder la République en France* which remained unpublished. Its title points to the tension between principles and circumstance, between abstract concepts and material events. Later, when she wrote *Considérations sur la Révolution française*, she included two chapters with similar headings: 'Des circonstances qui ont amené la convocation des Etats généraux' and 'Des circonstances qui ont accompagné le premier retour de la maison de Bourbon en 1814'. Here, abstract analysis is refined by the examination of individual cases and theory must be pragmatic in

---

21. Pierre Legay, *L'Infidèle par circonstance*, 3 vols (Paris, Marchand, an XI [1803], vol.2, p.342. In 1789 Nougaret had published *Le Danger des circonstances* (Brussels-Paris, Defer de Maisonneuve); there then appeared Joseph Raoul Ronden's *Henriette et Sophie, ou La Force des circonstances* (Paris, Fréchet, An XII [1804]), and the anonymous *Lucinde ou La Victime des circonstances, roman historique* (Paris, Vauquelin, 1819).
22. See Michel Porret, *Sur la scène du crime: pratique pénale, enquête et expertise judiciaires à Genève (XVIIIe-XIXe siècle)* (Montreal, 2008).
23. See C. P. Collart de Martigny, *Du système des circonstances atténuantes* (Paris, 1840); and Georges Imbart de La Tour, *Des circonstances atténuantes* (Paris, 1898).

taking account of details which vary from case to case. The novels of Charlotte Bournon-Malarme make overt reference to a moral Manichaeism that assumes humans to have essential qualities but they simultaneously sketch out an explanation of violence founded on circumstance. By taking historical conditions into consideration she colours the essentialist view of fixed individual character. In one view, violence is simply the expression of Evil; according to the other, it can have an historical explanation. In the accumulation of episodes, in the creation of intricate plots and in the staging of catastrophes on a spectacular scale, the novelist contrives to refrain from making the philosophical implications of her creations explicit.

Summaries

Gambling and violence: Loaisel de Tréogate as a neuroscientist?
John Dunkley

Clearly recognised in the eighteenth century, the links between gambling and violence were examined by moralists and by creative writers alike. In conformity with the prevailing religious mindset, the motives for gambling were identified as idleness and avarice, and the result to the individual was a loss of rational control. Recent neurological research and the development of sociological and medical perspectives allow us to move beyond religious explanations, to revisit the imaginative literature of the past, to see how writers of fiction documented the connections between gambling and violence, in a wide variety of manifestations, and to portray them in ways which surpassed the moralistic and philosophical explanations of the day and are more in harmony with the modern understanding of the gambler's mind.

Metaphors of popular violence in the revolutionary debate in the wake of Edmund Burke
Olivier Ritz

From 'cannibals' to 'torrents', from 'brigands' to 'barbarians', numerous metaphors are used to speak about the violent mob in the Revolution. This chapter examines the use of such metaphors in French translations of, and responses to, Edmund Burke's *Reflections on the Revolution in France*. These metaphors are more than rhetorical ornaments, for they serve to define and to delimit what is acceptable and unacceptable in popular political interventions. Linguistic violence played a key role in the normalisation of political life through the exclusion of the people.

Dreaming the Terror: the other stage of revolutionary violence
Stéphanie Genand

The Revolution demanded a new system of thought capable of ascribing a political and moral meaning to the violence that emphatically marked the collapse of the *ancien régime*. Whereas historiography relegates the massacres to the anthropological margins of a 'monstrous' Terror, narrative fiction portrays a palpable landscape of fear in which violence is no longer defined in terms of historical criteria. Several writers explore the possibilities of the dream which, in defying chronology and rational thought, may be the most effective means to think the unthinkable, and speak the unspeakable.

Gothic explosions: Révéroni Saint-Cyr's *Pauliska ou La Perversité moderne*
Pierre Saint-Amand

The question of whether violence can be modern is central to this chapter on Jacques-Antoine de Révéroni Saint-Cyr's novel *Pauliska ou La Perversité moderne* (1798). Situating the novel in turn-of-the-century scientific debates such as mesmerism, this contribution challenges Foucault's reading of this 'timeless' text, and argues instead that *Pauliska* can be situated among a group of contemporary works that were written under the influence of a crisis of Reason, transmitting not only an emerging irrationality but also a violence never before imagined.

The 'dix août' (10 August 1792) in literary texts
Catriona Seth

This chapter examines the literary responses to one of the key outbursts of revolutionary violence, which saw hundreds of people massacred at the Tuileries in 1792. This moment of excess and inhumanity changed the perception of the Revolution (both at home and abroad). In a grotesque carnivalesque spirit, conventional moral, familial and social bearings are inverted and overturned. Novels analysed include Louis de Bruno's *Lioncel ou L'Emigré*, Dumaniant's *Les Amours et aventures d'un émigré* and Mme de Staël's *Corinne*.

Violence in history and the rise of the historical novel: the case of the marquis de Sade
Michèle Vallenthini

This chapter examines the inherent link between history and violence in Sade's final three novels – *La Marquise de Gange*, *Adélaïde de Brunswick* and *Histoire secrète d'Isabelle de Bavière*. In these late novels, progress is not shown as a positive force but as an inevitable movement towards loss. Sade's lack of interest in contemporary events and his retreat into a version of the Middle Ages convey his resistance to history and his traumatised immobility in the face of progress.

The everlasting trials of Jean Calas: justice, theatre and trauma in the early years of the Revolution
Yann Robert

Between December 1790 and July 1791, three distinct plays recreated on stage the trial and execution of Jean Calas. Through a close reading of these plays, and of the ensuing debates in the press on the wisdom of reopening old wounds, this chapter argues that the Calas plays served two vital functions, linked to the two forms of violence intrinsic to any legal system – crime and punishment. Firstly, the plays aimed to heal the trauma inflicted upon the national psyche by the injustice and cruelty of legal proceedings under the *ancien régime*. Secondly, the plays presented themselves as a new and improved way of coping with violent crimes. Indeed, as much as the trial of individuals, these plays were the trial of their trials – that is, of the very workings of justice.

Violence in the theatre of the Revolution
Pierre Frantz

This chapter examines the risks inherent in commemorating revolutionary violence on stage. How does the tempestuous audience respond to staged violence? Does the representation of violence stoke further brutality, or can it serve to calm the audience through a process of catharsis? This chapter answers those crucial questions by means of a close reading of a number of tragedies, comedies and *faits historiques et patriotiques* in their political context. Dramatists analysed include Marie-Joseph Chénier, Sylvain Maréchal and Olympe de Gouges.

Violence, vulnerability and subjectivity in Sade
Thomas Wynn

Accounts of violence in Sade's work overwhelmingly assume that violence is the prerogative of the sovereign, autonomous self, and that the effect of that violence is to destroy the other, to reduce it to nothing. Using insights from Judith Butler's analysis of war and violence, this chapter offers a new reading of Sade's correspondence – and of Sadean subjectivity more generally – by contending that violence serves to constitute the victim as a subject. The pristine subject is a myth, for the self bears the traces of others' brutality.

The Bastille or the 'Enfer de Dutailli de Saint-Pierre'
Odile Jaffré-Cook

Violence is not always of a spectacular nature, for it can operate quietly as a coercive effect of power. Richly detailed and based on archival research, this chapter details how imprisonment acts upon the mind and body of the individual subject. Uncovering letters between Bernardin de Saint-Pierre and his brother Dutailli, imprisoned at the Bastille, this contribution reveals that the prison of the late Enlightenment was far from the reasonable site of correction it aimed to be.

Violence, terrorism and the legacy of the Enlightenment: debates around Jean-Jacques Rousseau and the Revolution
Ourida Mostefai

Focusing on the pantheonisation of Rousseau – a figure claimed by such diverse factions as the Girondins, the Montagnards and the Jacobins – this chapter analyses the debates on the legacy of the Enlightenment during the Revolution. This ceremony marked a key moment in the decade, and it must be seen in the context of the entry of Marat and the exit of Mirabeau from the Panthéon. A close analysis of a range of pamphlets and creative writing allows a keener sense of the condemnation of violence at the end of the century.

Violence in the work of Bernardin de Saint-Pierre
Malcolm Cook

This chapter explores how Bernardin de Saint-Pierre perceives the world as paradoxical, with immense natural beauty and yet containing inherent violence. Bernardin combines a picture of a violent and savage nature with the image of a man who is corrupt and vicious. The answer to this conundrum is to argue that natural violence can be majestic and sublime, and that man cannot find true happiness in a world which he alone has corrupted and yet which he cannot fully comprehend.

Violence and the monster: the *Private lives* of the duc d'Orléans
Rebecca Sopchik

There is an explosion of violence in the tone of political pamphlets over the course of the Revolution, as a previously bantering tone metamorphoses into a moralistic, crude and denunciatory style. While this accurately describes the tone of the pamphlets attacking the duc d'Orléans, we can note however that their major narrated events change little from 1784 to 1794. This observation prompts some key questions: if the actual events stay the same, why does the author suddenly denounce Orléans? How does this new rhetorical violence alter Orléans's character and the details of the events? This chapter examines four pamphlets against the duc d'Orléans dating from 1784, 1789, 1793 and 1794. The transformation in tone is accompanied by the addition of violent details that pervade the later texts, while also increasingly separating the duc from humanity itself.

'Avec une telle violence que...': Sade's use of the term *violence*
Jean-Christophe Abramovici

Violence is clearly at the heart of Sade's work, but critics tend to ignore the novelist's precise deployment and modulation of the phenomenon. Examining how Sade uses the term 'violence' in sexual and non-sexual contexts in *Les Infortunes de la vertu, Justine ou Les Malheurs de la vertu* and *La Nouvelle Justine* as well as in *Les Cent vingt journées de Sodome*, this chapter shows that Sade aims to position the reader carefully in two significantly different ways, as a privileged spectator and as a victim.

The sound of violence: listening to rape in Sade
Will McMorran

Under the enduring influence of Roland Barthes, literary critics since the 1960s have typically taken a linguistic approach to Sade's fiction that focuses on discourse rather than representation. While this approach has proved fruitful in many respects, it has signally failed to convey or address the violence which is arguably the defining characteristic of Sade's œuvre. One way of capturing the force of this violence is to shift focus from the words on the page to the mental imagery – auditory as well as visual – that these produce in the minds of their readers. This broadly cognitive approach is applied to a pivotal scene of brutal violence from *Justine, ou Les Malheurs de la vertu*.

Violence in the novels of Charlotte [de] Bournon-Malarme
Michel Delon

The early nineteenth-century novels of Charlotte [de] Bournon-Malarme depict personal and widespread violence across Europe. This chapter considers how these texts exorcise revolutionary violence through both a personal psychological explanation and its contextualisation in a wider European space. Offering both essentialist and historically contingent explanations for violence, these novels, characterised by their intricate plots and spectacular catastrophes, encapsulate some of the contradictions of the period's thought, fiction and culture.

Bibliography

Primary texts

Les Affiches, annonces et avis divers
La Chronique de Paris
La Feuille du jour
La Feuille du salut public
Le Journal de la montagne
Le Journal de Paris
Le Moniteur
Les Révolutions de Paris

Archives parlementaires, 100 vols (Paris, 1867–).

Azaïs, Hyacinthe, *Des compensations dans les destinées humainse* (Paris, Garnery, 1809).

Bachaumont, Louis Petit de, *Mémoires secrets, édités par P.-L. Jacob, bibliophile* (Paul Lacroix) (Paris, [1921]).

Barbeyrac, Jean, *Traité du jeu*, 2 vols (Amsterdam, Pierre Humbert, 1709).

Bardou, Abbé Jean, *Histoire de Laurent Marcel, ou L'Observateur sans préjugés* (Lille, Le Houcq, 1779).

Bernardin de Saint-Pierre, Jacques Henri, *La Chaumière indienne* (Paris, Didot le jeune, 1791).

–, *Paul et Virginie*, ed, J.-M. Racault (Paris, 1999).

–, *Œuvres complètes de Bernardin de Saint-Pierre*, ed. Louis Aimé-Martin, 2 vols (Paris, 1840).

Boissy d'Anglas, François-Antoine de, *Observations sur l'ouvrage de M. de Calonne intitulé De l'état de la France présent et à venir; et à son occasion, sur les principaux actes de l'Assemblée Nationale; avec un postscript sur les derniers écrits de MM. Mounier et Lally* (Paris, Le Boucher, 1791).

Bournon-Malarme, Charlotte (de), *Alicia, ou Le Cultivateur de Schaffhouse*, 2 vols (Paris, Cretté, An XIII [1805]).

–, *Lancelot Montaigu, ou Le Résultat des bonnes fortunes*, 3 vols (Paris, Pigoreau, 1816).

–, *Miralba, chef des brigands*, 3rd edn, 2 vols (Paris, Lecointe et Durey, 1821).

–, *Peut-on s'en douter? ou Histoire véritable de deux familles de Norwich*, 2 vols (Paris, Mme Masson, An X [1802]).

–, *Le Temps passé, ou Les Malheurs de Mad. de Mo*** émigrée*, 2 vols (Paris, Maradan, An IX [1801]).

–, *Les Trois Générations, ou Drusilla, Wilhelmina et Georgia*, 3 vols (Paris, Gérard, An XII [1804]).

Briois, le Citoyen, *La Mort du jeune Barra, ou Une Journée de la Vendée, drame historique en un acte* (Paris, Barba, An II).

Brissot de Warville, J. P. (ed.), *Bibliothèque philosophique du législateur, du politique, du jurisconsulte*, 6 vols (Paris, Desauges, 1782).

–, 'Discours de M. Brissot sur les causes des dangers de la patrie, et sur les mesures à prendre, etc. (Séance du 9 juillet 1792, An IV de la liberté)', in *Choix de rapports, opinions et discours prononcés à la Tribune Nationale depuis 1789 jusqu'à ce jour*, 21 vols (Paris, 1819-1825), vol.9, p.189-233.

Bruyère, Jean de la, *Les Caractères*, X, 29 [1692] (Paris, 1995).

Burke, Edmund, *A Philosophical enquiry into the origin of our ideas of the sublime and beautiful*, ed. Adam Phillips (Oxford, 1990).

–, *Reflections on the Revolution in France, and on the proceedings in certain societies in London relative to that event: in a letter intended to have been sent to a gentleman in Paris* (London, Dodsley, 1790).

–, *Réflexions sur la Révolution de France, et sur les procédés de certaines sociétés à Londres, relatifs à cet événement: en forme d'une lettre, qui avoit dû être envoyée d'abord à un jeune homme, à Paris*, 2nd edn (Paris, [1790]).

Calonne, Charles-Alexandre de, *De l'Etat de la France, présent et à venir* (London and Paris, Laurent, 1790).

Charrière, Isabelle de, *Réponse à l'écrit du colonel de La Harpe, intitulé De la neutralité des gouvernans de la Suisse depuis l'année 1789*, in *Œuvres complètes* (Amsterdam, 1979-), vol.10.

Chénier, Marie-Joseph, *Caïus Gracchus* (Paris, 1793).

–, *Jean Calas, tragédie en cinq actes* (Paris, Moutard, 1793).

–, *Timoléon, tragédie en trois actes avec des chœurs* (Paris, An III).

Le Comte d'Artois à l'agonie à la suite de sa confession, rêve d'un membre du clergé ([Paris?], 1789).

Damiens de Gomicourt, Augustin Pierre, *Dorval, ou Mémoires pour servir à l'histoire des mœurs au XVIIIe siècle*, 4 vols (Amsterdam and Paris, Mérigot jeune, 1769).

Dictionnaire de l'Académie Française, 5th edn, 2 vols (Paris, J. J. Smits, 1798).

Dubrail, *Grande dispute au Panthéon entre Marat et Jean-Jacques Rousseau* (Paris, 1794).

Dufey, *Descente de Louis Capet dans la région des ombres, ou rêve d'un citoyen philosophe* (Paris, chez les marchands de nouveautés, An VIII).

Dumaniant, A.-J., *Les Amours et aventures d'un émigré*, in Stéphanie Genand (ed), *Romans de l'émigration (1797-1803)*, p.71-154.

Encyclopédie, ou Dictionnaire raisonné des sciences, des arts et des métiers, par une société de gens de lettres, ed. Denis Diderot and Jean Le Rond d'Alembert, 17 vols (Paris and Neufchâtel, 1751-1765).

Etienne, Charles-Guillaume, *Le Rêve, opéra-comique en un acte et en prose* (Paris, Vente, An VII).

Etienne, Charles, and Alphonse Martainville, *Histoire du théâtre français, depuis le commencement de la révolution jusqu'à la réunion générale*, 4 vols (Paris, Barba, 1802).

Ferrière, Claude-Joseph de, *Dictionnaire de droit et de pratique, nouvelle édition*, 2 vols (Toulouse, Rayet, 1787).

Franklin, Benjamin, *The Papers of Benjamin Franklin*, ed. Leonard

W. Labaree, 40 vols (New Haven, CT, and London, 1950).

Genand, Stéphanie (ed.), *Romans de l'émigration (1797-1803)* (Paris, 2008).
Le Génie conciliateur: rêve d'un citoyen (n.p., 1789).
Genlis, Félicité de, 'Le malencontreux, ou mémoires d'un émigré, pour servir à l'histoire de la Révolution', *Nouveaux contes moraux et nouvelles historiques*, 3 vols (Paris, Maradan, An XI).
Gouges, Olympe de, *L'Esclavage des noirs, ou L'Heureux Naufrage* (Paris, 1792).

Hugo, Victor, *Les Contemplations* (Paris, 1856).
Hume, David, *A Treatise of human nature*, ed. David Fate Norton and Mary Jane Norton (Oxford, 2000).

Joigny, le Citoyen, *Le Siège de Lille, ou Cécile et Julie* (Paris, An II).
Jousse, Daniel, *Traité de la justice criminelle de France*, 4 vols (Paris, Debure père, 1771).

Lally-Tolendal, Trophime-Gérard de, *Défense des émigrés français, addressée au peuple français* (Paris, Cocherin, 1797).
–, *Lettre écrite au très honorable Edmund Burke, membre du parlement d'Angleterre* (n.p., 1791).
–, *Mémoire de Monsieur le Comte de Lally-Tollendal, ou Seconde lettre à ses commettans* (Paris, Desenne, 1790).
La Poix de Freminville, Edme de, *Dictionnaire ou Traité de la police générale des villes, bourgs, paroisses et seigneuries de la campagne* (Paris, Gissey, 1758).
La Salle, Antoine de, *La Balance naturelle* (London, 1788).
Laya, Jean-Louis, *Les Dangers de l'opinion: drame en cinq actes* (Paris, chez Maradan, 1790).
–, *Jean Calas, tragédie en cinq actes et en vers* (Avignon, chez Jacques Garrigan, 1791).
–, *Voltaire aux Français, sur leur constitution* (Paris, chez Maradan, 1789).
Lebrun-Tossa, Jean-Antoine, *La Folie de Georges, ou L'Ouverture du parlement d'Angleterre* (Paris, Barba, An II).
Legay, Pierre, *L'Infidèle par circonstance*, 3 vols (Paris, Marchand, Au XI [1803]).
Lemierre d'Argy, Auguste-Jacques, *Calas, ou Le Fanatisme, drame en quatre actes, en prose* (Paris, Imprimerie des Révolutions de Paris, 1791).
Lezay, Adrien, *Des causes de la Révolution et de ses résultats* (Paris, Desenne, 1797).
Linguet, Simon-Nicolas-Henri, *La Bastille dévoilée or receuil de pièces authentiques pour servir à son histoire* (Paris, Desenne, 1789).
Loaisel de Tréogate, Joseph-Marie, *Dolbreuse, ou l'homme du siècle, ramené à la vérité par le sentiment et par la raison*, 2 vols (Amsterdam and Paris, Belin, 1783).
Louvet, Jean-Baptiste, *Paris justifié, contre M. Mounier* (Paris, Bailly, 1789).

Mackintosh, Jacques [James], *Apologie de la Révolution française*

et de ses admirateurs anglais, en réponse aux attaques d'Edmund Burke; avec quelques remarques sur le dernier ouvrage de M. de Calonne (Paris, Buisson, 1792).
Mallet du Pan, Jacques, *Lettre de M. Mallet du Pan à M. D. B. sur les événemens de Paris du 10 août* ([Paris], 1792).
Malouet, Pierre Victor de, *Motion sur le discours adressé par le roi à l'Assemblée nationale, dans la séance du jeudi 4 février* (Paris, 1790).
Mercier, Louis-Sébastien, *L'An deux mille quatre cent quarante* (London, 1772).
–, *Annales patriotiques et littéraires de la France. Journal libre, par une société d'écrivains patriotes, et dirigé par M. Mercier* (Paris, 1789-1794).
–, *Le Nouveau Paris*, ed. Jean-Claude Bonnet ([1798], Paris, 1994).
Mirabeau, Honoré-Gabriel Riquetti, comte de, *Des lettres de cachet et des prisons d'état*, 2 vols (Hamburg, 1782).
Mémoires de Linguet sur la Bastille, et de Dusaulx, sur le 14 juillet (Paris, 1821).
Michelet, Jules, *Histoire de la révolution française*, 9 vols (Paris, 1888).
M. R. D. W., *Vie de Louis-Philippe-Joseph, duc d'Orléans, traduit de l'anglais* (London, Imprimérie du Palais Saint-James, 1789).
Mounier, Jean-Joseph, *Exposé de la conduite de M. Mounier, dans l'Assemblée nationale, et des motifs de son retour en Dauphiné* (Paris, Cuchet, 1789).

Nougaret, Pierre-Jean-Baptiste, *Le Danger des circonstances* (Brussels-Paris, Defer de Maisonneuve, 1789)
–, *Histoire du donjon et du château de Vincennes, depuis leur origine jusqu'à l'époque de la révolution*, 3 vols (Paris, 1807).

Paine, Thomas, *Les Droits de l'homme; en réponse à l'attaque de M. Burke sur la Révolution française* (Paris, Buisson, 1791).
Paré, Ambroise, *Des monstres et prodiges*, ed. Jean Céard (Geneva, 1971).
Philipon de la Madeleine, Louis, and Louis Emmanuel Jadin, *Agricol Viala, ou Le Jeune Héros de la Durance* (Paris, Duchesne, An VII).
Pixerécourt, René Charles Guibert de, *Théâtre choisi*, 4 vols (Nancy, 1841).
Polier de Bottens, Jeanne Françoise, *Félicie et Florestine*, 3 vols (Geneva, 1803).
–, *Mémoires d'une famille émigrée*, 3 vols (Hamburg, Fauche, 1798).
Le Pour et le contre: recueil complet des opinions prononcées à l'Assemblée Conventionnelle dans le procès de Louis XVI, 7 vols (Paris, Buisson, An I).
Priestley, Joseph, *Lettre au très honorable Edmund Burke, au sujet de ses réflexions sur la Révolution de France* (Paris, 1791).
Pujoulx, Jean-Baptiste, *La Veuve Calas à Paris, ou Le Triomphe de Voltaire* (Paris, Brunet, 1791).

Remarques historiques sur la Bastille: nouvelle édition, augmentée d'un grand nombre d'anecdotes intéressantes et peu connues (London, 1783).
Le Rêve d'un homme de bien, adressé

aux illustres représentants de la nation française, par M. Tri*** (Paris, Prudhomme, 1789).
Le Rêve d'un patriote éveillé (n.p., n.p., 1790).
Révéroni Saint-Cyr, Jacques-Antoine de, *Pauliska ou La Perversité moderne*, ed. Michel Delon (Paris, 1991).
Rousseau, Jean-Jacques, *Correspondance complète de Jean-Jacques Rousseau*, ed. R. A. Leigh, 52 vols (Oxford, 1965-1998).
–, *Œuvres complètes*, vol. 3, ed. Bernard Gagnebin and Marcel Raymond (Paris, 1966).

Sade, Donatien Alphonse François de, *Correspondance du marquis de Sade et de ses proches enrichies de documents, notes et commentaires*, ed. Alice Laborde, 20 vols (Geneva, 1999-).
–, *50 lettres du marquis de Sade à sa femme*, ed. Jean-Christophe Abramovici and Patrick Graille (Paris, 2009).
–, *L'Aigle, Mademoiselle...*, ed. Gilbert Lely (Paris, 1949).
–, *Œuvres*, ed. Michel Delon, 3 vols (Paris, 1990-1998).
–, *Œuvres complètes du marquis de Sade*, ed. Annie Le Brun and Jean-Jacques Pauvert, 15 vols (Paris, 1986-1991).
Sandras, Courtilz de, *Testament politique de Louvois* (Cologne, 1695).
Saulnier, Guillaume, and the Citoyen Darrieux, *La Journée du dix août 1792 ou La Chute du dernier tyran* (Paris, An II).
Sénac de Meilhan, Gabriel, *L'Emigré*, ed. Michel Delon (Paris, 2004).

Staël, Germaine de, *Considérations sur la Révolution française*, ed. Jacques Godechot (Paris, 2000).
–, *De l'Allemagne*, ed. Simon Balayé, 2 vols (Paris, 1968).
–, *Essai sur les fictions*, in *Œuvres de jeunesse*, ed. John Isbell and Simon Balayé (Paris, 1997).
–, *Œuvres complètes*, 5 vols (Paris, 2000-).

Théveneau de Morande, Charles, *Vie privée ou Apologie de très-sérénissime prince Monseigneur le Duc de Chartres* (Paris, A cent lieues de la Bastille [London, J. Hodges] 1784).
Turbat, Pierre, *Vie de L.-P.-J. Capet, ci-devant duc d'Orléans, ou Mémoires pour servir à l'histoire de la Révolution française* (Paris, Imprimérie de Franklin, 1793).

Valcour, Plancher, P.-A.-L.-P. Plancher de Valcour, dit, *La Discipline républicaine, fait historique, en un acte, en prose, mêlé d'ariettes* (Paris, Cailleau, 1794).
La Vie et les crimes de Philippe, duc d'Orléans (Cologne, 1793).
Vie secrète de Louise-Marie-Adélaïde Bourbon Penthièvre, duchesse d'Orléans, avec ses correspondances politiques (London, Imprimérie Werland, 1790).
Villemain d'Abancourt, François-Jean, *La Bienfaisance de Voltaire* (Paris, Brunet, 1791).
Voltaire, *Œuvres complètes de Voltaire / The Complete works of Voltaire* (Oxford, 1968-).
–, *L'Affaire Calas*, ed. Jacques Van den Heuvel (Paris, 1975).

Critical works

Abramson, Marianne, and Stephen D. Goldinger, 'What the reader's eye tells the mind's ear: silent reading activates inner speech', *Perception & psychophysics* 59:7 (1997), p.1059-68.

Adorno, Theodor W., and Max Horkheimer, *Dialectic of Enlightenment* (London, 1997).

Airaksinen, Timo, *The Philosophy of the marquis de Sade* (London, 1995).

Alexander, Jeffrey, 'Towards a theory of cultural trauma', *Cultural trauma and collective identity* (Berkeley, CA, 2004), p.1-30.

Andress, David, *The French Revolution and the people* (London, 2004).

–, 'Popular violence in the French Revolution: revolt, retribution and the slide to state terror', in *Cultures of violence: interpersonal violence in historical perspective*, ed. Stuart Carroll (Basingstoke, 2007), p.175-91.

–, 'La violence populaire durant la Révolution française: révolte, châtiment et escalade de la terreur d'Etat', in *Les Politiques de la Terreur, 1793-1794*, ed. Michel Biard (Rennes, 2008), p.69-80.

Andrews, Richard Mowery, *Law, magistracy and crime in Old Regime Paris, 1735-1789* (New York, 1994).

Andriès, Lise (ed.), *Cartouche, Mandrin et autres brigands du XVIIIe siècle* (Paris, 2010).

Apollinaire, Guillaume, *L'Œuvre du marquis de Sade* (Paris, 1909).

Arasse, Daniel, *La Guillotine et l'imaginaire de la Terreur* (Paris, 1987).

Arendt, Hannah, *On violence* (London, 1970).

Astbury, Katherine, *Narrative responses to the trauma of the French Revolution* (Oxford, 2012).

Astbury, Katherine, and Catriona Seth (eds), *Le Tournant des Lumières: mélanges en l'honneur du professeur Malcolm Cook* (Paris, 2012).

Baars, Bernard, *In the theatre of consciousness: the workspace of the mind* (New York, 1997).

Baczko, Bronislaw, *Politiques de la Révolution française* (Paris, 2008).

–, 'Thérèse, La Comtesse, Mme de Staël, Chateaubriand, et les autres', *Lire la correspondance de Rousseau*, ed. Jacques Berchtold and Yannick Séité, *Annales de la Société Jean-Jacques Rousseau* 47 (2008), p.5-74.

Baecque, Antoine de, *Glory and Terror: seven deaths under the French Revolution* (New York, 2001).

Barine, Arvène, *Bernardin de Saint-Pierre* (Paris, 1891).

Barthes, Roland, 'L'arbre du crime', in *Tel Quel* 28 (1967), p.23-37.

–, 'The death of the author', in

Image – music – text, trans. Stephen Heath (London, 1977), p.142-48.
–, *Sade, Fourier, Loyola* (Paris, 1971).
Bataille, Georges, *L'Erotisme* (Paris, 1958).
Beale, Sophia, *The Churches of Paris* (London, 1893).
Beauvoir, Simone de, *Faut-il brûler Sade?* (Paris, 1955).
Belmas, Elisabeth, *Jouer autrefois: essai sur le jeu dans la France moderne (XVIe-XVIIIe siècle)* (Seyssel, 2006).
–, 'Jeux d'exercice, divertissement et virilité', in *Histoire de la virilité 1: L'Invention de la virilité, de l'antiquité aux Lumières*, ed. Alain Corbin, Jean-Jacques Courtine and Georges Vigarello (Paris, 2011), p.445-65.
Bennington, Geoffrey, 'Sade: laying down the law', *Oxford literary review* 6:2 (1984), p.38-56.
Berchtold, Jacques, René Desmoris and Christophe Martin (eds), *Violences du rococo* (Bordeaux, 2012).
Bernard-Griffiths, Simone, and Jean Sgard, *Mélodrames et romans noirs* (Toulouse, 2000).
Berthevin, Jules-Julien-Gabriel, *Recherches historiques sur les derniers jours des rois de France, leurs funérailles, leurs tombeaux* (Paris, 1825).
Bianchi, Serge, *La Révolution culturelle de l'An II: élites et peuple (1789-1799)* (Paris, 1982).
Biet, Christian, and Laurence Schifano (eds), *Représentations du procès: droit, théâtre, littérature, cinéma* (Nanterre, 2003).

Binde, Per, 'Gambling, exchange systems and moralities', *Journal of gambling studies* 21.4 (2005), p.445-79.
Blackmore, Susan, *Consciousness: an introduction*, 2nd edn (London, 2010).
Blanchot, Maurice, *Sade et Restif de la Bretonne* (Brussels, 1986).
Blanning, Tim, *The Pursuit of glory: Europe 1648-1815* (London, 2007).
Bonnet, Jean-Claude (ed.), *La Mort de Marat* (Paris, 1986).
–, *Naissance du Panthéon: essai sur le culte des grands hommes* (Paris, 1998).
Brisolin, Viola, *Power and subjectivity in the late work of Roland Barthes and Pier Paolo Pasolini* (Bern, 2011).
Brown, Howard G., *Ending the French Revolution: violence, justice, and repression from the Terror to Napoleon* (Charlottesville, VA, 2006).
Butler, Judith, *Excitable speech: a politics of the performative* (New York and London, 1997).
–, *The Psychic life of power* (Stanford, CA, 1997).
–, *Precarious life: the powers of mourning and violence* (London, 2004).

Camus, Michel, and Philippe Roger (eds), *Sade: écrire la crise* (Paris, 1983).
Candler Hayes, Julie, *Identity and ideology: Diderot, Sade, and the serious genre* (Amsterdam and Philadelphia, PA, 1991).
Carlier, Christian, *Histoire du personnel des prisons françaises du XVIIIe siècle à nos jours* (Paris, 1997).

Caron, Pierre, *Paris pendant la Terreur: rapports des agents secrets du ministre de l'intérieur*, 2 vols (Paris, 1910).

Carroll, Noël, *Beyond aesthetics: philosophical essays* (Cambridge, 2001).

Castle, Terry, *Clarissa's ciphers: meaning and disruption in Richardson's Clarissa* (Ithaca, NY and London, 1982).

Cavell, Marcia, *Becoming a Subject: reflections in philosophy and psychoanalysis* (Oxford, 2006).

Chambers, R. Andrew, and Marc N. Potenza, 'Neurodevelopment, impulsivity, and adolescent gambling', *Journal of gambling studies* 19:1 (2003), p.53-84.

Chen, Thomas C. et al., 'Are dopaminergic genes involved in a predisposition to pathological aggression? Hypothesizing the importance of "super normal controls" in psychiatric genetic research of complex behavioral disorders', *Medical hypotheses* 65:4 (2005), p.703-707.

Chouliaraki, Lile, *The Spectatorship of suffering* (London, 2006).

Claverie, Elizabeth, 'Procès, affaire, cause. Voltaire et l'innovation critique', *Politix* 26 (1994), p.76-85.

Clay, Richard, *Iconoclasm in revolutionary Paris: the transformation of signs*, SVEC 2012:11.

Clemit, Pamela (ed.), *The Cambridge companion to British literature of the French Revolution in the 1790s* (Cambridge, 2011).

Cobban, Alfred (ed.), *The Debate on the French Revolution, 1789-1800* (London, 1950).

Collard de Martigny, C. P., *Du système des circonstances atténuantes* (Paris, 1840).

Cook, Malcolm, *Bernardin de Saint-Pierre: a life of culture* (London, 2006).

–, 'Bernardin de Saint-Pierre and Girodet: illustrating the "luxury" edition of *Paul et Virginie*', *The Modern language review*, 102 (2007), p.975-89.

–, *Fictional France: social reality in the French novel 1775-1800* (Oxford, 1993).

–, 'The first separate edition of Bernardin de Saint-Pierre's *Paul et Virginie*', *French studies bulletin* 109 (2008), p.89-91.

Cossy, Valérie, 'Des romans pour un monde en mouvement. La Révolution et l'émigration dans l'œuvre d'Isabelle de Charrière', *L'Emigration en Suisse (1789-1798): événements, récits, représentations: Annales Benjamin Constant* 30 (2006), p.155-78.

Cossy, Valérie, and Deirdre Dawson (eds), *Progrès et violence au XVIIIe siècle* (Paris, 2001).

Cotoni, Marie-Hélène, 'Image et discours de "Jean-Jacques" dans la *Grande dispute au Panthéon entre Marat et J.-J. R. de Dubrail* (1794)', in *Rousseau and the eighteenth century: essays in memory of R. A. Leigh*, ed. Marian Hobson, J. T. Leigh and Robert Wokler (Oxford, 1992), p.369-84.

–, 'Une tragédie de Voltaire en marge de toute règle: *Saül*', in *Marginalité et littérature:*

hommage à Christine Martineau-Génieys, ed. Maurice Accarie, Jean-Guy Gouttebroze and Eliane Kotler (Nice, 2001), p.407-21.

Cottret, Monique, *La Bastille à prendre: histoire et mythe de la forteresse royale* (Paris, 1986).

Craver-Lemley, Catherine, and Adam Reeves, 'How visual imagery interferes with vision', *Psychological review* 99 (1992), p.633-49.

Crocker, Lester, *Nature and culture: ethical thought in the French Enlightenment* (Baltimore, MD, 1963).

Cronk, Nicholas, *The Classical sublime: French neoclassicism and the language of literature* (Charlottesville, VA, 2003).

Cryle, Peter, *Geometry in the boudoir: configurations of French erotic narrative* (New York, 1994).

Currie, Gregory, *The Nature of fiction* (Cambridge, 2008).

Darlow, Mark (ed.), *Revolutionary culture: continuity and change*, Nottingham French studies 45 (2006).

–, *Staging the French Revolution: cultural politics and the Paris Opera, 1789-1794* (Oxford, 2012).

Darnton, Robert, *Mesmerism and the end of the Enlightenment in France* (Cambridge, 1968).

–, *The Devil in the holy water, or the art of slander from Louis XIV to Napoleon* (Philadelphia, PA, 2010).

Daumas, Maurice, *Le Syndrome Des Grieux: la relation père/fils au XVIIIe siècle* (Paris, 1990).

Deleuze, Gilles, *Présentation de Sacher-Masoch: le froid et le cruel* (Paris, 1967).

Delon, Michel, 'Les historiennes de Silling', in *L'Histoire au XVIIIe siècle* (Aix-en-Provence, 1980) p.101-13.

–, *L'Idée d'énergie au tournant des Lumières (1770-1820)* (Paris, 1988).

–, 'L'invention sadienne et les pamphlets révolutionnaires', in *Le Travail des Lumières, pour Georges Benrekassa*, ed. Caroline Jacot Grapa et al. (Paris, 2002), p.557-68.

–, 'Machines gothiques', *Europe* 659 (1984), p.72-79.

–, Sade autobiographe: les personnages de Valcour et de Rodin', in *Autobiography, historiography, rhetoric*, ed. Mary Donaldson-Evans, Lucienne Frappier-Mazur and Gerald Prince (Amsterdam, 1994), p.75-86.

–, 'Sade comme révélateur idéologique', *Romanistiche Zeitschrift für Literaturgeschichte* 5 (1981), p.103-12.

–, *Les Vies de Sade*, 2 vols (Paris, 2007).

Delon, Michel, and Catriona Seth (eds), *Sade en toutes lettres: autour d'Aline et Valcour* (Paris, 2004).

Dennett, Daniel, *Consciousness explained* (Boston, MA, and London, 1991).

Didier, Béatrice, *Ecrire la Révolution: 1789-1799* (Paris, 1989).

–, 'Sade dramaturge de ses carceri', *La Nouvelle Revue française* 216 (1970), p.72-80.

DiPiero, Thomas, 'Disfiguring the victim's body in Sade's

Justine', in *Body and text in the eighteenth century*, ed. Veronica Kelly and Dorothea Von Mücke, (Stanford, CA, 1994), p.247-65.

Dodd, James, *Violence and phenomenology* (New York, 2009).

Douthwaite, Julia, *The Wild girl, natural man, and the monster* (Chicago, IL, 2002).

Downing, Lisa, and Libby Saxton, *Film and ethics: foreclosed encounters* (London, 2010).

Du Bled, Victor, *Histoire anecdotique et psychologie des jeux de cartes, dès, échecs* (Paris, 1919).

Dubois, Maud, 'Le roman sentimental en Suisse romande, 1780-1830', in *La Sensibilité dans la Suisse des Lumières: entre physiologie et morale, une qualité opportuniste*, ed. Claire Jaquier (Geneva, 2005), p.167-256.

Dunkley, John, *Gambling: a social and moral problem in France, 1685-1792*, SVEC 235 (1985).

Dutray-Lecoin, Elise, and Danielle Muzerelle (eds), *La Bastille ou l'enfer des vivants'* (Paris, 2010).

Eaglestone, Robert, *Ethical criticism: reading after Levinas* (Edinburgh, 1997).

Farge, Arlette, *La Vie fragile: violence, pouvoirs et solidarités à Paris au XVIIIe siècle* (Paris, 1986).

Fauskevåg, Svein-Eirik, *Sade ou la tentation solitaire: étude sur l'anthropologie littéraire dans La Nouvelle Justine et l'Histoire de Juliette* (Paris, 2001).

Felman, Shoshana, 'Forms of judicial blindness, or the evidence of what cannot be seen: traumatic narratives and legal repetitions in the O. J. Simpson case and in Tolstoy's *The Kreutzer sonata*', *Critical inquiry* 23 (1997), p.738-88.

Ferret, Olivier, 'La *Vie privée... du duc de Chartres* et les *Mémoires secrets*', in *Le Règne de la critique: l'imaginaire culturel des Mémoires secrets*, ed. Christophe Cave (Paris, 2010), p.397-413.

Ferret, Olivier, Anne-Marie Mercier-Faivre and Chantal Thomas (eds), *Dictionnaire des Vies privées*, SVEC 2011:02.

Foucault, Michel, *Dits et écrits*, 2 vols (Paris, 1994).

–, 'So cruel a knowledge' in *Essential works of Foucault, 1954-1984*, vol.2: *Aesthetics, method, and epistemology*, ed. James D. Faubion (New York, 1997), p.53-67.

–, *Surveiller et punir: naissance de la prison* (Paris, 1975).

Fournel, Victor, 'Le parterre sous la Révolution', *Revue d'art dramatique* (July-September 1893).

Frappier-Mazur, Lucienne, *Sade et l'écriture de l'orgie* (Paris, 1991).

Friedland, Paul, *Seeing justice done: the age of spectacular capital punishment in France* (Oxford, 2012).

Funck-Brentano, Frantz, *Légendes et archives de la Bastille*, 4th edn (Paris, 1898).

Garapon, Antoine, *Bien juger: essai sur le rituel judiciaire* (Paris, 1997).

Gimenez, Raphaël, *L'Espace de la douleur chez Loaisel de Tréogate, 1752-1812* (Paris, 1992).

Girault de Coursac, Paul and Pierrette, *Enquête sur le procès du roi Louis XVI* (Paris, 1992).

Gobel, Gundula, and Albert Soboul, 'Audience et pragmatisme du rousseauisme: les almanachs de la Révolution (1788-1795)', *Annales historiques de la révolution française* 234 (1978), p.608-40.

González, Julio, Alfonso Barros-Loscertales, Friedemann Pulvermüller, Vanessa Meseguer, Ana Sanjuán, Vicente Belloch and César Avila, 'Reading cinnamon activates olfactory brain regions', *NeuroImage* 32:2 (2006), p.906-12.

Grant, Jon E., and Marc N. Potenza (eds), *Pathological gambling, a clinical guide to treatment* (Washington, DC, and London, 2004).

Gray, John, *Al Qaeda and what it means to be modern* (London, 2003).

Grussi, Olivier, *La Vie quotidienne des joueurs sous l'ancien régime à Paris et à la cour* (Paris, 1985).

Guénot, Hervé, 'De l'Ile des Peupliers au Panthéon: la translation des cendres de Rousseau', *Etudes Jean-Jacques Rousseau* 3 (1989), p.101-25.

Guermazi, Jamel, '*La Marquise de Gange*, un récit et un mélodrame', in *Mélodrames et romans noirs, 1750-1890*, ed. Simone Bernard-Griffiths and Jean Sgard (Toulouse, 2000), p.99-112.

Hartmann, Pierre, *Le Contrat et la séduction: essai sur la subjectivité amoureuse dans le roman des Lumières* (Paris, 1998).

Haywood, Ian, *Bloody Romanticism: spectacular violence and the politics of representation* (Basingstoke, 2006).

Hénaff, Marcel, *L'Invention du corps libertin* (Paris, 1978).

–, 'Sade, the mechanization of the libertine body, and the crisis of reason', in *Technology and the politics of knowledge*, ed. Andrew Feenberg and Alistair Hannay (Bloomington, IN, 1995), p.209-31.

Hinnant, Charles, '"The late unfortunate regicide in France": Burke and the political sublime', *1650-1850: ideas, aesthetics, and inquiries in the early modern era* 2 (1996), p.111-36.

Hobsbawn, Eric J., *Primitive rebels: studies in archaic forms of social movement in Europe in the 19th and 20th centuries* (Manchester, 1959).

–, *Bandits* (London, 1969).

Hraba, Joseph, and Gang Lee, 'Gender, gambling and problem gambling', *Journal of gambling studies* 12:1 (1996), p.83-101.

Huet, Marie-Hélène, *Monstrous imagination* (Cambridge, MA, 1993).

Jaquier, Claire, Florence Lotterie and Catriona Seth (eds), *Destins romanesques de l'émigration* (Paris, 2007).

J.-J. Rousseau et la Révolution française, *Etudes J.-J. Rousseau* 3 (1989).

Kivy, Peter, *The Performance of reading: an essay in the philosophy of literature* (Oxford, 2009).
Koselleck, Reinhart, 'Terreur et rêve', in *Le Futur passé: contribution à la sémantique des temps historiques* (Paris, 2000), p.249-62.
Kosslyn, Stephen M., William L. Thompson and Giorgio Ganis, *The Case for mental imagery* (Oxford, 2006).
Kozul, Mladen, 'L'inachèvement des *Cent vingt journées de Sodome* de Sade', *Cahiers d'histoires des littératures romanes/ Romanistische Zeitschrift für Literaturgeschichte* 1-2 (1995), p.60-71.

Laborde, Alice, 'La dialectique du regard dans *La Marquise de Gange*', *Romanic review* 60 (1969), p.47-55.
–, 'La notion d'isolisme et ses implications lyriques dans l'œuvre du marquis de Sade', *SVEC* 88 (1972), p.871-80.
Lacey, Simon, Randall Stilla and K. Sathian, 'Metaphorically feeling: comprehending textural metaphors activates somatosensory cortex', *Brain and language* 120:3 (2012), p.416-21.
Lajer-Burcharth, Ewa, *Necklines: the art of Jacques-Louis David after the Terror* (New Haven, CT, 1999).
La Tour, Georges Imbart de, *Des circonstances atténuantes* (Paris, 1898).
Laugaa-Traut, Françoise, *Lectures de Sade* (Paris, 1973).
Le Brun, Annie, *Les Châteaux de la subversion* (Paris, 1982).

–, *Soudain, un bloc d'abîme* (Paris, 1993).
Lehrer, Jonah, *Proust was a neuroscientist* (Edinburgh, 2011).
Lely, Gilbert, *Vie du marquis de Sade* (Paris, 1982).
Lescure, Mathurin de, *Bernardin de Saint-Pierre* (Paris, 1892).
Leung, K. S., and L. B. Cottler, 'Treatment of pathological gambling', *Current opinion in psychiatry* 22:1 (2009), p.69-74.
Lever, Maurice, *Donatien Alphonse François, marquis de Sade* (Paris, 1991).
Lévy, Maurice, *Le Roman gothique anglais 1764-1824* (Paris, 1995).
Lindsay, Suzanne, 'Mummies and tombs: Turenne, Napoleon, and death ritual', *The Art bulletin* 82 (2000), p.476-502.
Lüsebrink, Hans-Jürgen, *Kriminalität und Literatur im Frankreich des 18. Jahrhunderts* (Munich, 1983).
Lüsebrink, Hans-Jürgen, and Rolf Reichardt, *The Bastille: a history of a symbol of despotism and freedom*, trans. Norbert Schürer (London, 1997).
Lynch, Lawrence W., *The Marquis de Sade* (Boston, MA, 1984).
–, 'Sade and the case of *La Marquise de Ganges*: sources, adaptations and regressions', *Symposium* 41 (1987), p.188-99.

MacKinnon, Catherine A., *Only words* (Cambridge, MA, 1993).
Martin, Jean-Clément, *Violence et révolution: essai sur la naissance d'un mythe national* (Paris, 2006).
–, 'Violence et révolution', in *Historiographies, concepts et débats, II*, ed. Christian

Delacroix, François Dosse, Patrick Garcia and Nicolas Offenstadt (Paris, 2010), p.1276-83.

Marty, Eric, *Pourquoi le XXe siècle a-t-il pris Sade au sérieux?* (Paris, 2011).

Mathiez, Albert, 'Le coût des fêtes publiques à Paris en 1794', 'Notes et glanes', *Annales historiques de la Révolution française* 6 (1929), p.501-505.

Mauzi, Robert, 'Ecrivains et moralistes du XVIIIe siècle devant les jeux de hasard', *Revue des sciences humaines* 90 (1958), p.219-56.

Maza, Sarah, *Private lives and public affairs: the causes célèbres of prerevolutionary France* (Berkeley, CA, 1993).

McCallam, David, 'The terrorist earth? Some thoughts on Sade and Baudrillard', *French cultural studies*, 23:3 (2012), p.215-24.

Mercken-Spaas, Godelieve, 'Some aspects of the Self and the Other in Rousseau and Sade', *SubStance* 20 (1978), p.71-77.

Messiaen, Jean-Michel, 'Violence et son réseau lexical (1600-1800): prémisses sémasiologiques', in *Violence et fiction jusqu'à la Révolution*, ed. Martine Debaisieux and Gabrielle Verdier (Tübingen, 1998), p.33-41.

Michel, Pierre, *Un Mythe romantique, les Barbares, 1789-1848* (Lyon, 1981).

Miller, Mary Ashburn, *A Natural history of Revolution: violence and nature in the French revolutionary imagination, 1789-1794* (Ithaca, NY, 2011).

Miller, Nancy K., *French dressing: women, men and ancien régime fiction* (London and New York, 1995).

Monnier, Raymonde, 'L'apothéose du 20 vendémiaire An III (11 octobre 1794). Rousseau revisité par la République', *Annales J.-J. Rousseau* 42 (1999), p.403-28.

Muchembled, Robert, *Une Histoire de la violence de la fin du moyen âge à nos jours* (Paris, 2008).

Noiray, Michel, 'L'opéra de la Révolution (1790-1794): un "tapage de chien"?', in *La Carmagnole des muses: l'homme de lettres et l'artiste dans la Révolution*, ed. Jean-Claude Bonnet (Paris, 1988), p.359-79.

Peurot, Jean-Luc, *Tombeau du marquis de Sade* (Paris, 2012).

Pinker, Steven, *How the mind works* (London, 1998).

–, *The Better angels of our nature: the decline of violence and its causes* (London, 2011).

Porret, Michel, *Sur la scène du crime: pratique pénale, enquête et expertise judiciaires à Genève (XVIIIe-XIXe siècle)* (Montreal, 2008).

Proust, Jacques, 'La diction sadienne: à propos de *La Marquise de Gange*' in Michel Camus and Philippe Roger (eds), *Sade et la Crise* (Paris, 1983).

Quétel, Claude, *Histoire véritable de la Bastille* (Paris, 2006).

Radford, Colin, and Michael

Weston, 'How can we be moved by the fate of Anna Karenina?' *Proceedings of the Aristotelian Society, supplementary volumes* 49 (1975), p.67-93.

Reinhardt, Mark, Holly Edwards and Erinna Duganne (eds), *Beautiful suffering: photography and the traffic of pain*, (Williamstown, MA, 2007).

Robespierre, Maximilien, *Virtue and Terror*, ed. Jean Ducange, with preface by Slavoj Žižek (London, 2007).

Roger, Philippe, *Sade: la philosophie dans le pressoir* (Paris, 1976).

–, 'Note conjointe sur Sade épistolier', in *La Fin de l'ancien régime: Sade, Rétif, Beaumarchais, Laclos*, ed. Béatrice Didier and Jacques Neef (Saint-Denis, 1991), p.45-53.

Ronzeaud, Pierre, *Peuple et représentations sous le règne de Louis XIV: les représentations du peuple dans la littérature politique en France sous le règne de Louis XIV* (Aix-en-Provence, 1988).

Roussel, Jean, *Jean-Jacques Rousseau en France après la Révolution 1795-1830: lectures et légende* (Paris, 1972).

Saint-Amand, Pierre, *The Laws of hostility: politics, violence and the Enlightenment* (Minneapolis, MN, 1996).

Saint Girons, Baldine, *Fiat lux: une philosophie du sublime* (Paris, 1993).

Salvadori, Philippe, *La Chasse sous l'Ancien Régime* (Paris, 1996).

Sandrier, Alain, '"Si j'avais écrit *L'Embrasement de Sodome*": Voltaire et le théâtre manuscrit de la philosophie clandestine', *Revue Voltaire* 8 (2008), p.49-65.

Schlanger, Judith, 'Théâtre révolutionnaire et représentation du bien', *Poétique* 22 (1975) p.268-83.

Sclippa, Norbert, *Pour Sade* (Paris, 2006).

Searls Giroux, Susan, 'Sade's revenge: racial neoliberalism and the sovereignty of negation', *Symposium* 44:1 (2010), p.1-26.

Seifert, Hans-Ulrich, *Sade: Leser und Autor* (Frankfurt, 1983).

Seth, Catriona (ed.), 'Dire l'indicible: description et peinture dans *L'Emigré* de Sénac de Meilhan', in *Destins romanesques de l'émigration*, ed. Claire Jaquier, Florence Lotterie and Catriona Seth (Paris, 2007).

–, *Imaginaires gothiques: aux sources du roman noir français* (Paris, 2010).

–, *La Fabrique de l'intime. Mémoires et journaux de femmes du XVIIIe siècle* (Paris, 2013).

Sgard, Jean (ed.), *Dictionnaire des journalistes*, 2 vols (Oxford, 1999).

Shapiro, Barry M., *Traumatic politics: the deputies and the king in the early French revolution* (University Park, PA, 2009).

Shattuck, Roger, *Forbidden knowledge: from Prometheus to pornography* (San Diego, CA, 1997).

Shepard, Roger, and J. Metzler, 'Mental rotation of three-

dimensional objects', *Science* 171 (1971), p.701-703.
Smith, Jay M., *Monsters of the Gévaudan: the making of a beast* (Cambridge MA, 2011).
Soble, Alan, *Pornography, sex and feminism* (New York, 2002).
Soboul, Alain, *La Révolution française* (Paris, 1984).
Souriau, Maurice, *Bernardin de Saint-Pierre d'après ses manuscrits* (Paris, 1905).
Sozzi, Lionello, 'Interprétations de Rousseau pendant la Révolution', *SVEC* 64 (1968), p.187-223.
Stafford, Barbara Maria, *Body criticism: imaging the unseen in Enlightenment art and medicine* (Cambridge, MA, 1991).
Steintrager, James, A., *Cruel delight: Enlightenment culture and the inhuman* (Bloomington, IN, 2004).
Svagelski, Jean, *L'Idée de compensation en France 1750-1850* (Lyon, 1981).

Tilby, Michael, 'Ducry-Duminil's *Victor ou L'Enfant de la forêt* in the context of the Revolution', *SVEC* 249 (1987), p.407-38.
Trouille, Mary, *Wife-abuse in eighteenth-century France*, *SVEC* 2009:01.
Trousson, Raymond, 'Histoire d'un fait divers du marquis de Sade à Charles Hugo', on http://www.bon-a-tirer.com/volume9/rt.html (24 December 2003).

Urmson, J. O., 'Literature' in *Aesthetics: a critical anthology* ed. George Dickie and Richard Sclafani (New York, 1977), p.334-41.
Van Crugten-André, Valérie, 'Syncrétisme et dérision parodique dans *Pauliska ou La Perversité moderne* de Révéroni Saint-Cyr', *Revue d'histoire littéraire de la France* 6 (2001), p.1551-72.
Villiers, Patrick, 'Redécouvrir la justice d'ancien régime', in *Aventures et dossiers secrets de l'Histoire* 52 (2004).

Wahnich, Sophie, 'De l'économie émotive de la Terreur', *Annales HSS* 4 (2002), p.889-913.
Walton, Kendall, *Mimesis as make-believe: on the foundations of the representational arts* (Cambridge, MA, 1990).
Wievorka, Michel, *Violence: a new approach*, trans. David Macey (London, 2009).
Williams, Linda, *Hard core: power, pleasure, and the 'frenzy of the visible'*, 2nd edn (Berkeley and Los Angeles, CA, 1999).
Wilson, Margo, and Martin Daly, 'Competitiveness, risk-taking and violence: the young male syndrome', *Ethology and sociobiology* 6 (1985), p.59-73.
Wittgenstein, Ludwig, *Zettel*, 2nd edn (Oxford, 1981).
Wynn, Thomas, 'Masochisme et le tableau sadien', in *Lire Sade*, ed. Norbert Sclippa (Paris, 2004), p.245-57.
–, *Sade's theatre: pleasure, vision, masochism*, *SVEC* 2007:02.

Index

10th August, 46-47, 75-92, 114-15, 117, 119, 129-30, 133

bandits and brigands, 40-42, 128-29, 254-57
Bardou, Jean, 26, 28-30
Barthes, Roland, 143, 229-33, 245-59
Bernardin de Saint-Pierre, Jacques Henri, 161-75, 191-202
Boissy d'Anglas, François-Antoine de, 36, 44
Bournon-Malarme, Charlotte de, 251-62
Briois, le Citoyen, 132-33
Bruno, Louis de, 76, 79-80, 90
Burke, Edmund, 7-8, 35-38, 42-43, 46, 239
Butler, Judith, 143-45, 150, 156-57

Calas, Jean, 1, 103-19
Calonne, Charles-Alexandre de, 36, 39, 44
catharsis, 3, 110-11, 113, 116-17, 122, 125, 131
Charrière, Isabelle de, 81-82
Chénier, Marie-Joseph, 103, 111, 113, 124-25

Damiens de Gomicourt, Augustin Pierre, 26-28
Dumaniant, A.-J, 79, 84-88, 89-91
Dutailli de Saint-Pierre, Joseph, 161-75

emigration, 12, 79-83, 89-92, 251-54
ethics and morality, 5-8, 17-33, 79, 83-92, 227-28, 229-49, 251-62

Foucault, Michel, 49, 63, 70, 163, 185, 251

Genlis, Félicité de, 82-83, 95, 251
Girondins, 115-17, 179, 181
Gouges, Olympe de, 127
guillotine, 10, 54-56, 94, 119, 126, 128, 135, 203, 213, 257

imprisonment, 65-72, 100, 142-60, 161-75, 253-54
inhumanity, 7, 41-42, 77-78, 183-84, 203-20

Jacobins, 114-19, 129-30, 178-83, 253-60

La Barre, chevalier de, 1, 104
Lally-Tollendal, Trophime-Gérard, 36-37, 92
Lamballe, prince de, 208-14
Laya, Jean-Louis, 103, 104n, 106, 112
Lebrun-Tossa, Jean-Antoine, 130-31
Lemierre d'Argy, Auguste-Jacques, 103, 106n, 111n, 112
Loaisel de Tréogate, Joseph-Marie, 26, 30-32
Louis XVI, 55-59, 75-78, 114-19
Louvet, Jean-Baptiste, 42

Mackintosh, James, 35-36, 39, 43-44, 46
Mallet du Pan, Jacques, 77-78, 90-91
Marat, Jean-Paul, 179-80, 181-84, 186-87
Marie-Antoinette, 56, 80, 118, 131

martyrdom, 97, 104-105, 131-33, 182
Mercier, Louis-Sébastien, 45-46, 53, 104n, 178-80
Montagnards, 124-25, 128, 132, 179-80
Mounier, Jean-Joseph, 36, 40-42

National Assembly, 35-36, 113, 185
National Convention, 114-14, 118, 124, 133, 181
neuroscience, 17-22, 24-25, 32-33, 237-38, 246-47
Nodier, Charles, 121-22
novels, 17-33, 54-60, 61-72, 78-92, 93-102, 200-202, 221-28, 232-49, 251-62

October Days, 36, 38, 41, 45-47
Orléans, Louis Philippe, duc d', 203-20

Paine, Thomas, 35, 42-44
pamphlets, 35-47, 180-87, 203-20
Polier de Bottens, Jeanne Françoise, 75n, 78-82
Priestley, Joseph, 35, 39-40

Révéroni Saint-Cyr, Jacques-Antoine de, 61-72, 257
Robespierre, Maximilien, 47, 51, 114-17, 125, 181
Rousseau, Jean-Jacques, 177-87, 193, 196, 201

Sade, Donatien-Alphonse-François de, 8, 57
  Adélaïde de Brunswick, princesse de Saxe, 97-98
  Aline et Valcour, 141-42, 155, 232
  Les Cent vingt journées de Sodome, 140-41, 158, 160, 221-24, 226, 228, 233-35
  Correspondance du marquis de Sade, 101, 141-44, 147-51, 153-58
  Histoire de Juliette, 8, 146, 158, 236, 240
  Histoire secrète d'Isabelle de Bavière, 98-99
  Justine ou les malheurs de la vertu, 158, 225-26, 229-33, 236-37, 243-45
  La Marquise de Gange, 95-98, 158
  La Nouvelle Justine, 226-28, 233-34
sans-culottes, 76, 80, 90, 123, 129, 131, 179, 183, 186
Saurin, Bernard-Joseph, 23-26
Sénac de Meilhan, Gabriel, 54-56, 80-81, 84, 88-89, 92
Staël, Germaine de,
  Considérations sur la Révolution française, 59, 261
  Corinne ou l'Italie, 78, 83-84
  De l'Allemagne, 56
  De l'influence des passions, 50-52
  Réflexions sur la paix adressées à M. Pitt et aux Français, 51
suicide, 19, 23-24, 104n, 225-26, 255, 257, 258

theatre, 2-5, 49, 103-19, 121-35
torture, 64-67, 157, 224, 233
trauma, 11-12, 93-94, 100-101, 108-109

violence
  and commemoration, 75-92, 103-19, 121-35, 177-87
  as a creative force, 8-10, 46, 142-45, 154-60
  and history, 49-51, 63, 75-92, 93-102, 114-16, 203-20, 251-62
  and the mob, 35-47, 77-79, 84-89
  and nature, 9, 36-40, 191-202
  and pathology, 17-23

and rhetoric, 35-47, 202-20, 221-28
and spectatorship, 5, 103-19, 121-35

Voltaire, 1-5, 106, 108, 124, 126, 183, 186
Saül, 2-5